Child Protection

Child Protection:
An Introduction

Chris Beckett

SAGE Publications

London • Thousand Oaks • New Delhi

First published 2003

SAGE Publications Ltd
6 Bonhill Street
London EC2A 4PU

SAGE Publications Inc
2455 Teller Road
Thousand Oaks, California 91320

SAGE Publications India Pvt Ltd
32, M-Block Market
Greater Kailash – I
New Delhi 110 048

British Library Cataloguing in Publication data

A catalogue record for this book is available from the British
Library

ISBN 0 7619 4955 0
ISBN 0 7619 4956 0 (pbk)

Library of Congress Control Number: 2002111623

Typeset by Mayhew Typesetting, Rhayader, Powys
Printed and bound in Great Britain by Athenaeum Press, Gateshead

Contents

Contents

Introduction

This book is aimed in particular at social work students and at social workers embarking into the field of child protection work – by which I mean the tasks carried out by field social workers who follow up on concerns about the abuse and neglect of children. Specifically it addresses child protection work as it is constituted in England and Wales, but much of its content is applicable to other parts of the English-speaking world, where similar legal systems and child protection systems exist. Much of the research quoted in this book comes from North America, and the English and Welsh framework that I describe is currently undergoing a period of reappraisal.

Of course child protection work in a broader sense embraces not only social workers but a whole range of other professionals, such as doctors, nurses, police officers and lawyers – and of course teachers, who arguably have the most important role in protecting children, since they are the only profession which has an overview, on a daily basis, of almost all the children in the country. Child protection work also embraces many other kinds of social worker. Residential social workers, adoption and fostering specialists and, indeed, social workers in other specialisms not directly concerned with children (notably mental health, learning disability and drug and alcohol services) often play crucial roles in child protection work. I hope that parts of this book will be of interest to all these groups too. My particular focus on the work of the child protection social worker should not be taken as implying that I see these other groups as secondary in the child protection system.

I also hope that this book will be of interest to more experienced child protection social workers because, though it is presented as an introduction, it is also an attempt at a distillation of some of my own experience in this field. I myself now teach social work students, but I was involved in child protection social work for some 18 years, first as a social worker and latterly, as the manager of a children and families fieldwork team. What I have done with this book is to try to draw together as much as possible of what I think I have learnt from my experience, and to relate this to the research findings and ideas of other commentators.

Part I of the book is about what the job of child protection social work entails and what it demands of the worker. Part II looks at the different ways in which children can be abused and neglected and considers the indicators and warning signs in each case, as well as the long-term consequences. It includes a chapter on the abuse of children with disabilities.

Part III considers the causes of abuse and neglect. What leads adults to mistreat their children or fail to provide the care and protection they need? It includes a chapter on the relationship of drug abuse to child abuse and neglect, and a chapter on parents with learning disabilities.

Finally, in Part IV, I look at some of the difficulties and dilemmas involved in child protection social work.

Each chapter in the book begins with a list of points to be covered, and concludes with a summary. The text is interspersed from time to time with what I have called (for want of a better word) 'exercises'. These invite the reader to reflect on what is being discussed and to relate the discussion to specific situations such as might be encountered in practice and in everyday life. If you prefer not to break the flow of your reading by pausing to work on exercises of this kind, then of course you do not need to do so. You should read, however, through them rather than skip over them, because I will often refer to them in the subsequent text.

Many of these exercises are based around case examples. I should emphasize that these examples are fictional. Real-life elements have been included but they have been combined together, modified and mixed with imaginary elements, and names have been chosen at random. In short, these case examples are intended to be realistic, but *none* of them is a portrait of real-life human beings.

In the text, for the sake of simplicity, I tend to refer to 'parents' when talking about the adult carers of children. Of course in many families children are cared for by step-parents, grandparents, foster-parents and others, and the word 'parent' can generally be taken as including any adult acting as a carer of a child. I also tend to refer to social workers as 'she' because in England the majority of social workers are women. No disrespect is intended to my fellow-members of the male minority.

My thanks are due to Anglia Polytechnic University and to my colleagues there for providing me with an environment in which it has been possible to reflect and write about my experience in practice, and to all my former colleagues for helping to provide me with that experience in the first place. I am also very grateful to my parents and to my three children, Poppy, Dominic and Nancy, who have taught me so much about childhood and parenthood, and not least to my dear wife, Maggie, for all her strength and support.

Part I

Doing Child Protection Work

Different Perspectives 1

The modern child protection system •
The historical context in Britain •
International comparisons •
Cross-cultural complexities •
Different disciplines •

Children are mistreated by adults. Sometimes they are killed or badly injured. Sometimes they are used for sexual gratification, or to meet other adult needs that are contrary to their own. Sometimes they are so poorly cared for that their basic requirements for safety, warmth and nutrition go unmet. Often they are treated in ways that may not do any obvious physical harm, but which have long-term emotional and psychological consequences. This happens in Britain and in other countries. It happens now and it happened in the past. And I suspect that every society, at every stage in history, has recognized to some degree that this is a problem about which 'something should be done'.

In Britain today, as in the USA and many other countries, there is now a complex, professional child protection system, set up and regulated by the state, which is expected not only to respond to incidents of child abuse, but also to anticipate and prevent serious harm being done to children. It is a system which provides work to thousands of social workers, doctors, nurses, judges, lawyers, police officers, civil servants, academics and many others, and a system upon which high expectations are placed by the community at large. It is the work involved in running this system, and specifically the role within it played by the child protection social worker that is the subject of Part I of this book. This chapter takes a broad overview. Chapter 2 looks in more detail at the task of the child protection social worker as it is defined specifically in the law of England and Wales (there are many parallels, but also differences, in the task assigned to social workers in other parts of the English-speaking world). Chapter 3 looks at what is entailed in doing the job of child protection social worker at a more personal level.

The modern child protection system

In the next chapter I will describe the child protection system that operates in England and Wales – a system which shares many features with those that operate in North America and other English-speaking countries. For the present, here is a brief summary of the system's essential elements:

1. All agencies involved with children, including social work services, the police, state and private schools, churches, the probation service, the health service, housing departments, various voluntary organizations and others, are expected to share information about children who may be at risk, if necessary within the formal framework of a child protection conference. This obligation is generally seen as over-riding each agency's duty of confidentiality towards its service users.
2. Central government provides detailed guidelines as to the duties of the various agencies and the arrangements for them to cooperate.
3. At the local level agencies are required to establish collaborative structures within which to coordinate and develop local child protection strategies and procedures.
4. Social work agencies and the police have a joint responsibility to investigate incidents of abuse, and police services have special units for this purpose.
5. Social work agencies have legal duties to investigate families causing concern, and if necessary, to seek powers from the courts allowing them to intervene and impose solutions, which can include temporarily or permanently removing a child from her carers.
6. Incidents where a child dies at the hands of carers are often presented in the media as serious failures of the child protection system, meriting detailed scrutiny. When the child protection system is seen to have behaved overzealously, this is also seen as a matter of serious public concern.

As I have said, I will be looking in more detail in the next chapter at how this complex multidisciplinary system operates. For the present I simply want to draw your attention to the fact that in England at present there is a particular system, and a particular way of looking at child protection. It has not always been so, and it is not so in other places.

Much of the rest of this book will take the existing system as a given, and look at how to operate effectively within this system, but it is useful to bear in mind at the outset that the system as it now operates is only one of many possible approaches. Reminding ourselves of this, it seems to me, enables us to think creatively about our own system, and be more open to the possibility of changing and improving it.

The following, for instance, are objections that might legitimately be raised to the system I have described:

1. Historically it would have been the extended family and the community that dealt with abusive parenting. The more the state intervenes in family life, the less the extended family and the community become involved, so that, in the long run, in trying to help, the state ends up weakening society's informal protective networks. In short, if concerned neighbours can pick up their telephones and report their concerns about a child, they may well feel they have discharged their responsibilities to that child. If the option of reporting it to a professional agency was not available, they might feel that they needed to take more action themselves.
2. If children are neglected or abused then a crime has been committed, and it should be the responsibility of the police to deal with it. Involving social workers in the investigation process compromises social work and makes it more difficult for social workers to be accepted as a source of help for families. Many social workers comment on the irony that, having gone into the profession because they wanted to help people, they find themselves to be widely feared by those they hoped to help.
3. Most of the abuse and neglect that is detected occurs in poor families. One of the main factors in abuse and neglect is poverty and social exclusion. Therefore if child abuse and neglect are really to be tackled, we need to do something about social exclusion, rather than add to the oppression of the poor (and, incidentally, of those ethnic minorities who are overrepresented in lower income groups). It is possible to argue that social workers provide a fig leaf for structural injustice by making people into 'cases' and their problems look like individual failings, rather than the result of structural inequality and oppression. (For more on this see Chapter 10.) It is also possible to argue that the inter-agency information sharing involved in the child

protection system, overriding confidentiality, constitutes a form of state surveillance to which the poor are subjected, but which more powerful members of society would not tolerate if it was routinely applied to them.

4. The child protection system in Britain has, in many ways, been shaped by a series of public inquiries about child deaths – and by newspapers and public opinion demanding that child deaths should not happen again. Trying to predict child deaths, though, is like trying to find a needle in a haystack and there is not much evidence that it has been successful, in spite of all the changes. The whole system has been shaped by a goal which will never be reached, and is arguably set up to fail. (For further discussion on this, see Chapter 12.)

5. The system is geared towards detecting abuse, but much less thought has been given to how to help abused children once their abuse has been detected. For example, there are nothing like enough treatment facilities available to aid the recovery of victims of sexual abuse. In recent years more and more children have been taken into care. But the care system is often not very successful. Abuse can occur in care too, for one thing, and the care system often fails to provide children with the security and stability that they need. Repeated placement breakdowns, for example, may simply confirm and reinforce negative and rejecting messages that a child received at home. In all kinds of ways the system itself may be harmful to children. (For more on this see Chapter 11.)

All these arguments, I would suggest, have validity, though they are all rather one-sided. The difficulty of course is trying to construct an alternative system that retains the benefits of the present system without suffering from any of the disadvantages.

The historical context in Britain

Ideas about how children should be treated by adults, and about the community's responsibilities towards children, have naturally changed over the centuries, although this is not to say that in the past adults were not concerned to protect children from harm. The fact that it was a serious matter to harm children in Biblical times, two thousand years ago, seems to me to be illustrated, for example, by the following famous verse:

> And whosoever shall offend one of these little ones that believe in me, it is better for him that a millstone were hanged about his neck, and he were cast into the sea. (Mark 9:42)

It would be impossible to establish the prevalence of child abuse in historic times with any degree of certainty, since even today much abuse is never discovered, and until very recently only a tiny proportion of sexual abuse in particular ever came to light. And attitudes as to what *constituted* abuse and what constituted appropriate chastisement have also changed. Take, for example, another Biblical quote: 'He that spareth his rod hateth his son' (Proverbs 13:24).

During the nineteenth century the industrial revolution in Britain led to the growth of big cities and new state institutions began to appear. It was in 1856, for instance, that it became mandatory for local authorities to set up police forces and 1870 that the first state elementary schools appeared. Attitudes to child welfare changed over the course of the century. The 1833 Factory Act prohibited children under nine from working in factories and restricted the hours that could be worked by 9- to 13-year-olds, but the employers of nine-year-olds could still quite legally expect them to work a *48-hour week*, with a 69-hour maximum working week for 13- to 18-year-olds.

State regulation of childcare began with efforts to regulate the practice of 'baby-farming', common in the nineteenth century ('baby farmers' being essentially private foster-parents). A series of pieces of legislation, beginning in 1872 with the Infant Life Protection Act, laid down requirements for baby-farmers to register with local authorities and to meet certain minimum standards.

In 1889, the Prevention of Cruelty to Children Act empowered police to search premises for children thought to be in danger and to remove them if necessary to a place of safety (a power which continues to exist under section 46 of the 1989 Children Act). Meanwhile, in the 1880s, the precursor organizations to the modern NSPCC – the National Society for the Prevention of Cruelty to Children – had begun to take shape. The NSPCC was really the first child protection social work agency in England.

However, although what we now call the 'welfare state' had been developing over the previous century, the period after 1945 is generally seen as representing a sea change in welfare provision in Britain, the so-called 'post-war settlement'. The establishment of the National Health

Service is probably the best-known achievement of that period, but another change was the requirement on local authorities under the 1948 Children Act to set up Children's Departments employing welfare officers. These Child Welfare Officers – children and family social workers – were subsequently incorporated (along with welfare officers for the elderly and others) into the new generic Social Services departments in the 1970s. Over the past decade or so we have seen these generic departments reorganizing themselves once again on client group lines.

During the 1960s, there was a growing awareness of the prevalence of physical abuse of children ('the battered baby syndrome' as it was originally described). The death of Maria Colwell in 1973 was the first of many cases which brought child abuse, and the professional agencies, into the spotlight. It was also the first of many which were presented in the media as failures by gullible or incompetent social workers to protect children. Following the public inquiry into this case, much of the framework was put in place that British social workers would still recognize as the modern multi-agency child protection system. The *child protection register*, the *case conference* and the *Area Child Protection Committee* were key elements of a system that was supposed to ensure an efficient flow of information between the various agencies and a sharing of expertise. Many other public inquires over the next decade emphasized again and again the importance of detecting indicators of abuse, improving communications between agencies and acting decisively to protect children from harm.

In 1987, however, there was a quite different kind of outcry about the activities of social workers:

> If previous inquiries demonstrated that welfare professionals, particularly social workers, failed to protect the lives and interests of children and intervened too little too late into the private family, the concerns focussed around Cleveland seemed to demonstrate that professionals . . . paediatricians as well as social workers, failed to recognise the rights of parents and intervened too soon and in too heavy-handed a way into the family. (Parton, 1991: 79)

In Cleveland social workers were castigated for removing children from their families too readily on the basis of advice from doctors that there were indicators of sexual abuse. In the media families were presented as innocent victims and the social services department was compared by at least one MP to the Nazi SS (*Hansard*, 29 June 1987).

The public reaction in this case may reflect in part the fact that what was at stake here was *sexual* and not physical abuse. Professional awareness of the sexual abuse of children had been growing in the 1980s, just as awareness of 'battered babies' had emerged in the previous two decades, but it was a form of abuse whose prevalence the general public found much harder to accept. However, in the wake of the Cleveland affair, the pendulum of child protection practice in general swung once again away from intrusive intervention and towards supporting families.

Part of the legacy of this swing can be found in the 1989 Children Act (which actually came into effect in October 1991): the legislation under which childcare social work in England and Wales still operates. The Children Act was supposed to strike a new balance between support and compulsory intervention in families. 'The most important and far-reaching reform this century of the law on children', said *The Times* newspaper when the Act came into effect, 'a fundamental shift from the adversarial legal system. The new emphasis is away from courts imposing solutions or orders and towards parents, relatives and local authorities working in partnership . . .' (*The Times*, 8 October, 1991).

In spite of these expectations, though, since the Act came into force the pendulum again swung back in the direction of more intervention into families. For example, the number of children made subject to Care Orders steadily increased (Beckett, 2001a). I suspect the pendulum will continue to swing to and fro because, ever since its beginnings in Victorian times, the British child protection system has always struggled to reconcile two desirable but ultimately incompatible goals: on the one hand protecting children against their carers, and on the other hand protecting the privacy and autonomy of the family and the individual against the state.

International comparisons

We've seen how the growth of the formal child protection system in Britain did not emerge until the country industrialized in the nineteenth century. Very similar developments were occurring at the same time in other industrialized countries, and essentially the same difficulties and dilemmas were being encountered. Neil Guterman describes the early child protection movement in nineteenth-century America, and observes that:

a schism arose between the investigative, protective and 'child rescue' approach taken by the New York SPCC and an approach that emphasized family strengthening and abuse prevention, as represented by the Massachusetts SPCC. (Guterman, 2001: 79)

But of course there are still many countries in the world which have not yet industrialized or are still in the process of industrializing. And in many of these countries, as in pre-industrial Britain, the regulation of family life is left much more to informal systems, with much less of a role for the state.

Even in the industrialized world, there are differences between different countries as to how the problem of child abuse is seen and responded to. Cooper et al. (1995), for instance, offer a comparison between the British and French child protection systems, and suggest that there are quite significant differences in approach at either end of the Channel Tunnel. 'They don't seem to have to panic', commented one British social worker enviously about French child protection social workers (1995: 11), while a French social worker was struck by 'a semi-obsession with getting evidence' that seemed to preoccupy the British child protection worker, who seemed to have become 'a bit like a detective' (1995: 10).

Guterman (2001) makes an interesting observation which may help to explain the contrasts between the French and the British systems. American law, he writes, operates on the same principles as English law, and American child protection systems are therefore, like the English one, based on the legal doctrine of *parens patriae*, which requires the state to accumulate evidence in order to allow it to intervene at all. As Waldfogel (1999) comments, this has the result that an initial contact with a family by the child protection services is

> reactive and investigative, concentrating on gathering information to confirm or disprove the allegations . . . Investigators and families are also keenly aware that the information being collected during the investigation might be used as evidence in future court proceedings . . . Thus the model for CPS [child protection service] operations, particularly at the investigative stage, is adversarial. (Waldfogel, 1999: 69)

By contrast, French child protection workers operating, like most of continental Europe, under the very different framework of Roman Law, 'do not need to obtain legally admissible evidence of abuse before they can refer a case to a judge, and equally they do not have to experience themselves as "destroying families"' (Cooper et al., 1995: 10).

Cross-cultural complexities

For a child protection social worker in modern Britain – and indeed in most other countries – there are more immediate reasons for being aware of the different attitudes of different cultures to children, families and child protection. A child protection social worker in Britain may be involved in decision-making about children and families from a huge range of cultural backgrounds. She may find herself dealing, for example, with a Sudanese family for whom clitoridectomy of little girls is normal, or a Bangladeshi family where the mother married the father at the age of 12, or Romany families who choose to keep their children out of school because they are opposed to sex education in any form. Belief systems may not always differ quite so obviously from the norms of white British culture as in the examples above, but any British social worker – along with social workers in America, Australia and other parts of the English-speaking world – will certainly find herself working with families from diverse traditions with profoundly different attitudes, for example, to discipline and parental authority, physical punishment, sex, the role of men and women, and the nature of the obligations that exist between parents, children and the extended family. Even attitudes to educational achievement may be very different, with some migrants from poor countries placing an emphasis on their children's educational achievement that may look like undue pressure, and even cruelty, to European, Australian or North American eyes, though they themselves may see themselves as ensuring that their children can provide for themselves and avoid destitution.

These cultural differences have led to a fair amount of heart-searching in child protection social work about practices which, in one cultural context would be defined as abusive, but in another cultural context would be seen as normal.

Exercise 1.1

The following behaviours are regarded as normal in various cultures, or are methods of punishment used by families in this society. How should we respond to them when they occur in this society?

- Circumcision of boys (the cutting off of the foreskin either in infancy, in the case of Jewish or Muslim culture, or in adolescence, in the case of some African cultures).

- Arranged marriages of 12-year-old girls (normal in many Asian and African societies).
- Beating with a stick (accepted as a normal method of punishment in many cultures).
- Clitoridectomy (removal of the clitoris, or 'female circumcision', common in Middle Eastern and African cultures).
- Locking a child into a room (quite commonly used as a punishment in this country).

Comments on Exercise 1.1

It is difficult to take an entirely consistent view of these things. It seems reasonable on the one hand that a society should have a consensus view of minimum standards which apply to everyone in it, regardless of their culture of origin, and in fact at least two items on this list are quite simply illegal under English law. On the other hand, it is important to be aware that every culture has its own system of values and meanings.

It is also important to be aware that the abusiveness of any act cannot be understood except in context. Being beaten with a stick may be undesirable in any context, but its meaning will be very different for a child who knows that all his friends are punished in the same way, and that his parents love him and genuinely believe it is for his own good, than for a child who knows that none of his friends are beaten, and that his parents seem to do it as an expression of feelings of rage and hatred. The latter would feel more abusive to the child, even if the actual physical severity of the beatings was the same.

Likewise, for a Muslim child circumcision is a normal part of being a boy. Circumcision performed for no reason at all, however, and out of the blue, by a parent with no cultural reason for doing so, would be a bizarre and very abusive act.

It is important to bear in mind too that differences in parenting practices, and views about what is appropriate, exist not only between different ethnic groups but also within the same ethnic group, between different neighbourhoods and social classes. One Israeli author, observing that the importance of cultural factors in child maltreatment has been increasingly recognized, comments that 'the focus of this increased cultural awareness has been on cultural differences among ethnic groups and not among socio-economic groups' (Shor, 2000: 165). Shor finds significant differences in attitudes towards things like parental authority and the use of corporal punishment between low-income and middle-income groups, with the former being more supportive of more authoritarian methods. He suggests that some parenting behaviour considered excessively punitive or authoritarian by middle-class parents may, in fact, be appropriate in the context of preparing children for life in a 'deprived' neighbourhood.

Different disciplines

As well as different approaches to child abuse and child protection in different places, different times and different cultures, different perspectives and approaches are also taken by different professional disciplines within a single culture. Each discipline has its own particular approaches, its own characteristic ways of understanding the world.

The medical approach

Naturally enough a medical approach to child protection, an approach led or inspired by the medical profession, will tend to place emphasis on those aspects of the problem that are clearly in the province of medicine: the interpretation of physical symptoms. This means that, even when talking about those aspects of the problem that are not specifically physical, it will tend to use the language of illness and treatment. For an example, consider the term 'battered baby syndrome' introduced by C. Henry Kempe and his colleagues in 1962. These doctors did a service to the cause of child protection by drawing attention to the fact that many supposedly accidental injuries to young children were, in fact, the result of being hit by adults. But 'battered baby syndrome' is, when you think about it, a curious use of the word 'syndrome'. It treats the consequences of violent behaviour – hitting children – as if they were a medical condition. (Would we speak of the 'playground punch-up syndrome', or 'pub brawl syndrome'?)

Social work practice has been heavily influenced over the years by the medical model. Words like *treatment*, *therapy*, *pathology*, *prognosis*, all borrowed from medicine, are often used by social workers in case discussions that have nothing to do with any kind of organic illness. But if we use medical language and medical analogies, we need to be aware that these are not the only possible analogies that can be used, and may not always be the most useful. For instance, if we describe battering babies as a 'syndrome', are we inadvertently constructing it in our minds as something outside the control of the individuals concerned: a matter for professionals and not for ordinary people?

There are many areas in which doctors do indeed possess special expertise, but we should not assume that this expertise extends to all aspects of the problem. There is no reason to assume that a doctor should be seen as having special expertise into *why* a parent injured a child, for example, even if the doctor is better qualified than others to tell us *how* the parent did so. Child protection social workers should also be careful not to assume that medicine is more of an exact science than it is, even within its own particular area of expertise. Many physical symptoms are hard to interpret, and two doctors will often disagree as to how they were caused.

In the Cleveland report, social workers were criticized for accepting too readily the diagnosis of sexual abuse made by two paediatricians, who relied in particular on the so-called anal dilation test to conclude that anal penetration had taken place. As Nigel Parton puts it: '*Medical diagnosis* not only dominated and prescribed *social assessment* but it predetermined the form any social work response would take' (1991: 97, his italics). One thing that Cleveland social services did not take into account was that there was controversy within the medical profession about the reliability of the anal dilation test.

More recently, medical 'arrogance' and uncritical acceptance of medical opinion by others have been features of the criticism levelled at professionals in the cases of Victoria Climbié and Lauren Wright, whose deaths at the hands of their carers in London and Norfolk respectively have been well-publicized in the British media.

The report made a series of recommendations – the main one being that professionals in any child care agency should challenge decisions that do not accord with their professional judgement. (*Guardian* Society, 1 October 2001, summarizing a report prepared on the Lauren Wright case for Norfolk Area Child Protection Committee)

Early suspicions of non-accidental injury were overruled by consultant paediatrician Dr Ruby Schwartz, who diagnosed scabies . . . Another doctor wrote on the notes that there were 'no child protection issues', a phrase repeated in the referral letter to social services . . . Inquiry counsel criticised both Hines [senior social worker] and Dewar [police officer] for accepting Schwartz's diagnosis without question. (*Community Care*, 21–27 February 2002: 18–19, on the Victoria Climbié inquiry)

Psychological perspectives

It is difficult to draw a hard-and-fast line between medical and psychological approaches, because psychological theories are often influenced by the medical model. For example, classical Freudian theory draws extensively on medical language, using words such as *pathology*, *neurosis* and *trauma* that were used originally in medicine, and adopts a model in which the sick patient comes to the trained expert for treatment.

Psychology, however, concerns itself with the workings of the mind, not of the body, and psychological theory provides a range of ideas that can be used to try and make sense both of why child abuse happens and what its effects are. Indeed it would be impossible for any social worker to work with abusive and neglectful families – or abused and neglected children – without having *some* sort of psychological theories in her mind about abuse, even if those theories were only derived from her own life experience. If you had no ideas about what makes people abuse children, or what abuse does to children, how could you decide what action to take?

I will be drawing on various psychological approaches to abuse in this book, particularly in Chapter 6, where I consider the long-term consequences of abuse for children, and Chapter 7, where I discuss the origins of abusive and neglectful behaviour by adults.

Sociological perspectives

Important though a psychological understanding is, the big limitation of psychological theories is that they locate the origins of the problem at the level of the individual or the family, and therefore are in danger of ignoring the wider social and structural factors. Exactly the same criticism can be made of traditional social work practice, based as it is on casework with individuals and with families.

In reality, child maltreatment takes place within a social context. To fully understand child abuse we need to look beyond the particular individuals involved, or the particular family, and think about the workings of a society in which individuals and families are only tiny parts. We need to think of things like the way that relationships between adults and children are constructed in this society, for example, and about power differences between men and women. Why is it that more abusers are men than women, for example? When looking at abuse involving black children or black adults, we need to consider the question of racism, as well as being aware of the possibility of different cultural norms and expectations.

In particular, a hugely important issue that is left out of the equation by a purely psychological approach is that of class, poverty and structural inequality. As I will discuss more fully in Chapter 10, abuse and neglect are linked to poverty and social exclusion. This has major and difficult implications, for if one looks at abuse and neglect as being in large measure a consequence of poverty and social deprivation, it is possible to argue that the kind of intervention that is typically carried out in the USA and Britain in child protection cases is not only inappropriate, but may actually make the problem *worse*. Intervention may simply add to the feelings of powerlessness and alienation that lead parents to physically abuse or neglect their children in the first place.

The police and the legal profession

Two other professional groups closely involved with the child protection process are the police and the legal profession.

The police approach in child protection, as it is in other areas of police work, tends to be geared to establishing whether an offence has taken place and, if so, prosecuting the offender. Such an approach has an important place in a society that wants to give a clear signal that mistreatment of children is a crime. But in individual cases, the police approach can cut across the interests of a child. An abused child, for example, may want the abuse to stop, but she may not want her abuser to go to jail.

Lawyers play an important role in our child protection system, and one of the benefits of their involvement is to ensure that all parties, including parents and children, have articulate advocates who are conversant with the law. On the minus side, the adversarial British legal system can result in polarizing views, turning the process into a battle. One of the problems with the system in Britain, which I will return to in Chapter 11, is that the court process has become extremely long, so that children are kept waiting for long periods in temporary care while legal arguments go on about their future (see Beckett, 2001b). A preoccupation with 'looking good in court' can also seriously distort an agency's child protection practice, because the issue then becomes 'What will show our agency in the best light?' rather than 'What is best for this child?'

In this chapter I have tried to sketch out the context of child protection social work, and a variety of perspectives that can be applied to it. I have considered:

- the development of the child protection system as we know it in the UK over the past century and a half
- the differences between child protection systems operating in different countries
- the particular issues raised by different cultural attitudes to children and families
- the viewpoints of different professional disciplines. I considered in particular medical, psychological and sociological approaches, but also drew attention to the standpoints of the police and the legal profession.

In the next chapter I will focus on the specific legal and procedural framework that exists in England and Wales at the present time, and at the specific social work task that it defines.

The Child Protection Task 2

In the previous chapter I tried to look at the modern child protection system from the *outside*, as it were, looking at it from different perspectives, comparing it with other approaches and considering various objections that could be raised to the modern child protection system as it stands. In this chapter I want to look at it from the *inside*, considering how it operates now and what the role of the child protection social worker is within it. I will look specifically at the system that operates in England and Wales at the time of writing, though there are many parallels with systems that operate in other parts of the English-speaking world.

The legal context

In England and Wales the implementation of the 1989 Children Act means that almost all the relevant law relating to child protection social work, and social work with children and families in general, has been brought together in one piece of legislation. There are a number of books that explain the workings of the Children Act in detail (see for example Allen, 1998), but the following are a few key points.

General principles of the Children Act

Section 1 of the Act makes clear that the child's welfare should be the paramount consideration in all court proceedings carried out under the Act. It provides a checklist for the courts to use in determining what is for the child's best interests and, for the first time in English law, it specifically states that delays in court proceedings is harmful to a child and should be avoided. In spite of this, however, court proceedings have grown steadily longer since the Act came into effect (Beckett, 2001b).

Crucially, section 1 (5) states that the court must not make an order 'unless it considers doing so would be better for the child than making no order at all'. This means that when a local authority takes a case to court it needs to prove not only that a child is being harmed in her family, but that the local authority *will be able to do better if an order is made*. Child protection social workers should always bear this in mind, because they will often find themselves in the position of being under pressure (perhaps from other agencies, family members or neighbours) to act. Other people, perhaps powerful, angry people, are demanding that '*Something must be done!*' and in such a situation it is very easy to be pressured into taking *any* action rather than doing nothing. 'Yes, something *must* be done,' we may find ourselves thinking, 'and this is something. Therefore it must be done.' But of course there is only ever any point in doing something if it is likely to make things better rather than worse.

The duty to investigate

Sections 37 and 47 set out a local authority's duties to investigate cases of alleged harm to children. Section 37 relates to situations where a court decides that an investigation is needed in relation to a case which is before the court for other reasons (for example, a divorce case).

Section 47 relates to the more common scenario where a local authority receives information about a child within its area who may be suffering, or likely to suffer, 'significant harm', and sets out the action the local authority should take:

- It should make sufficient enquiries to allow it to determine what action needs to be taken to protect the child.

- It should arrange for the child to be seen, unless sufficient information can be obtained without doing so.
- If denied access to a child, or refused information about the child's whereabouts, it should apply for a court order (an emergency protection order, a child assessment order, a care order or a supervision order).
- More generally it should decide whether it is in the interests of the child whether to initiate court proceedings.

The police also have duties to investigate such concerns because intentionally or avoidably harming children is a criminal matter. As a result local agreements exist throughout England and Wales under which joint investigations by police and social services are carried out. The NSPCC can also be involved, and is the only body, other than local authorities, specifically authorized under the Act to initiate care proceedings.

Immediate protection

If immediate action is needed to protect a child – for example, removing a child from a parent's care, or preventing a parent from removing a child from hospital or from a foster-home – then a social worker can apply for an Emergency Protection Order (EPO), under section 44. To grant the order the court must be satisfied that there is good cause to believe that the child will suffer significant harm if the order is not made. NSPCC officers can also apply for an EPO, as can other professionals, though the latter is rare. The EPO *is* only a provision for use in *emergencies*. If you consider that a child is at risk of significant harm but that risk is not immediate (i.e., the risk is *chronic* rather than *acute*, to slip into medical language for a moment), then you should not apply for an EPO but for an Interim Care Order.

Police officers have another method of protecting a child in an emergency, which is to take a child into police protection, under section 46 of the Act. This they can do, without going to court, if they believe that a child needs to be removed to a place of safety, or that parents should be prevented from removing a child from a hospital or a foster-home. This order lasts a maximum of 72 hours. The police can also obtain a warrant allowing them to force entry and search for a child. A social worker can apply for a police warrant at the same time as applying for an EPO if she has reason to believe that she is likely to be refused access to a child and that police assistance will be required.

Neither an EPO nor police protection automatically confer powers to insist on a medical examination of a child. If permission is refused for a medical by the parents or child, then it is necessary to seek specific directions from the court.

Children in need

The Act also places a duty on local authorities to assess and meet needs. These are set out in part III of the Act, with the general principles being set out in section 17. There is a large grey area between 'children in need' and 'children in need of protection'. In many cases there will be a question as to whether a referral should be followed up under section 47 or section 17 (that is, by a child protection investigation or by a needs assessment.) Since it can be a very traumatic experience for both parents and children to be on the receiving end of a child protection investigation, however sensitively it is handled, I suggest we should take very seriously the following point made by Neil Guterman:

> The most potent origins of the problem [of child abuse and neglect] stem from ecological factors that are exogenous to the parent-child relationship and that erode parents' control and power, leading to an unfolding pattern toward abusive and/or neglectful parenting . . .
> Protective services . . . interviews only *after* parents have lost control in the parenting process, and it does so in an involuntary and adversarial fashion . . . The adversarial and stigmatizing nature of protective services intervention, although aimed at promoting children's safety, can rather jeopardise parents' feelings of support and confidence during a highly vulnerable time. To the extent that such intervention thus engenders in parents deeper feelings of powerlessness and adds additional ecological challenges, it may even heighten the risk of child maltreatment – precisely the opposite of the stated purpose of the intervention. (Guterman, 2001: 49)

It is important to try and minimize the number of cases which are subjected to the child protection investigation process, if a child's needs can be adequately met by a gentler and less intrusive process. As far as possible, social work 'intervention' should take a form which will be experienced as positive by families, and not as an attack.

The multidisciplinary system

No one profession can claim child protection as its own, and failures in the child protection system are often in part failures of different professional groups to collaborate effectively together. Before going on to look at the multidisciplinary system, it is worth noting that, not only is child protection not the province of a single profession, but that the entire professional child protection system is in reality a small adjunct to the informal and non-professional system that protects the majority of children, most of the time. Most children, after all, look to their parents first for protection, and to neighbours, friends and other members of their families. Many situations that might have come to the attention of child protection agencies are headed off through the intervention of families, neighbours and friends in ways that professionals may never get to hear about, except when they happen in the families and neighbourhoods of the professionals themselves.

Exercise 2.1

The following are some questions about what it might be like to be on the receiving end of a child protection investigation:

- Have there ever been any situations in your own extended family that could possibly have resulted in child protection issues, but were in fact dealt with within the family? (A young mother suffering severe post-natal depression, for example, or parents at the end of their tether because of a marital crisis, or a crisis brought about by external factors such as redundancy.) If you can think of a situation of that kind, consider what kind of professional intervention might have been helpful, and what would have been unhelpful.
- If a teacher at your children's school was concerned about one of your children and decided to inform social services, how would you feel if they did so without consulting you?
- How would you feel if you were to discover, long after the event, that one of your children had been the subject of discussions between their school, social services and your family doctor without you being informed?
- What would your first feelings be if you received a telephone call from a social worker who wanted to interview your child at school without you present?

- What would your feelings have been, when you were a child of, say, 10, if a social worker you had never met before was to come to your school and ask you questions about the way that you were treated by your parents?

Comments on Exercise 2.1

It is important, I suggest, from time to time to ask yourself how you would like to be treated and how you would like your children to be treated if your family became the subject of a child protection investigation, and checking whether your own practice is actually consistent with this.

It is also important to consider how you would react. It is easy to label people as 'awkward', 'unco-operative' or 'anti-authority' when they behave in an angry or difficult or aggressive way during an investigation, but I suggest that professionals would be more careful about applying such labels if they considered how they would react in the same situation. While it isn't possible or desirable always to avoid upsetting people, it is important to think about why people get upset, so that you are able to acknowledge and allow for it.

Although child protection social workers are given a key role in the child protection system, and are the group of professionals who seem to be most commonly held to account when the system fails, child protection is not solely or even mainly the responsibility of social workers. Teachers, for example, pick up the early signs of abuse and neglect far more often than social workers and are the only professional group that has an overview of almost all children. In fact in the great majority of cases social workers have to rely on the expertise of others to provide them with information about children causing concern.

In England and Wales, the framework within which professionals are required to operate is described in the Department of Health's publication *Working Together to Safeguard Children* (Department of Health, 1999). Like the Children Act, this is a document with which child protection workers should be familiar at first hand, rather than relying on second-hand accounts like this one, but the following are some key points.

Local arrangements

The arrangements under which the different agencies work together are not precisely the same from one part of England or Wales to another.

This is because the guidelines allow for – and expect – each area to work out the details of how its multidisciplinary system is going to work. This means that, in addition to *Working Together*, child protection professionals need to be familiar with their local child protection procedures. *Working Together* (pp. 33–7) sets out guidelines as to the form and function of the Area Child Protection Committees, multi-agency bodies which have the job of agreeing and monitoring local inter-agency procedures.

The strategy discussion

Paragraph 5.28 (p. 46) states that 'Whenever there is a reasonable cause to suspect that a child is suffering, or is likely to suffer significant harm, there should be a strategy discussion involving the social services and the police, and other agencies as appropriate (e.g. education and health).' It is a striking feature of the English and Welsh child protection system that it ties social services and the police very closely together at the outset of an investigation.

The purpose of the strategy discussion, which can if necessary take place over the phone, is to share information, decide whether section 47 enquiries should be initiated, or continued if they have already started, plan how the enquiries will be carried out and by whom (including the need for medical treatment), agree what action is needed immediately to protect the child, and determine what information about the meeting will be shared with the family. Information should be shared, the guide says, 'unless such information sharing may place a child at risk of significant harm or jeopardise police investigations into any alleged offence(s)'.

Race and ethnicity

Among the relevant matters to be discussed in the strategy meeting, *Working Together* includes, 'in the light of the race and ethnicity of the child and family, considering how this should be taken into account in enquiries, and establishing whether an interpreter will be needed'.

But how should race and ethnicity be 'taken into account'?

Exercise 2.2

I suggested earlier that you consider how you would like to be treated – and how you would like your children to be treated – if you were on the receiving end of a child protection investigation. What I would like you to do now is consider that question again, but this time imagine that you are a parent in a country where:

- The language spoken by the majority, and by public officials, is different from your own, and you are not able to speak it very well, if at all.
- The dominant culture is different from your own and you are well aware of the fact that this culture disapproves of many things that you regard as normal, and tolerates many things that you regard as wrong.
- You are aware that there is widespread prejudice against your ethnic group, and you have been treated rudely by public officials in the past.
- You are visibly different from the majority population, so you can be immediately identified as not belonging to the majority before you have opened your mouth.

(I appreciate that some readers of this book will not need to imagine these things, but will have experienced some or all of them at first hand.)

What would your fears be about the way the system would treat you and your child, if you heard that you had been reported to the authorities for suspected child abuse, and that the authorities were following it up? What would you hope for, or want from the investigating authorities?

Comments on Exercise 2.2

I don't know, of course, what your fears would be, but I would be fearful that I would not understand what was going on, and that my child would not understand either and would be frightened. I would also fear that the authorities would not understand me, or listen to me properly, or that they would believe the worst of me. I would be concerned that they would be prejudiced against me. I would fear that the situation would be completely out of my control and that I would be prevented from providing reassurance to my child at a time when she really needed it. I would perhaps be frightened of ending up in jail or of having my child removed from me.

The sorts of things that I imagine would help would be:

- If a good interpreter was provided, who could not only translate words for me, but also explain the cultural differences.
- If the public officials carrying out the investigation acknowledged to me and my child that they could see this was difficult for us, and assured me that they would do their best to take the cultural differences into account.

The purpose of this exercise, obviously, was to look at what a child protection investigation would feel like if you were a member of an ethnic minority. It is an important question, but professionals operating in areas where there is only a very small ethnic minority population may be tempted to think that it is not important to them. But this is very mistaken, since it may well be *precisely* in situations where members of ethnic minorities feel themselves to be in a very small minority, that they are most likely to feel vulnerable. And it may be precisely in such situations that, if a professional is a member of the ethnic majority, she will be *most* in danger of being taken by surprise.

Initial child protection conferences

The initial case conference (*Working Together*, paragraphs 5.53–5.74) is the formal inter-agency meeting that is supposed to take place within 15 working days of the strategy discussion. It brings together all the relevant agencies and members of the family concerned. Its purpose is to share information about the child and the care the child is receiving, to look at the level of risk to a child, and to decide *what* action needs to be taken to protect the child, *who* will take that action and with what *goals* in mind. In different areas there are different arrangements as to who should chair the conference, but the guidance lays down that the chair should not be involved in dealing with the case, either directly, or as a line manager.

Paragraphs 5.64–5.70 of *Working Together* set out in detail what the conference should make decisions about. Among these are deciding whether the child's name should be placed on the *child protection register*. If the child *is* registered, the conference also needs to appoint a *key worker* (this is always a social worker), and it needs to set up a *core group* of professionals and members of the family. It also needs to agree timescales for the meetings of the core group, for the completion of the child protection plan (which the conference will have agreed in outline), and for the setting up of a *review case conference.*

In some cases an initial child protection conference may be held before the actual birth of a child.

The child protection register

The register is a list which must be maintained in each social services area, and which is meant to include all the children in that area who are considered to be at risk of significant harm and for whom there is a child protection plan. Children are placed on the register under one or more of the categories of abuse (physical abuse, sexual abuse, emotional abuse and neglect). The register must be accessible to the relevant agencies not only in working hours but out of them, so that, for example, when a child is admitted at eight o'clock at night to an accident and emergency department in a hospital with an injury which could be non-accidental, the staff can check the register. And when children on the register move from one area to another, then they need to be placed on the register in the new area.

Placing children's names on a child protection register tends to have the effect of reducing professional anxieties about a case (see Farmer and Owen, 1995: 85–6). It is therefore important to bear in mind that being on the list does not, in itself, protect children against *anything.* Whether children are on or off the register, the risk of their being maltreated depends entirely on the behaviour of those who actually look after them. What being on the register *does* do is help to ensure first, that a level of inter-agency liaison takes place, and secondly, that existing concerns are flagged up when new situations arise, as in the hospital example I've just given.

Having a child's name on the register is almost inevitably going to be a humiliating and distressing experience for families, and therefore placing a child's name on the register is not something to be done lightly. It is likely that in some instances registration may actually *increase* risk to a child, by increasing the stresses on the family. For these sorts of reasons there has been an emphasis in Britain, since the publication of *Child Protection: Messages from Research* (Department of Health, 1995), on trying to reduce the number of cases dealt with under child protection procedures.

The key worker role

The social worker who is appointed key worker for a child on the register has responsibility for making sure that the outline of the child protection plan agreed in the conference is developed into a detailed inter-agency plan. She is required to complete the 'core assessment' of the child and family, drawing as necessary on the assistance of other agencies. She is also the 'lead worker' for the inter-agency effort, and is supposed to coordinate the efforts of the family members and agencies involved in the child protection plan, making sure that the plan is carried out and that its progress and effectiveness are properly reviewed.

The core group

The first meeting of the core group is supposed to take place within 10 days of the initial conference. The group should then continue to meet regularly in order to coordinate efforts and share information. The members should include the key worker, the family members and those professionals (including foster-parents) who will have direct contact with the child or the family during the implementation of the child protection plan. The first task of the core group is to 'flesh out' the plan agreed at the child protection conference. Paragraphs 5.75–5.89 of the guide cover the role of the core group, the contents of the protection plan and the contents of the *core assessment*.

Core assessment

The core assessment must be completed by the social services department within 42 working days of completing the initial assessment, and should be carried out within the prescribed assessment framework, on the lines laid out in the so-called 'Lilac Book' (Department of Health, 2000a). Even if a child is not placed on the child protection register, social services are required to complete a core assessment of the child – as a child in need – within this timescale, if that is wanted by the parents.

Review child protection conferences

With the same membership as the initial conference (subject, of course, to any changes that have occurred in the interim in the personnel involved in working on the case), a review case conference should be convened within three months of the initial conference, and thereafter at a minimum of every six months while the child's name remains on the register. As with the initial conference, the review conference discusses the risks to the child and reaches a decision on registration, though in this case the decision is whether or not to *de*-register the child. (See paragraphs 5.90–5.95.)

Family group conferences

The idea of family group conferences is discussed approvingly in *Working Together* (on p. 78). It is a model developed in New Zealand where it was intended to draw on the strengths of the strong extended family networks that exist in the Maori and Pacific Island communities, and it has been adopted in some parts of the UK. Basically it is a framework within which the extended family is provided with as much support as possible to come up with their own solutions to child protection problems (or other child care problems). An account of this approach is given by Morris et al. (1998).

The social work role

Within the multiprofessional system that I have just described, there are a number of different roles played by social workers. These include the following:

- Taking child protection referrals from the public and other agencies, and following them up appropriately. This of course includes many referrals which may or may not most appropriately be viewed as child protection cases, so that the task includes determining at what level to respond.
- Carrying out initial investigations on suspected child protection referrals, usually jointly with the police. This includes setting up and participating in strategy discussions.

- In the event of an investigation coming to the conclusion that no further action needs to be taken under child protection procedures, trying to reassure the family and checking whether there is any other help that they need.
- Taking any immediate action necessary to protect the child, which in some circumstances could include going to court for an EPO.
- Requesting an initial child protection conference and providing the conference coordinator with preliminary information and details of those to be invited. In some cases the request for a conference may come from other agencies initially.
- Undertaking an initial assessment and providing a report to the initial child protection conference.
- Informing the family and child about the case conference and the child protection process. Preparing the family and child for the child protection conference.
- In the event of a conference deciding not to put the child's name on the register, following up with the family and discussing whether they need other help.
- In the event of registration, taking on the key worker role, and carrying out the following tasks:
  a   carrying out a core assessment within the prescribed timescale
  b   taking a lead role within the core group in the development of a child protection plan
  c   ensuring that there is good communication between the family, yourself as key worker and the other agencies (and other parts of your own agency who may be involved in the child protection plan, such as family aides, family centres, residential homes and foster-homes) – and ensuring in particular that the child is consulted and informed about what is going on in a way that is consistent with her age and understanding
  d   taking a lead role in the implementation of the care plan. This may include direct work with the child, direct work with the family or a care management role, in which you are involved in recruiting and supervising input from others
  e   preparing reports for review case conferences.
- If any court proceedings are required, initiating them, working with lawyers in the preparation of statements and giving evidence in court.
- If a child is removed from the family home (whether as a result of a court order, or by being accommodated in foster- or residential care on a voluntary basis), ensuring that the necessary visits, reviews and paperwork is completed, and (most importantly) that the child's

needs are met as far as possible, that the child is kept informed about what is happening, and that the child's views and wishes are sought and taken into account.

Working to change things

An outsider, unfamiliar with British social work, might read through the list above and feel that they still didn't know what it is that social workers actually *do*.

'The list is strong on assessment and investigation, planning and coordinating, reviewing and writing reports,' this imaginary outsider might observe, 'but once they have done their assessments, how do social workers actually *change things*?' We would think it an odd description of a doctor's job, after all, if we were told of the procedures doctors use to investigate patients' illnesses, but were told nothing about medicines or surgery.

The reality is that what social workers actually do to make things better is rather less clear-cut than what a surgeon or a physician does. Some would argue that this lack of clarity reflects a weakness of social work in Britain: there is too much emphasis on assessment, the social work equivalent of 'diagnosis', and yet relatively little on 'intervention', the social work equivalent of 'treatment'. Nigel Parton (1994: 30) has written of 'a hole at the centre of the enterprise of social work' and, with Patrick O'Byrne (Parton and O'Byrne, 2000), has proposed a new 'Constructive social work', drawing on ideas from therapists such as Steve O'Shazer and Michael White to provide social work with new tools to help its service users towards solutions to their problems.

The purpose of this book is not to propose a new model of child protection work, however, but to describe and discuss the existing one. So what I will now do is consider the ways in which child protection social workers typically do 'intervene' with families in order to try to reduce the risk of harm to children.

Methods of 'intervention'

Family social work in Britain, and in many other countries, is in many ways a strange hybrid of a job, containing elements of policeman, therapist, negotiator, troubleshooter, forensic psychologist, mediator, administrator, advice worker, legal assistant, spy, civil servant and entrepreneur.

The most extreme intervention that a child protection social worker may be involved in is the removal of a child from a family and the permanent placement of that child elsewhere. This is, of course, the exception rather than the rule, but it is something that in many ways casts a shadow over the other activities of social workers. On the one hand, awareness that this is one of the options in a social worker's tool kit can, naturally enough, make parents and children wary of getting involved with social workers. On the other, the existence of this possibility means that many families who might otherwise refuse to work with social workers at all, may feel that they have no choice but to do so. Even when a social worker has not obtained any kind of court order, she still has considerable power over families because of the possibility of *applying* for such an order. This is something that we should be aware of when we talk about 'working in partnership' with families, or drawing up 'agreements' with them.

The other techniques which social workers, in collaboration with other professionals, commonly use to try and bring about change in child protection cases could, I suggest, be divided into:

1. 'Boundary setting'
2. 'Practical assistance'
3. 'Therapy'

'Boundary setting'

Along with the other professional agencies involved in a child protection case, social workers try and provide a framework for change by agreeing/ setting goals and ground rules with parents – and then monitoring progress while trying to encourage parents to achieve those goals and operate within those ground rules. Goals might include anything from 'excluding adult A from the household', 'providing new bedding for the children', 'finding new means of disciplining the children', 'completing a programme of treatment for drug addiction', 'spending time each day playing with the children' or 'attending an anger management course'. Ground rules might include 'ensuring that the children are never left on their own unsupervised', 'remaining sober when in charge of the children' and so on.

I call this 'boundary setting' because the intervention is based on the idea that the parents have crossed some boundary of acceptable parental behaviour, and the aim of the work is to re-establish that boundary. The goals and rules are, at least partly, imposed rather than negotiated. Sticking to certain agreed rules may be presented as a requirement if a child is not to be removed from the family home, or as a precondition for a child to be *returned* to the home, or as a precondition for a child's name to be removed from the child protection register. But such work is more likely to achieve long-term change if the goals are agreed to be sensible by the parents (or other carers), and if they agree that there is a problem that needs to be addressed.

In 'boundary setting' it is important to be clear about 'bottom-line' positions (for example: 'your child will be removed from you if you do not do X') without presenting the bottom-line simply as a threat or as punishment for failure. It is important, too, not to set goals that are higher than is necessary, or to set families up to fail by asking for the impossible. And it is important to offer support, encouragement, praise and recognition of where service users are coming from. An intervention which simply has the effect of further undermining confidence and self-esteem, as Neil Guterman pointed out in the passage I quoted earlier, is not only ineffective but could have the effect of actually *increasing* the risk to the child.

'Practical assistance'

There are a range of practical ways in which social workers try to help resolve family problems. They may give financial assistance under section 17 of the Children Act, for example to help a family purchase new bedding for a child, or to pay for a playgroup place. They can act as advocates on a family or child's behalf with other agencies, for example by negotiating a house move if the family lives in social housing, or by resolving a problem with the Benefits Agency.

Social workers commonly also arrange for practical assistance with parenting skills to be provided. British social services departments typically employ 'family aides' who may offer this sort of help, and have 'family centres' that families can attend for help with parenting skills. (Family centres are commonly also used for the purposes of 'assessment', which presents them, like social workers, with a difficult combination of tasks.) In some circumstances, social workers may arrange respite care for children as a service for families. Social workers may also recruit additional help by referring on to other agencies, or enlisting the support of other agencies who are already involved in the care planning process, or, on occasion, by 'buying in' services, such as input from a therapist. It may be that some of the services that social workers arrange in these ways may be things that the family are *required* to cooperate with as part of a child protection plan. Attendance at a drug rehabilitation unit, or an anger management programme, are typical examples of this.

While practical support can be exactly what is required, it is important not to overdo it. When the professionals around a family become anxious, they may be tempted to recruit ever greater 'help' for the family, and subject them to more and more monitoring, until their time is dominated by a bewildering array of professional visitors and appointments. An invasion of this kind is undermining by its sheer volume, but it is also likely to include a confused variety of different approaches that have the effect of cancelling each other out.

'Therapy'

Much of the work involved in what I have called 'boundary setting' could arguably be seen as a form of 'therapy', in so far as it is aimed at changing the functioning of families. Social workers engaged in it may draw on ideas from a variety of sources that overlap with those employed by therapists, such as cognitive-behavioural approaches, psychodynamic approaches, approaches drawing on family systems theory or humanistic psychology (in other words, the range of approaches that are presented in social work textbooks such as Payne, 1997).

We should not lose sight of the fact that the work of a child protection social worker is *very* different from that done by a professional therapist or counsellor. A professional therapist sees clients for the sole purpose of engaging in a therapeutic conversation in a context where this is understood by all parties to be the case. Conversely, a child protection social worker who tries to work in a 'therapeutic' way has to juggle this role with many others. Probably many social workers would agree with the comment made by one social worker interviewed in Andrew Pithouse's study of a social work team, that 'We don't as a rule have time for therapeutic work, we may try to connect clients to that, but we don't do it' (Pithouse, 1998: 87).

Nor is lack of time the only problem, for if *social workers* find it difficult to combine a therapeutic role with their other tasks, we should not forget that social work *service users* may well have reservations about doing 'therapy' with a professional who also provides reports to case conferences and to courts, or is their access point to other services.

Whatever the difficulties entailed in doing 'therapy', the fact is that simply setting boundaries and monitoring adherence is, on its own, a pretty blunt instrument. Sometimes it works very well, but we cannot expect it to bring about change in many cases where problems are deep-rooted and long lasting (abuse in some families is a pattern that has persisted literally for generations). We should also bear in mind that research on the effects of abuse tends to show that the long-term harm is done not so much by particular incidents, but by the *kind of relationship* in which abuse takes place (this will be discussed more fully in Chapter 6), so that merely persuading the family to stop one particular kind of behaviour may not result in any major change in the child's experience.

There is also a real danger that, in the absence of 'therapeutic' alternatives, child protection workers will resort more and more to the courts as a means of stopping the abuse of children, as would seem to have been the trend in Britain in recent years (see Beckett, 2001a). Removal of children into care creates many new problems and can cause much new suffering – and it does not in any case take away the need for skilled 'therapeutic' work, since many children do not settle in the care system. (Children who have experienced rejection, for instance, will often act in ways that invite further rejection and so result in placement breakdown.) It would be tragic if children were being removed into care in situations where skilled work could have allowed them to live safely within their own families. So, as Margaret Lynch (1992: 19) observes, 'assessment has got to lead somewhere other than the courtroom'.

'Therapeutic' work

I would suggest that the following principles need to be borne in mind by the child protection social worker in relation to the 'therapeutic' aspects of the social work task.

Promoting change

The purpose of any intervention is to bring about change, and specifically (a), to reduce the likelihood of a child being subject to maltreatment and/or (b), to assist recovery from the experience of maltreatment. Every interaction between the social worker and the service user should be about facilitating change – and should therefore be, in a very broad sense, 'therapeutic'. The social worker therefore needs to consider what it is she is tying to achieve in each interaction, and how she is proposing to achieve it. Some questions that she might ask are:

- What messages am I trying to give?
- What messages do I wish to avoid giving?
- How do I communicate in a way that will allow me to be clear and honest about boundaries and the consequences of crossing them, but yet at the same time encourage, rather than discourage, the service user to believe in her own capacity for change?

How to do this is not something that can easily be taught – and is certainly not something that is easily taught in a book – since everyone has to find his or her own way of doing it: it is an art rather than a science. (Research comparing different therapeutic approaches has tended to conclude that 'the client's experience . . . is much more related to the personal qualities of the therapist than to the techniques he or she employs', Howe, 1993: 11.) I hope, though, that the examples given in this book will provide opportunities for readers to think about their own approaches.

Clarity

It is important for a social worker to be clear about what *kind* of conversation she is having at any given moment when she is with service users, and to clearly differentiate between conversations whose primary purpose is 'therapeutic' and those which are related to practical arrangements. Thus, for example, a social worker might say, 'I thought that we could start by talking about the transport arrangements for the family centre and any other practical problems you are having with the care plan, and then spend the rest of the session talking about the work you have been doing yourselves and how you feel you are doing with it.' When the part of the conversation dealing with the practical arrange-ments is completed, she can then clearly signal that the session is now moving into a different area. Or she might prefer to have separate sessions for different kinds of business. Again, each social worker has to find her own way of doing this, but if different aspects of the role are not in some way clearly delineated, there is a danger of real confusion on all sides about the purpose of a meeting, and about what the social worker's role really is.

Limits to confidentiality

A child protection social worker, like other professional participants in the child protection system as it is currently constituted, cannot give a guarantee of confidentiality. A social worker cannot tell a child or parent that what he says will go no further, because the social worker is obliged to record the content of her discussions, and may be obliged to share that content much more widely too, for example in case conference reports or court reports, or in discussions with other professionals. This is very different from, say, a therapist in private practice, and it inevitably constrains what service users will be prepared to share with social workers. However, it is the reality, and it is important to be completely honest about it. Much more trust is lost by allowing a client to believe that something can be shared in confidence, and then subsequently have to share it with others, than is lost by being honest at the outset about what information is recorded and the circumstances under which information will be shared, and with whom. This helps to establish trust of a limited but realistic kind.

Limitations of the social work role

There is a debate to be had about the compatibility of the various roles that a modern child protection social worker attempts to juggle, but there is no doubt that there are areas of 'therapeutic' work that a child protection social worker cannot realistically undertake because of lack of specialist skills and experience, and/or lack of time. Examples might be:

- Work with perpetrators of sexual abuse.
- Work with children who have serious difficulties in forming attachments.
- Work with children and their families where there are extreme behavioural problems.
- Work on addictions (drugs, alcohol, gambling, etc.) that are affecting family functioning.

It is also often impracticable – and even unethical – for a social worker to attempt 'therapy' with a family when the social worker is also in a position of conflict with that family, through the child protection process or the courts. Families may agree to work with social workers under such circumstances, but agreement may be based not so much on a genuine wish to work with the social worker, as on the perception that the social worker is in a powerful position and is best mollified.

It has sometimes struck me that, in such circumstances, a social worker should really begin each session with the warning: 'You have the right to remain silent, but anything you say will be taken down and may be used in evidence against you.' And this is not a very promising basis for therapeutic work.

In this chapter I have looked at the framework within which a child protection social worker operates and at the elements of the social worker's task. Discussion has been focused specifically on social work in the legal and administrative framework that exists, at the beginning of the twenty-first century, in England and Wales. However, this has much in common with child protection social work elsewhere in the English-speaking world. Topics covered included:

- the legal framework provided in England and Wales by the 1989 Children Act
- the multidisciplinary system in England and Wales, as prescribed by the *Working Together* guidance
- the diverse tasks undertaken by social workers within this system
- the nature of social work intervention
- 'therapeutic' work and its relationship with the social work role.

In the next chapter I will consider questions, already touched upon in this chapter, about what it means from a personal point of view to be a child protection social worker.

Doing the Job 3

Child protection work is uniquely difficult because it involves operating at a point where two of the most strongly held beliefs in our
society meet and clash: the belief that children should be protected
against harm, and the belief that outsiders should not intrude into
personal relationships. A child protection social worker is at the heart of
what has been 'a major tension for the liberal state since the late
nineteenth century: how can we devise a *legal* basis for the power to
intervene into the family which does not convert *all* families into clients
of the state?' (Parton, 1991: 2).

Because of this tension, child protection workers often feel that,
whatever they do, they will be criticized. They can be criticized for
failing to intervene to protect a child (as in the Jasmine Beckford case,
for example (London Borough of Brent, 1985)). But they are also
frequently characterized as 'interfering do-gooders' and castigated for
removing children from their families (perhaps most famously in
England in the 'Cleveland crisis' (Butler-Sloss, 1987)). Child protection
social workers can expect some uncomfortable reactions in a social
context when asked what they do for a living. Even social workers from
other specialisms may at times seem to want to distance themselves from
the 'dirty work' that is involved in child protection.

What is more, the clashing values I have just described - the belief that
children should be protected against harm and the belief that outsiders

should not intrude into personal relationships - do not just exist as something to be dealt with *out there*. They exist also within each social worker as an individual. One social worker involved in a case where the removal of a baby at birth was being considered, commented that it felt like going 'against the laws of nature' (Corner, 1997: 25). Child protection work can feel like transgressing against deeply embedded taboos. It can also touch very deep personal emotions, linked to social workers' own life experiences. Corner goes on to observe that contemplating removing a child at birth was particularly difficult for the professionals who were mothers.

It is this complex interaction between the child protection worker as a human being, and the child protection worker as a professional, that is the subject of this chapter.

Personal feelings and professional practice

It is commonly acknowledged that child protection social workers can feel that they will be criticized whatever they do. It is perhaps less often recognized that they may often find themselves in positions where any course of action *feels* wrong. It does indeed feel 'like going against the laws of nature' to remove a baby from a mother, but to leave a baby at risk of violence feels equally contrary to our basic sense of what is right and natural. It can be deeply uncomfortable to visit a family you have never met before and insist on answers to very personal questions about the way they relate together. It can feel equally uncomfortable to wake up in the night and wonder if you missed some warning sign, and if a child may be badly hurt as a result.

The best way to steer a way through all this will be different for each individual, depending on temperament and personal experience. Indeed, each individual will have different areas of difficulty and different trigger points depending on her own history. Every social worker has had different experiences of childhood and (if a parent) of parenthood. Some have experienced abuse at the hands of parents or other adults. All will have had at least some childhood experience of being let down by adults - and all who are parents will have had at least some experience of having been less good a parent than they would like. Some will have personal experience of poverty, or single parenthood, and will perhaps more easily identify with others in the same position. Some will have personal experience of drug abuse, or alcoholism, or domestic violence, or mental illness, or disability, or racism. Men will have had different experiences to women.

It is extremely important for social workers to reflect on their own personal style, their strengths and weaknesses, their priorities, and how these relate to their own experience. Social workers should be aware, for instance, of which kinds of parental behaviour they find most unforgivable and which kinds they find easiest to understand, or what kinds of situations arouse in them in particular the desire to 'rescue', and to have some sense of why they feel as they do. We cannot necessarily change our feelings, but professional priorities should not automatically be based on them.

It is also important for child protection social workers to be aware of what aspects of the work they find the most painful, uncomfortable or frightening. It is normal for human beings to try and avoid things that they find painful – that, after all, is the *function* of pain – but this very natural impulse can be very dangerous in child protection work, because it can make child protection professionals avoid seeing things that are important, or avoid doing things that need doing. Most social workers in my experience will admit to having once or twice knocked very quickly on the door of a house and then hurried back to their office to record 'Visited. No answer.' In the Jasmine Beckford case, a social worker visited Jasmine's family several times when Jasmine was present and still managed to avoid noticing that Jasmine had several broken bones (London Borough of Brent, 1985). Perhaps she could not bear to let herself see it?

Exercise 3.1

Have a look at the statements below. They represent various stances in relation to child protection work.

For each statement consider (a), what might be a *strength* of a social worker taking the stance which it represents, and (b), what might be a weakness. (For example, in the case of the first statement you might think that a *strength* of a social worker taking this stance would be that she would work hard to make service users feel listened to and involved. A weakness might be that she might be reluctant to take any step which might result in an angry and hostile response, even if this was necessary for the safety of the child.)

Notice also which statements seem closest to your own viewpoint.

- I do not like to be seen as the 'bad guy' and I want to work *with* people not against them.
- I am repulsed and appalled by the idea of adults abusing children.
- I was abused myself as a child; I know how awful it is and I just want to stop any other child going through what I went through.
- I am a parent and can very easily understand why some people lose their temper with their children and go over the top.
- I think most children engage in sexual play. I know I did. It doesn't mean they have been abused.
- I came into social work to help and empower people, not to do police work.
- I was sometimes beaten as a child, but I don't think it did me any harm.
- I identify very strongly with the powerless position of a child in an abusive family.
- I don't feel it is my job to order people around or to tell other people how they should live their lives.
- I think that heavy-handed intervention can often increase the risk of abuse.
- I feel strongly that middle-class values should not be imposed on poor working-class families.
- I think child abuse, like many other 'social problems' is often the result of social injustice: the abusing parents are often as much victims as children.
- I can understand why a parent might hit a child, but sexual abuse I will never understand.
- I think different cultures have different ways of disciplining children, and we should be very wary about defining abuse in white European terms when dealing with black or Asian families.
- I am there to protect children, not to help parents.
- I think the child protection system is there to protect agencies, not to protect children. I am therefore very sceptical about the system.

Comments on Exercise 3.1

Good child protection work does involve striking a balance. Any of these stances has its strengths, but can be dangerous if not balanced by other considerations.

For example: if you can identify with abused children and their powerless position, this may help you to be clear about your priorities and help you to avoid being deflected by the needs of carers and others. But, even though protecting children is the first priority in child protection, there are dangers in overidentifying yourself with the child. The child is not you and has her own needs and loyalties (including perhaps to the abuser), which you will not necessarily understand from your own experience. If you try to form an alliance with the child against the carers, this can have effects within the family which may make things worse for the child rather than better.

Likewise, if you can identify with the feelings that lead parents to abuse children, then this may help you to establish a rapport with the parents and to work constructively with them to improve things for the child. But you need to be careful not to enter into a 'cosy' or collusive relationship with the parents that makes you overlook or minimize the harm they are doing to the child.

Again, it is true that many children engage in sexual play and it would clearly be a pity to overreact to this and so make the children feel they have done something terribly abnormal or wrong. But equally, oversexualized behaviour is a common indicator of sexual abuse, so you need to consider any sexual behaviour by children carefully, and not be too quick to dismiss it as 'normal childhood exploration'.

You will doubtless have been able to come up with similar 'pros' and 'cons' for the other statements.

I suggest you take particular note of those statements with which you identified personally, and give some thought to what that tells you about possible strengths and weaknesses in your own practice. Awareness of possible strengths and weaknesses allows you to avoid pitfalls, and to seek help when you are entering an area of work that is difficult for you.

The list of statements in Exercise 3.1 highlighted a number of themes or dilemmas that are commonly entailed in child protection work, which I might summarize as follows:

- Avoiding over- and underreaction. Being clear about what is seriously abusive and what is not, in the context of cultural differences.
- Working in partnership with parents, and avoiding being oppressive, while keeping a focus on the child and giving priority to the child's needs.
- Working as part of a bureaucratic system.

The first point I will return to in the next chapter. The others I will consider now.

Working in partnership

In Britain government guidance on child protection, and on family social work generally, gives considerable weight to the idea of 'working in partnership' (see, for instance, pp. 75–7 in *Working Together* (Department of Health, 1999)). People tend to become social workers because they like the idea of helping other people and the idea of working in partnership sits very comfortably with this. However, although child protection work *is* of course intended to help other people – namely children – it is not always experienced as helpful by parents and carers who are suspected of neglect or abuse, or even necessarily by children themselves. Most parents will probably not find it hard to imagine just how frightening it would be to be visited by a social worker or a police officer and accused of mistreating their children. Indeed, most of us would surely find it threatening and intrusive to be questioned in detail about a very personal aspect of our lives by a powerful official who made it clear that she did not necessarily believe what we were telling her. If the allegations against us were not true, we would feel very angry, and also scared that we might not be believed. If the allegations were true, we might still feel that our actions were being judged out of context, or by unrealistic criteria – or that our own perspective was being disregarded.

Child protection work, then, often involves working in conflict with adults. It often involves confrontation. And it often involves dealing with anger and hostility, which may be overt, or may be hidden, because people do not always show their feelings when dealing with people they perceive to be powerful and feel they must placate. All of this is uncomfortable for most social workers and there are various defences that we commonly put into place to try and deal with it. These defences, if not recognized can lead to bad, and perhaps dangerous practice:

1. *Over-placatory or evasive practice.*
   In a desire to placate the angry and distressed carer, or to avoid difficult confrontations, a worker may:
   - avoid asking difficult questions, or challenging inconsistencies and evasions
   - give assurances that cannot realistically be given (for example, saying, 'this will definitely not result in your child being taken into care' when in fact that is a possibility)
   - cross professional boundaries inappropriately in a desire to establish her credentials as 'caring' or 'human' (for example, by discussing her own personal problems)

- avoid meeting particularly hostile family members, and thereby miss out on part of the picture
- go into 'denial' about what she has observed (for example, in giving an account of the case to her supervisor, she may avoid giving the full story, or try to put a favourable gloss on it – much as the parent may have done to her)
- avoid the child who is the subject of concern, and form a kind of alliance with the parents.

2. *Punitive practice*

Another way of dealing with discomfort at distressing and confrontational situations is going to the opposite extreme of the overplacatory stance, and, for instance:

- adopting a cold, 'official' persona
- making threats
- dealing with parents as if they had forfeited the right to actually be treated as parents, or to have an opinion as to what is right and best for their own children.

3. *Hiding behind the system*

There are also ways in which a social worker may 'hide behind' procedures or behind the organization in which she works. While it is perfectly appropriate – and indeed very important – for any professional to acknowledge that she is part of an organization and that the organization places certain requirements upon her, 'hiding behind the system' involves the social worker effectively subverting that system in order to ward off hostility:

- 'Of course, if it was down to me I wouldn't make you go through this.'
- 'I don't want to call a child protection conference, but my boss says I've got to.'
- 'I know these are a lot of stupid questions, but I'm afraid we've got to fill in this form for the file.'

Such evasions are very human and understandable, but they are potentially dangerous, resulting first in seriously skewed perspectives, and secondly in ineffective and dishonest working relationships. It is therefore important for practitioners to be alert to these patterns. 'Am I doing this for the right reasons, or am I doing this so as to avoid doing something difficult?' is, for instance, a good question for social workers to ask themselves. Or 'Is there something else I would be doing now if I did not find it so scary?'.

But it is also important to remember that feeling frightened is perfectly normal and legitimate, and that it is also legitimate to ask for help. If a particular parent is very intimidating, for instance, it is reasonable and sensible to ask for a colleague to do a joint visit.

Focusing on the Child

It is very easy for a social worker to become engrossed in the complexities of her working relationship with parents (or foster-parents or other agencies) to the point where the child's needs end up being a secondary concern. This can happen for a number of reasons. For one thing, as the social worker is an adult, she may well find it easier to identify with adult carers and their needs than with children, particularly if she finds the problems of the adults interesting in some way (perhaps because they resonate with her own experience). If adults are very hostile and intimidating, then the social worker may put all her energies into coping with this, whether by trying to placate them, or trying to overpower them in the sorts of ways described above, and this may leave little mental space for thinking about the child. Alternatively, some parents may be grateful to be helped and may be extremely rewarding to work with. And some children may be difficult, resistant and unrewarding.

It is also possible to become so preoccupied with the logistics of the case, or become so preoccupied with the issues that the case raises, that you forget that the child is not just a 'case' or a 'cause', but a human individual – a danger well-described in the inquiry report on the Cleveland affair:

> There is a danger that in looking to the welfare of the children believed to be the victims of sexual abuse the children themselves may be overlooked. The child is a person and not an object of concern. (Butler-Sloss, 1987: 245)

In many cases it is perfectly appropriate for a social worker to do most of her work with the parents or carers, rather than directly with a child. Indeed there are times when a social worker can do *too much* direct work with a child for reasons to do with her own needs rather than those of the child. It is not helpful to a child, for instance, if a social worker effectively undermines the parents by giving rewarding attention to the child in ways that the parents cannot compete with. But if it is the case that the social worker's plan does not involve much contact with the child, then she needs to find ways of checking that what she is doing is still focused on the child's needs, and has not become deflected by her own needs, the needs of the parents, or the needs of others.

Whatever the protection plan, it is important for the social worker to ensure that she hears the child's own view of things, and makes sure that the child is kept informed of what is going on in a way that is appropriate to her age. This involves having some competence in and confidence about working with children.

Most of the basic principles involved in working with children are, of course, the same as those involved in working with adults but there are particular issues involved in working with children, which I will now briefly summarize.

Developmental issues

Typically adults make one of two incorrect assumptions about children's understanding of the world. On the one hand adults sometimes act as if children think and understand just like they do, whereas in fact there are concepts that children simply cannot grasp – and children have ways of thinking that adults may have forgotten about. Social workers will encounter parents, for example, who assume that their children are perfectly capable of understanding the intricacies of their love-life, or parents who assume that a small child is just as capable as they are of realising that an 18-rated horror video is fiction, not fact. Yet on the other hand adults – perhaps even the *same* adults at different times – often behave as if children don't think at all about the world around them. A social worker expressing some discomfort about discussing an adult matter with a child present, will often get the response: 'Oh don't worry about him, he doesn't understand all this!'

Adults often seem to move between these assumptions according to what is convenient for them at the time. One day a child is expected to understand adult matters perfectly well, the next day the child is expected to allow adult matters to pass over her head and to be untouched by them. But in fact, while children do think *just as much* as adults, they don't think *in the same way*. In particular, small children have a very different understanding of time and space from adults ('next week' means very little to a four-year-old, for example), and very different ideas about cause and effect.

So, to communicate properly and respectfully with children, it is necessary to take into account their level of understanding. This is not a matter of intelligence – it is important not to make the mistaken assumption that a bright articulate child can think like an adult, just because she is intelligent – and it is not just a matter of information. There is some information which a child simply will not be able to grasp as an adult can.

In general children think in more concrete terms than adults, which is one reason why it it is often useful to use concrete things such as toys, drawings, books and puppets as an aid to understanding, particularly with younger children. Such tools also make the process less threatening because they allow the child to explore their situation as if it was happening to a third person.

Power issues

To a six-year-old child a typical grown-up looks as big as a twelve foot, twenty stone giant would look to an adult. All children are used to deferring to adults, being told what to do by adults, and being told off by adults. Smaller children are used to being picked up and carried from place to place by adults. They are dependent on adults to meet their most basic needs, for food, for clothing, for comfort, and even just to open doors and get them from A to B. Adults often forget just how powerful they are in relation to children, but an important part of effective work with children involves finding ways of reducing the discomfort arising from the power imbalance. Getting physically down to the child's level is one simple example.

Children in abusive situations are, of course, also aware of the potential for adults to misuse their power. They may have learnt – or been explicitly taught – not to speak their own minds but rather to try and guess what adults want them to say. They may have learnt that it is unwise to say anything at all. On the other hand, children in neglectful situations may also have a lot of experience of adults failing to use their power appropriately. An example of this might be a four-year-old who is allowed to wander round the streets on her own and to cross busy roads, or is allowed to watch 18-rated sex and horror videos if she chooses. Such children may see any exercise of authority by adults as threatening or intrusive.

Children who have been abused in an extreme, systematic way by adults may need specific help in recognising that one particular adult – the abuser – is not in fact all-powerful and that other adults, be they other family members or professionals, are powerful enough to protect them. But it is important to bear in mind that most children, even children in families where there is some abuse, do look to their parents for protection, and therefore need to see their parents as powerful. For this reason professional interventions should not humiliate and undermine the parents unnecessarily in the eyes of their children, or indeed in their own eyes, and do not put children in a position where they are made to feel they are betraying someone whom they care about.

Finally, it is important to remember that all the other power issues that apply in all areas of social work (including issues to do with ethnicity, class, gender and disability) also apply equally to work with children, over and above the adult–child power issues that I have been discussing. A child may see a social worker as a frightening or threatening figure not only because you are an adult, or because you seem to be a threat to her relationship with her parents, but because you are a member of a group that the child sees as alien or perhaps hostile. Consider, for example, the case of a white social worker dealing with a Bangladeshi child who has had very little contact with anyone outside her own Bangladeshi Muslim community . . . or a male social worker investigating a case of suspected sexual abuse to a girl whose experience of men is almost entirely confined to violent and abusive ones.

Adult inhibitions

Something that often gets in the way of professionals consulting children is that many adults are quite shy of children, or feel foolish trying to get down to a child's level. Such feelings may be difficult for a childcare professional to own up to, but I believe they exist and that they can lead to professionals failing to adequately consult children.

It is not always the social worker who is best placed to talk to a child. A social worker's task is to make sure that the work gets done – not necessarily always to do it herself – and there may be others with an easier, closer relationship with the child who can do it better. However, it is important not to use this as a rationale for always avoiding working directly with children.

Perhaps one of the dangers of writing about 'direct work' with children as a specific skill is that it can make some professionals unnecessarily fearful that they do not possess those skills. I would suggest, therefore, that we should be careful not to create a mystique about working with children. We have all been children and so we know what it is like to be a child. If you ask children what they like from adults, they will say things like:

- Speaking to me, rather than over my head to an adult.
- Making sure that I understand.
- Not using long words that I don't understand, but not being patronizing either.
- Taking my viewpoint seriously.
- Explaining things and not trying to conceal things from me.
- Giving me time and realizing that I may not want to talk when you want to talk.

Respecting family relationships

Being respectful of the position of parents is not incompatible with making the child's needs paramount. In fact, to fail to respect the importance of parents and family to a child or to acknowledge their role would, in the great majority of cases, be to ignore one of a child's most basic needs.

What can be forgotten by child protection professionals is that most parents, including those who are sometimes abusive, see themselves as the primary protectors of their children against external threats. So parents who are resistant to intervention by child protection agencies may in fact be trying to protect their children. If, for instance, parents show some reluctance to a social worker interviewing their child, this does not necessarily indicate that they have something to hide, or that they are reluctant to let the child have her say. Most parents would be hesitant about letting their children be interviewed about personal matters by a complete stranger, and there are perfectly good reasons for this, such as concern about the worry it will cause the child, or doubts that the stranger will handle it properly, or distrust of the stranger's motives.

Even parents who have abused or mistreated their children have a relationship with them which is deeper and longer-lasting than the relationship between the social worker and the child. Although there are some very cold and rejecting families, in most cases the love and concern that parents – even abusive parents – feel for their children is something of an altogether different order than the professional concern felt by a social worker or other professional, however committed and caring.

Social workers should therefore be cautious about talking to parents about what is in the best interests of their own children. The child protection social worker is intruding, perhaps necessarily, but still intruding, into the intimate relationships of others.

It is sometimes tempting, when a child is being treated badly within his family, for a social worker to view her role as one of 'rescuing' the child. Clearly there *are* circumstances in which it is right to remove a child from his family, but even in these situations, the child's family of origin is important to him, a part of his identity, and not something that can be erased or swept aside.

In most cases children are not removed from their families, and in these circumstances, for a social worker to simply form an alliance with a child against the rest of the family is likely to isolate that child and create more problems for him. To make things better for a child in a family requires helping the whole family change the way it operates. Although social workers cannot necessarily be family therapists, I suggest that they should have some understanding of the idea of families as systems. (See, for example, Franklin and Jordan, 1999. I gave a brief summary of this idea in Beckett, 2002a: 154–72.)

Exercise 3.2

Johnston Williams, aged 11, is noticed by his PE teacher at school to have several linear bruises across his back, and in some places actual broken skin. When questioned about it he eventually says that he was beaten by his father with a belt in the course of a row.

His parents do not deny that his father beat him. They say that Johnston's behaviour is impossible. He is disobedient. He stays out late and defies any attempt to 'gate' him as a punishment. He steals and tells lies. Johnston is the fourth in a family of five. His three older sisters and one younger brother are described by his parents as no problem at all, but, according to the entire family, Johnston's behaviour has been so difficult and distressing for Mrs Williams, that her health, never very good, has suffered and she has 'been close to a breakdown'. She has been put on antidepressants by her doctor, after admitting to suicidal thoughts.

Mr Williams is a businessman building up his own company: a travel agency. He normally works very long hours, is away several nights a week and often weekends. Because of Johnston's behaviour and Mrs Williams's health, he has been obliged to cut his working hours in order 'to keep the family going'.

'This is a hardworking family,' says Mr Williams, 'trying to do the best we can, and this selfish little boy is ruining things for everyone. I know I shouldn't have beat him but I came in to find my wife in floods of tears because Johnston had just had a tantrum and smashed a fruit bowl that was given to us as a wedding present. It was the last straw.'

Mr and Mrs Williams are both the children of African-Caribbean immigrants and Mr Williams adds that, for his parents' generation, a 'good beating' was considered the best way of dealing with naughtiness. 'Perhaps that was where we went wrong with Johnston,' he says, 'not being strict enough. We've tried everything else and he just laughs at us.'

Asked why he smashed the bowl and why he is behaving in ways that the rest of the family find so difficult, Johnston shrugs and says he doesn't know.

As a social worker looking into this case, how would you begin to approach this?

Comments on Exercise 3.2

Beating a child so hard as to produce bruising and break the skin is not a form of discipline that is acceptable in Britain or elsewhere. However I think that in this case, you would not get very far in improving life for Johnston if you were to focus too narrowly on this particular incident or to allow yourself to get too side-tracked, for example, into debates about whether or not this was acceptable in African-Caribbean culture. It seems to me that you would only be able to begin to address this situation by looking at what is going on in the whole family.

Mr Williams sees the beating as a desperate reaction to the problem of Johnston's behaviour. But why was Johnston behaving like that? What was the pay-off for him in making himself so unpopular with the rest of the family? Two other family issues are visible in the information we already have. First, Mr Williams has been in the habit of being absent a great deal of the time. Second, Mrs Williams suffers from poor health. (Johnston's behaviour is said to have caused her to have a 'near breakdown', but in fact her health problems pre-date the current crisis.)

One effect of Johnston's behaviour has been to bring his father home more. A possible pay-off for Johnston in behaving badly, therefore, is in achieving this. If Johnston was worried about his mother's mental health, or whether she was going to commit suicide, or perhaps the survival of his parents' marriage, the pay-off for him in terms of reduced anxiety might be considerable. There might also be a considerable pay-off for other members of the family – perhaps all of them – in treating Johnston as 'the problem', and perpetuating his behaviour, if this allowed them to avoid looking at other, more disturbing possibilities.

And there will be other, as yet invisible, dynamics at work in the family. Suppose, for instance, that Mr Williams, known to his wife but unknown to the rest of the family, had been having a long-standing affair with another woman, and that Johnston had somehow found out about it . . .

A single incident, directed at a single child, is usually the tip of an iceberg.

Bureaucracy

Child protection social work takes place within a tight procedural framework and under much external scrutiny. The advantage of this is that it provides checks and balances on individual practice, and sets some minimum standards.

A disadvantage is that meeting the needs of the system – completing records, filling in the prescribed forms, compiling the prescribed reports – takes up a significant proportion of a social worker's time, and takes time away from direct work with service users. Another disadvantage is that the system places many limits to the social worker's autonomy. This means that social workers may at times have to work in ways that they do not necessarily agree with. Sometimes it can feel as if a child protection agency's priorities are as much about protecting the agency itself as about protecting children, and there are times when the relative inflexibility of the bureaucratic system can seem oppressive, even abusive, in itself. Sometimes the need to do things 'by the book' may have the effect of inhibiting professionals from using their own judgement, even their own common sense. So part of the challenge for a child protection social worker is to find her own way of operating as part of this system, without sacrificing her judgement, her own values and her common sense.

There are times when it is just not practicable to adhere to an agency's procedures. There may simply not be enough hours in the day. In such cases it is important to be clear with agency managers that this is the case, and why. If this is not done not only do social workers make themselves vulnerable to disciplinary action, but the agency begins to function in a dangerous way because no one knows what is really going on. There will also be times when following the procedures as laid down may be counterproductive. But again, it is important that a decision to set them aside is collectively taken.

Safe, balanced practice requires that child protection workers do not attempt to work in isolation. And this applies not only to individuals but to agencies, which also need to avoid trying to work in isolation or assuming that their particular perspective is the 'right' one. The failure of agencies to communicate with each other (or of different parts of the same agency to do so) has been a frequent factor when serious abuse has failed to be picked up.

Inter-agency systems, like individual agencies, will not work if their individual participants act in isolation, but they will not work either if their participants operate like cogs in a machine, without using their own judgement or initiative, or without standing up for their own views. One point that is sometimes forgotten is that arrangements such as case conferences, core group meetings and so on, are means to an end, not ends in themselves. They will only help to protect children if effective, protective action flows from them. Calling a meeting, transferring a case to another agency, placing a child's name on a register, or seeking the involvement of yet another professional can all seem attractive propositions when a case is difficult – and they feel like *doing something*. But they can, in fact, be substitutes for real action, or a way of deferring decisions, and can therefore in themselves become dangerous. The only actions that will protect children are those which result in some actual positive change in the child's environment.

This point is well made by Sheryl Burton:

> When procedures become the primary focus of concern, a dangerous and false sense of security can develop. Professionals then have a tendency to invest faith in the formal processes, as if these structures, and not the work done with and by families and communities, actually decrease risk. (Burton, 1997: 6)

The worker's own needs

Child protection is a difficult and distressing area to work in. Confronted with tragic tales of abuse, neglect and misery, it is quite easy for a social worker to feel that her own needs are unimportant compared with those of the children with whom she works, and to end up working excessive hours or neglecting her own private life. But of course social workers and other professionals need to be given support, and to look after themselves – not only for their own benefit but for the benefit of the children and families with whom they work. It is worth remembering that no one would want to be operated on by a doctor who was not thinking straight because of exhaustion (though I fear that it often happens), or their teeth drilled by a dentist who could not keep his eyes open. By the same token, a professional who is stressed and exhausted is not likely to be of much help in resolving the intricacies of family relationships.

Child protection social workers need to be assertive in demanding a reasonable workload. They also need proper professional supervision if they are to disentangle personal feelings from professional judgement. This means establishing a clear understanding with their supervisors about what supervision is to consist of, and to be clear about what each party can expect from the other. Supervision must be an opportunity to share doubts, fears and emotional reactions, as well as to discuss the practical nuts and bolts. I believe that *any* social worker, however experienced, who does not regularly check out her own thinking with someone else is likely to make serious mistakes.

In this chapter, I have looked at some of the ways in which doing the job of a child protection social worker is especially challenging, and at the ways that personal and professional issues can interact. I have looked at:

- the ways in which personal experience affects how social workers approach their job, the things that they notice and the things they fail to notice
- the idea of 'working in partnership' and how it fits in with an area of work where professionals and service users are often in conflict
- the difficulties involved in staying focused on the child
- the importance of family relationships, and of taking family relationships seriously
- the issues involved in working as part of a bureaucratic system
- the fact that professionals have their own needs which must be met if they are to offer the best service.

In the next chapter I will move on to the second part of this book, which considers the nature of child abuse.

Part II

The Nature and Consequences
of Child Maltreatment

Recognizing Child Abuse and Neglect   4

Physical abuse •
Sexual abuse •
Emotional abuse and neglect •
Indirect abuse •

Introduction

This is the first of three chapters that will look at the nature of abuse and neglect. In this chapter I will discuss definitions of the different forms of child abuse and neglect, and at the signs which suggest that abuse is going on. The next chapter, Chapter 5, will consider particularly the case of disabled children, and then Chapter 6 will look at the consequences for children of abuse and neglect – the harm that it does.

This chapter will be organized under the headings of 'physical abuse', 'sexual abuse' and 'emotional abuse and neglect', but it is important to be aware that the conventional separation of abuse into 'physical', 'sexual', 'emotional' and 'neglect' is often quite difficult in practice, since different kinds of maltreatment often coexist, and the boundaries between one and another are often blurred. The chapter will conclude by drawing attention to 'indirect abuse', the exposure of children to violence between *adults* in a family.

When we are trying to determine whether abuse has taken place – or to assess the *severity* of abuse that has taken place – we can't expect to rely simply on visible physical symptoms. First of all there are many injuries that may be symptomatic of abuse, but may also have a non-abusive explanation. Secondly, many forms of abuse do not result in any physical symptoms at all. And thirdly, even if we have established that an injury does have a non-accidental explanation, we still need to understand the *social context* in order to get a measure of the nature and the severity of the abuse, and to decide whether it is helpful to view it as abuse at all.

The following exercise illustrates this point.

Exercise 4.1

The following are two imaginary scenarios involving physical abuse. Which one seem to you to be the most abusive? Which one seems more dangerous?

1. A nine-year-old boy ('David') is presenting a lot of management problems to his (single) mother. He has got into the habit of making demands, and then flying into a temper when refused. One day, when she is walking back from a park with him (pushing his two sisters, one aged two years and one aged six months, in a double buggy), he demands to be allowed to go to the sweetshop across the road to spend his pocket money. His mother refuses because she is late for an appointment. He runs off and is very nearly run over when he steps out into the road without looking. (A car has to make an emergency stop and the car behind almost runs into the back of it.) The mother, very frightened, as well as angry and embarrassed, drags him home by the collar and, when she gets inside, slaps him repeatedly on the legs as hard as she can. Next day he has scratch marks and bruises on his neck where she grabbed him, and several large hard-print bruises on his legs. His school reports this to social services.

2. A nine-year-old boy ('Peter') is very well-behaved and hard-working at school, very attentive to the teachers and always well turned-out. He is the adopted only child of a professional couple. One day in school, he does uncharacteristically badly in a spelling test, getting 9 marks out of 15. He is very distressed and agitated about this. His teacher takes time to explore this with him. Eventually he tells her that when he has a spelling test in school, his mother always asks him how he got on. And, if he obtained less than 100 per cent, she makes him stand in a corner until his father gets home, perhaps an

hour later. His father then sends Peter to fetch a ruler and smacks him on the back of the hand with it – one smack for each incorrect answer – before setting him some revision work to do, which he will be tested on later. 'We will not allow you to degenerate into an idle good-for-nothing illiterate like your real mother,' his parents tell him. No visible injury has ever been seen at school.

Comments on Exercise 4.1

The information given above is sketchy and you would certainly need to look into both these cases much more carefully before you reached any firm conclusions.

However, on the information so far available, you will probably agree that, while David's injuries were more severe than Peter's, the incident described seems less abusive than Peter's treatment. David's mother seems to have 'lost it' as a result of fear and a feeling of impotence. The biggest problem here seems to be her difficulty in managing his behaviour, and if she could be given help with that, then quite possibly such incidents as this would not occur.

The physical abuse involved in Peter's case (hitting with a ruler) is not violent enough to cause a visible injury. Yet his treatment by his adoptive parents seems calculated to deeply undermine his confidence and his sense of self-worth. This sort of thing seems to me to raise real questions as to whether Peter should be in this family at all, though (to repeat myself) we would clearly require much more information to get a proper picture, and it is entirely possible that either of these cases might turn out to be very different from what they first appear.

Again, when we consider the dangerousness of the two situations, perhaps it is David who is more at risk of serious injury, through a road accident, perhaps, or through his mother losing her temper again.

It would appear that the harm done to Peter is more of a psychological nature than a physical one (though one would want to consider whether other, more extreme punishments do also occur in what sounds a highly punitive environment). But psychological harm can be as devastating as any other kind of harm, and both boys seem likely to suffer psychological harm if their present circumstances do not change. David will find it very hard to grow up and form relationships if he does not learn about boundaries. Peter will find life very hard indeed if he is not given some more positive images of himself.

Physical abuse

Physical abuse is defined by the Department of Health's guide *Working Together* as:

> hitting, shaking, throwing, poisoning, burning or scalding, drowning, suffocating, or otherwise causing physical harm to a child. (Department of Health, 1999: 5)

This definition does not, however, clarify what degree of physical harm is to be considered abusive. Smacking, for example, is not treated as abuse in England and is regarded by many, if not most, of the population as an acceptable form of punishment, though in Sweden it is an offence. It could be argued that, although smacking is certainly a kind of hitting, it does not do physical harm and therefore falls outside of the definition of physical abuse defined above. But, as I have already said, the degree of physical harm is not necessarily an accurate measure of 'abusiveness'. Context is also important. So is *intention* and *premeditation*.

The *Working Together* definition of physical abuse goes on to say that:

> Physical harm may also be caused when a parent or carer feigns the symptoms of, or deliberately causes ill-health to a child. (Department of Health, 1999: 5)

This phenomenon is sometimes called 'Münchhausen's syndrome by proxy' (as opposed to Münchhausen's syndrome *per se*, where a person deliberately harms *herself* to feign illness). Although it is not as common as other kinds of physical abuse, it is something that child protection workers do encounter. Parents may poison and even kill a child in order to gain sympathy or attention.

So, if we look at physical abuse *as a behaviour*, we can see that it covers a very broad spectrum. At one end of this spectrum we might put unplanned acts of anger and exasperation, which probably most parents can identify with, even if they themselves have never been violent towards a child. But these unplanned acts themselves range from excessively hard smacks to fatal assaults.

At the other end of the spectrum there are very deliberate, premeditated acts, which many people find not only shocking but also bizarre

and inexplicable. Again, these premeditated acts range fr
behaviour that is described as Münchhausen's syndron
deliberate acts of punishment.

Recognizing physical abuse

Examining injures and determining what caused them is, of course, a
job for a doctor and not a social worker. Having said this, though, we
should remember that

- children sustain many injuries, most of which are accidental and
  most of which do not require medical attention. This means that
  other professionals, such as teachers and social workers, do have to
  exercise some judgement as to which injuries should be regarded as
  suspicious, and which injuries merit asking for a medical opinion
- doctors are not infallible, and social workers have been criticized for
  relying too heavily on medical opinion (as I discussed earlier)
- doctors are trained primarily to examine physical symptoms. The
  precise cause of many injuries cannot be determined by examining
  the physical symptoms. For example, a bruise caused by a child
  accidentally banging her head on the corner of a table is not
  necessarily physically distinguishable from a bruise caused by the
  child being hit on the head with an object. Often we can get some
  sense as to whether an injury is accidental or not, only by looking at
  the social context and the history.

Certain injuries are pretty clearly indicative of abuse, including hand-
shaped bruises, bite marks, multiple cigarette burns and the long bruises
and/or lacerations caused by blows from sticks or other implements.
This is not to say, however, that there may not sometimes be innocent
explanations for most of these injuries. It can be hard, for example, to
distinguish cigarette burns from scabies scars.

Another very serious injury that is very unlikely to occur accidentally is
internal bleeding in the head caused by shaking, which can result in death
or permanent brain damage. Cuts, fractures or bruising on babies who
are too small to move about are obviously also very suspicious. Bruising
and lacerations on soft parts of the body and parts which are unlikely to
be injured as the result of falling over or walking into something, are also

spicious: bruises on the face, buttocks, or back of the thighs for example. Although a black eye can be sustained accidentally, it is not easy to sustain two black eyes accidentally at the same time.

Patterns of injury can also be suspicious. It is worrying when a child may have far more bruises than average, even if none of the individual injuries clearly points to abuse. Some children do, however, suffer from medical conditions which result in their bruising very easily.

Often concern that an injury is not accidental arises not so much from the nature of the injury itself, but because of circumstances. The following are some examples:

- There is a previous history of abuse.
- The child is evasive about how the injury occurred, or gives an account of it that he seems to have been taught to say.
- The child tells contradictory stories about the injury, or gives a different story to the one given by a carer.
- A child returns to school after time off and there are signs of a fading injury.
- The child is frightened when questioned about the injury.
- The injury occurs in a context where there are already concerns about a child's relationship with her carer(s). For example, the child may seem frightened or uncomfortable with a carer, or the carer may speak of the child in an angry, rejecting or punitive way. Or angry altercations may have been seen or heard between the child and a carer.
- A carer has a previous history of violence. A person who is violent towards adults, or indeed towards animals, is also likely to be violent towards children.
- There is a history of marital violence.
- The family is known to be under exceptional stress.
- The carers are known to have difficulties managing the child's behaviour.
- Injuries seem to coincide with other events in a child's life: the arrival of a new adult in the family home, for example, or weekends spent staying with a non-custodial parent.
- The injury occurs in a context where there have been causes for concern about a child's emotional well being. Children who are being physically abused may show low self-esteem or seem to avoid social contact. They may be excessively anxious to please, or show excessive anxiety about being told off. In extreme cases, physically abused children may also show 'frozen watchfulness': they have learnt not to do anything or to show any feelings, but simply to watch those

around them and try and anticipate further mistreatment. Alternatively, children who are being abused may show an extremely short concentration span, and be very restless or hyperactive.

Exercise 4.2

Robert, who is nine, turns up at school with a large, unusually shaped bruise on his back. A teacher notices this when Robert is getting changed for gym. It strikes her as an unusual injury for which she can think of no obvious explanation.

If you were the teacher, what sorts of additional information might reassure you that this was an accidental injury?

What sorts of additional information might make you feel that this could be a non-accidental injury and an indicator of possible abuse?

Comments on Exercise 4.2

I would be much less concerned about this injury if Robert was able to give a plausible explanation of it without any sign of discomfort or embarrassment. ('Oh yes, I was climbing in a tree and I slipped and this branch stuck into my back. It really hurt.') I would also be reassured if I heard him give the same explanation to his friends, or if I heard the same explanation from whichever of his parents came to collect him at the end of the day.

I would also not be very worried about this injury if Robert was a confident sociable boy, who was popular with his peers, seemed to have a good relationship with his parents, and did not have a history of other injuries outside of the normal range of childhood bumps and bruises.

I would be much more concerned about the injury if Robert avoided looking me in the eye when I asked about it, gave an explanation reluctantly and tried to get away from me as quickly as possible. I would also be concerned if he seemed to have given different explanations to different people and (of course) if the explanation he gave did not seem to fit the injury.

I would be even more concerned if Robert had a history of injuries for which there had not been clear explanations, or if I observed Robert to be (or to have recently become) an unhappy or anxious child. I would also be more concerned if I was aware of particular relationship difficulties between him and his parents or carers, or if I had other reasons to be concerned about the level of care he was getting at home (for example, if he habitually came to school without having eaten, or in dirty clothes), or if I had noticed him being uneasy in the company of a carer.

Sexual abuse

The definition of sexual abuse in *Working Together* is:

> forcing or enticing a child or young person to take part in sexual activities, whether or not the child is aware of what is happening. The activities may involve physical contact, including penetrative (e.g. rape or buggery) or non-penetrative acts. They may include non-contact activities, such as involving children in looking at, or in the production of, pornographic material or watching sexual activities or encouraging children to behave in sexually inappropriate ways. (Department of Health, 1999: 6)

One issue that is not covered by this definition is age. I think it would be generally agreed that two seven-year-olds examining each others' genitals is not 'abuse', although an excessive preoccupation with sexual play on the part of children *can* be symptomatic of their having been sexually abused, or abused in other ways. But what if one of the children was seven and one was nine? Or one was seven and one was thirteen? Or one was seven and one was seventeen? Probably most people would agree that for a 13-year-old or a 17-year-old to take part in sexual play with a seven-year-old is a form of sexual abuse.

What is missing perhaps from the Department of Health definition is the question of unequal power which is central to sexual abuse and to other kinds of abuse. Non-consenting sex is always abusive. Consenting sexual activity between two little children is not abusive (even though it may be a cause for concern), and consenting sex between two adults is likewise not abusive. But sex between an adult and a child *is* abusive, *whether 'consenting' or not*, because of the huge differences in power and understanding between the two parties.

Recognizing sexual abuse

In the case of sexual abuse, physical symptoms are not likely to be the signs that first draw the attention of an outside observer. Many forms of sexual abuse do not result in any physical evidence. Where there *is* physical evidence, which is mainly when abuse has involved penetrative sex, then this is usually something that is identified after the likelihood of abuse has come to professional attention in another way. The interpretation of medical evidence is also sometimes controversial, as in the case of the 'anal dilation' test which caused such a lot of controversy in the 'Cleveland affair' – see, for example, Parton 1991: 79–115.

The signs and symptoms I will now look at, therefore, are mainly the behavioural and circumstantial ones that can alert us to the possibility that sexual abuse is taking place. The other way in which it sometimes comes to our attention is, of course, when the child herself – or someone who knows the child – makes a specific allegation of abuse.

Among the observable effects of sexual abuse on children are the following:

- Depression and social withdrawal.
- Anxiety.
- Self-harm.
- Inappropriate sexual behaviour towards adults. For example, touching adults in the genital area or on breasts, inserting the tongue when kissing, striking 'seductive' poses.
- Age-inappropriate sexual behaviour with other children. Although some sexual play is normal for children, it is suspicious when small children lie on top of one another and simulate sexual intercourse, or attempt to penetrate themselves or others with objects. (See Calder et al., 1997: 10, for an overview of studies looking at the spectrum of sexual behaviour by children.)
- Age-inappropriate sexual knowledge or preoccupation with sex.
- Sexually abusive behaviour towards other children.
- Behaviour problems or learning problems in school.
- Aggressive or anti-social behaviour.
- Frequent urinary tract infections (UTI).

This is not to say that any one of these symptoms necessarily indicates that sexual abuse is going on (urinary tract infections, for example, are quite common among small girls generally), but a combination of several of these together should certainly alert professionals to the possibility of sexual abuse.

For example, the profiles in the following exercise would suggest to me a child who may well be the victim of sexual abuse.

Exercise 4.3

Dana, aged seven, is difficult in school, unpopular with other children and socially isolated. When her teacher tries to get her to sit and read with her, Dana is restless and several times has touched her teacher's breasts, asking 'Do you like that?' She also tells her teacher, 'I fancy you, I want to give you a kiss.'

Helen, aged 13, is very thin, pale and withdrawn. Reports from primary school suggest that she has not always been so. But now she is dreamy and pays little attention in class. She has lost weight. She is frequently absent from school with headaches and similar minor complaints. She has deep scratches on her arms where she has cut herself. 'Because I was bored,' she says when asked by her class teacher. When the class teacher suggested meeting and talking with her mother and step-father she was tearfully adamant that she did not want this to happen, but will not say why. Her step-father joined the family about two years ago.

Suppose that in both these cases, the respective schools had contacted social services for advice as to how to proceed. What approach might you take?

Comments on Exercise 4.3

Both these children are clearly unhappy and it is obvious that something is not right with their lives. The pattern of behaviour of both of them certainly suggests that they may be being – or have been – sexually abused, though it is impossible to say categorically that this is the case.

Neither of them has, however, made an allegation of sexual abuse and there is no single piece of evidence that points unambiguously to it. In the absence of other information it is not clear that a formal abuse investigation is warranted, or would be productive, but you will want to try and find out more.

The task of trying to look into this further is a delicate one, since in both cases it seems likely that, if abuse is going on, then it will be going on in the family home.

I would suggest that this would require close cooperation with the respective schools. The next step might be for someone who each girl knows, to try and find ways of talking to them and giving them opportunities to talk about what is happening to them. The person best placed to do this might well be a teacher, though the teacher would need to be clear about her role and her boundaries.

Emotional abuse and neglect

It is commonly said that emotional abuse and neglect are harder to prove than physical or sexual abuse because they do not necessarily involve injuries or specific abusive acts. In some ways, though, emotional abuse and neglect can actually be *easier* to detect. You are unlikely to actually witness a child being beaten or sexually abused, after all, but emotional abuse and neglect may well take place right in front of you.

In spite of this, these forms of maltreatment tend to have a lower profile on the child protection agenda, perhaps because it is easier to respond to abusive *events* than to intervene in an abusive *relationship*. It is important, therefore, that we are aware of the very serious long-term consequences of emotional abuse and neglect.

In the Department of Health's *Working Together* guide, emotional abuse is defined as:

the persistent emotional ill-treatment of a child such as to cause severe and persistent effects on the child's emotional development. It may involve conveying to children that they are worthless or unloved, inadequate, or valued only insofar as they meet the needs of another person. It may feature age or developmentally inappropriate expectations being imposed on children. It may involve causing children frequently to feel frightened or in danger, or the exploitation or corruption of children. (Department of Health, 1999: 5–6)

The definition of neglect in *Working Together* is:

persistent failure to meet a child's basic physical and/or psychological needs, likely to result in the serious impairment of the child's health and development. It may involve a parent or carer failing to provide adequate food, shelter and clothing, failing to protect a child from physical harm or danger, or the failure to ensure access to appropriate medical care or treatment. It may also include neglect of, or unresponsiveness to a child's basic emotional needs. (Department of Health, 1999: 6)

You can see that the definition of neglect shades into the definition of emotional abuse. It may also have occurred to you that, while both these definitions make sense, they are distinctly blurred round the edges. What constitutes '*serious* impairment'? How bad is '*severe*'? (Presumably so bad as to constitute 'significant harm' in the language of the 1989 Children Act, but this still leaves the vexed question as to what constitutes '*significant*'!) Such difficulties are among the biggest challenges of identifying neglect and emotional abuse and deciding whether, and at what level, to intervene.

A further complication arises from the need to balance the possible harmful effects of any intervention with the likely benefits. A poorly thought-through intervention in an abuse case of any kind runs the risk of making things worse, not better, for the victim, if it just has the effect of stirring things up, without reaching any sort of resolution. Intervention in neglect and emotional abuse cases can be particularly difficult in that respect.

Recognizing emotional abuse

I've said that neglect and emotional abuse shade into each other. The following exercise illustrates this:

Exercise 4.4

Francesca (aged ten) suffers with cystic fibrosis. One of the features of this degenerative illness is that unusually thick and viscous mucus is secreted in the lungs. In order to prevent this from building up too much, it is necessary for a child's carers to carry out a physiotherapy procedure several times a day, involving rigorous pummelling on the back. Failure to do this means the mucus builds up, resulting in a persistent cough and serious chest infections – and, ultimately, a shorter life expectancy. It is also necessary for sufferers to take special enzymes before every meal.

Francesca's parents are very preoccupied with their own exciting and highly turbulent personal lives, and consistently fail to provide the necessary physio or to give the correct dosage of enzymes. Although they express affection for Francesca when they see her, they refuse to make her medical needs a priority, though this has a demonstrable effect on her health and on her life expectancy. Francesca's place in their order of priorities is perhaps illustrated by the fact that, when she is admitted to hospital, it is four days before either parent visits.

Would you describe the behaviour of the parents as emotionally abusive or neglectful?

Comments on Exercise 4.4

The failure of the parents to provide the necessary physiotherapy is a form of neglect – a form sometimes categorized as 'medical neglect'. In this case it is potentially fatal. But it is surely also a form of emotional abuse, as is the failure to visit Francesca in hospital, since emotional abuse includes 'conveying to children that they are worthless or unloved, inadequate, or valued only insofar as they meet the needs of another person'.

Such messages can be conveyed in words, but they can also – and probably much more powerfully – be conveyed in deeds. Few of us would accept that someone loved us just because they said so, if in fact they consistently treated us with indifference and contempt.

The fact that Francesca's parents do not make the effort to visit her in hospital is giving her a message that she is not important to them, and that her needs are much less important to them than their own. The fact that they are not prepared to provide her with the help she needs at home not only places her health at risk, it also gives her a rather clear message as to her own value to her parents.

Any kind of neglect, physical abuse or sexual abuse, in fact conveys to a child a negative message about her worth to her parents – and this is why emotional abuse is present in all forms of child abuse and neglect, and is therefore, in a sense, the primary form of abuse.

Emotional abuse is about *messages*, verbal or non-verbal, given by a carer to a child. The fact that long-term psychological and physical harm can result from emotional abuse decisively refutes the saying 'sticks and stones may break my bones but words can never hurt me'. Words can do as much harm as sticks and stones. Non-verbal messages may hurt even more than words. Inconsistency between verbal and non-verbal messages may also be particularly confusing and disturbing.

One difficulty with emotional abuse is that unlike sexual or physical abuse, almost all children are subjected to it to some degree. If you are a parent or carer of children, or if you look at parents or carers among your friends, you will probably agree that even the most caring of carers does at times give children quite negative messages. When we are pre-occupied, or tired, or busy, children may find that it is hard to interest us in their issues, or are made to feel that they are a nuisance and that we would rather they were not there. Probably most parents have at some time also said or done hurtful things to their children in anger, which they later regret.

A key word in the definition therefore is *persistent*. All children have some resilience, and are capable of understanding that even loving adults lose their temper, get tired and have bad moods. It is when the negative message becomes the predominant one that the situation becomes seriously abusive. In practice it is really when (a), the negative message can be seen to be persistent and (b), when the child's behaviour is such as to suggest that the negative messages are doing real psychological harm, that professional intervention under a child protection remit starts to be indicated.

The following are some parental behaviours that would generally be considered emotionally abusive. It is not an exhaustive list.

- Deliberately humiliating a child.
- Making a child feel ashamed for not being able to do or understand something which she is, in fact, developmentally incapable of.
- Expecting a child to put the needs of other family members before her own, and dismissing the expression of her own needs or wishes as selfish. This might involve consistently singling one child out, like Cinderella in the story, for inferior treatment as against her siblings.
- Shutting a child into a small space.
- Persistently verbally abusing a child.
- Persistently threatening to leave a child on her own as a punishment. This is abusive whether or not the threat is actually carried out, but obviously more so if a child is actually left alone.
- Making threats of other cruel and excessive punishments and/or carrying them out. A very extreme example of this that I am aware of is a case where a father killed family pets in front of his children, with the implication that the same might be done to them too.
- Telling a child that he was not wanted, was a mistake, or was the wrong gender. ('I never wanted a boy.')
- Exposing a child to age-inappropriate activity. For example, exposing a small child to horror videos (exposure to pornographic videos is generally regarded as sexual abuse).
- Isolating a child, preventing him from socializing with his peers.
- Persistently putting a child under unfair moral/emotional pressure. ('Go and out play with your friends by all means, but I always

thought you were the sort of caring boy who would want to stay in with your poor old mum'.)

The sort of evidence that might suggest that the abuse was doing significant harm to the child would be:

- The child is depressed, or withdrawn, or very passive, or has very low self-esteem.
- She is excessively anxious to please others and very frightened of criticism.
- The child is socially isolated.
- The child has behaviour problems.
- The child is underachieving.
- The child seems reluctant to go home, or shows signs of fear in the presence of a carer.
- Some children who behave in ways that seem indicative of sexual abuse (for example, compulsive masturbation) may in fact be *emotionally* abused rather than sexually, and may be seeking some way of providing the comfort to themselves that their carers are not providing.

As with sexual abuse, there will be times when children choose to disclose emotional abuse that is happening at home. The following exercise provides an example of this.

Exercise 4.5

At school Harriet (11) is an exceptionally hard-working and well-behaved child in the classroom, though quiet, serious and hard to get to know. She and her older sister (Dawn, aged 14) live with their mother, Ruth. Ruth is divorced from their father, who lives in another part of the country. Ruth is seen by the school staff as a 'difficult' parent, who is prone to come in and 'make a scene' when something happens at school which she disagrees with. She is also known to suffer with depression.

One day at school, Harriet spills some ink over her dress. To her teacher's surprise Harriet's reaction is one of utter terror. The teacher finds an opportunity to take her aside and ask her what the matter is, and eventually Harriet tells the teacher that her mother hates dirt of any kind and is furious when Harriet gets any kind of mark or stain on her clothes. Last time something like this happened (a glue stain on a tee-shirt), her mother screamed and shouted at her that she was a thoughtless, selfish little slut. She made Harriet scrub the tee-shirt at the sink for more than an hour, and then threw it out and said that she would not be giving Harriet a birthday present this year because the money would go on a new tee-shirt.

Harriet also tells the teacher that her mother makes her get up at 6 a.m. every day and hoover the house from top to bottom, and that her pocket money is stopped if her mother does not regard the house as cleaned to an acceptable standard.

She also says that she longs to see her father, whom she has not seen for several years, but that her mother flies into a rage if she or her sister Dawn so much as mention him.

Harriet agrees to the teacher talking about this with Social Services, but she begs for a reassurance that her mother will not be told that she has complained about her.

As a social worker responding to a call from the teacher, what would your thoughts be about the next step?

Comments on Exercise 4.5

Ruth will doubtless have a different story and we should not assume that Harriet's story is the only legitimate version of events. But I think there can be little doubt that Harriet is being emotionally abused, since her distress at spilling the ink was not premeditated or staged. Indeed, even if she has made up some of this story, why would she wish to do so unless she was very unhappy with her relationship with her mother?

It would appear that unrealistic demands and expectations are being placed upon Harriet, cruel and disproportionate punishments are being meted out, and that she is being given negative messages about herself.

The difficulty, of course, is that, as Harriet fears, any intervention will have to be carefully planned if it is not to result in making Harriet's situation even more difficult. This is a case that one would not wish to rush into. On the other hand, Harriet is frightened about what is going to happen tonight.

As much information as possible needs to be gathered (for example, from Dawn and her school, from the family doctor) and Harriet herself – as well as professionals with knowledge of the family – need to be properly consulted before any intervention in the family. (How is it going to be presented to Ruth? How, as far as possible, is Harriet not going to be put in the position of the one whose fault it is?)

Recognizing neglect

To recap on the *Working Together* definition given earlier, neglect is 'persistent failure to meet a child's basic physical and/or psychological needs'. It can include:

- Failure to feed a child adequately. For example: some children are not provided with regular meals, or are left to fend for themselves, or are fed on a diet of crisps and sweets.
- Failure to provide appropriate clothes or bedding. For example: a girl is sent to school in mid-winter in a thin summer dress and sandals; a boy wears the same clothes to school the next day, even though he wet himself in them and make him stink of urine; a girl goes to school in crumpled clothes, some of which she has put on backwards; three children sleep on a dirty mattress without sheets and with only a single blanket.
- Failure to provide basic physical care. For example: a girl of four has never been helped to wipe herself after using the toilet or brush her teeth, and has never been taught how to do so; a six-month-old baby is left in dirty nappies for many hours, resulting in very severe nappy rash.
- Failure to provide a routine. For example: children aged five and six are allowed to stay up until the early hours of the morning; a child of eight is habitually late for school, and often also has to wait for up to an hour to be collected from school.
- Failure to provide boundaries or consistency. For example: a mother finds it amusing that her seven-year-old son smokes and watches his parents' collection of adult movies; a family of children are described by neighbours as completely wild and 'like little wild animals', whose parents do not seem to enforce any kinds of rules of behaviour; a baby is passed around to numerous different carers.
- Failure to provide safety. For example: a small child is in the habit of climbing outside his upstairs bedroom window, and nothing is done to prevent him; children aged seven and nine are left alone all evening while their parents go out.
- Failure to attend to medical needs. For example: a child of seven is fed a diet of sweets all day and all her front teeth are visibly rotten, but her parents do not take her to the dentist.
- Failure to meet or recognize a child's emotional needs. For example: a mother seems indifferent to her child's crying, or not to notice his

repeated attempts to ask a question; a little girl is expected to call her mother's new boyfriend 'daddy' on the second time of meeting him, even though her real father was a member of the household only two weeks previously.

One problem with identifying and responding to neglect is the thorny question of *cultural differences*. I am not referring here only to differences between the cultures of different ethnic communities, though there certainly are differences of that kind, but also the cultural norms of different social classes, and indeed of different individual families.

One example of this is in attitudes to risk-taking. Every parent has to strike a balance between allowing their child some freedom to grow and enjoy life, and providing their child with protection against danger. To try and protect a child against all external dangers might, in an extreme form, itself be a kind of emotional abuse. Imagine a 16-year-old who is not allowed to ride a bicycle, or to go out on her own, and is accompanied by a parent on all shopping trips and on the way to and from school. But failure to protect a child at all would clearly be neglect. The difficulty is that we do not all choose the same point inbetween these two extremes. Middle-class social workers, for example, may sometimes regard as neglectful a practice that is seen as normal in poor working-class communities: letting children play on their own in the street, for instance.

Statistics collected in Britain in the 1970s found that, for boys, fatal accidents (in proportion to population), were five times greater for social class 5 as compared to social class 1. The figures were, respectively, 122 per 100,000 and 25.8 per 100,000. The comparable figures for girls were 63.1 and 18.8, so that for girls there is a threefold difference between the two ends of the class spectrum. This may reflect different class attitudes to risk-taking and to parental supervision. It may also reflect other things such as a lack of safe play facilities, or the cost of safety equipment (Green, 1995).

The following exercise invites you to reflect on your personal stance in these matters.

Exercise 4.6

Looking through the following list, pick out the practices that you would see as instances of parental neglect, as against those that you would see as acceptable:

- Leaving a 10-year-old alone in a house for an hour.
- Leaving a three-year-old alone in the house for an hour.
- Leaving a 10-year-old alone in a house for an evening.
- Sending a seven-year-old to school on her own, which involves a pelican crossing over a main road.
- Letting a six-year-old play with other children in a street which is used as a through-route by traffic.
- Letting 13-year-olds smoke and providing them with places where they can do so.
- Letting a ten, eight and seven-year-old (all swimmers) spend a whole day on their own in a meadow next to a river, providing them with a picnic and swimming things.
- Leaving an eight-year-old to play on her own in a public park.
- Letting a seven-year-old boil a kettle and make a cup of tea.
- Leaving a baby in the charge of a 12-year-old babysitter for two hours.
- Leaving an eight-year-old in hospital for three days without visiting him.
- Leaving an eight-year-old in a private boarding school for four weeks without visiting him.
- Letting children play in a park where there are dog faeces and therefore a small risk of picking up a disease that will cause blindness.
- Letting children get involved in (a) rugby football or (b) boxing.
- Allowing a 15-year-old girl to be driven to the seaside in her 18-year-old boyfriend's car.

Comments on Exercise 4.6

I have purposely chosen examples here which are not as extreme as those given earlier. I don't think any of these behaviours, taken on its own, would provoke formal intervention under child protection procedures. What you may notice is that there are quite sharp differences of views between people, including between responsible, thoughtful parents, about what is acceptable and what isn't.

It is also noticeable that views have changed over the generations. For example, in the 1950s it was considered kinder by many people not to visit children in hospital, and parents were actually advised not to do so. Nowadays a parent who would let small children spend a day by themselves swimming and picnicking by a river would be frowned on by many people, but a generation or two ago this was much more normal – and it could be argued that modern parents are exposing their children to new risks by restricting them more to the home.

The point of the above is not to suggest that neglect is impossible to define, but to demonstrate that neglect cannot necessarily be defined in absolute terms. Like other forms of child mistreatment, neglect needs to be interpreted in context. The following are some questions that may help you consider this:

- Is the behaviour normal in the community where it is taking place? If an entire neighbourhood regards a certain practice as normal and acceptable, it would be inappropriate to try and deal with individual instances on a casework basis.
- Is the behaviour (a) pretty certain to be harmful, or (b) risky, in that it may cause no harm at all but carries some risk of a very serious negative outcome? An example of the former would be sending children to school in dirty urine-smelling clothes, which is fairly certain to result in the children being stigmatized. An example of the latter would be letting children swim on their own, or play in the street, which can be fatal, though only in a minority of cases.
- In the case of behaviour which is certain to be harmful, what is the extent of the harm and the evidence for it? Is it such as to warrant intervention, bearing in mind that intervention itself can have negative effects?
- In the case of risk-taking behaviour, you could ask the following: is the risk proportionate to the benefit? Have the risks been properly thought through or is the risk-taking being allowed only as a result of parental indifference or resignation?
- Is the parents' overall *relationship* with the child neglectful? Do the particular instances of apparently neglectful behaviour reflect a more pervasive parental indifference?

Indirect abuse

I will conclude this chapter by drawing attention to the violent abuse of *adults* (usually women) by other adults (usually men) within families. On a superficial view, this may seem to be a separate question to that of child abuse since the victim of the violence is an adult, but in fact, as I will discuss in Chapter 6, the effects on children of exposure to such violence are very similar both in kind and severity to the effects of abuse specifically directed at the child. It is only quite recently that the impact of such violence on children has been widely researched. For this reason some commentators have referred to such children as 'the "forgotten", "unacknowledged", "hidden", "unintended", and "silent" victims' of adult violence (Holden, 1998: 1).

An adult who violently assaults another adult in the home is, in fact, also abusing children who may see, hear or be aware of that violence. (Hughes, 1992, found that in 90 per cent of cases of domestic violence, children were in the same or the next room.) This 'indirect abuse', as I will call it, is a form of emotional abuse, and actually one of the more severe forms. (Bearing in mind that emotional abuse and neglect are closely related, we might also see it as neglect of the child's needs.) Children are exposed to feelings of terror, grief, impotence, and to the realization that adults on whom they may rely for safety, security and protection are either (a), incapable of protecting even themselves, or (b), capable of dangerous violence towards those they are supposed to protect. Children can also themselves be actively involved in violent incidents, for example by intervening in some way to protect their mother who is being abused, or by being encouraged by the abuser to 'support and/or participate in the abuse and degradation of their mother' (Kelly, 1994: 44).

'Indirect abuse' is very harmful in its own right, but it is also commonly associated with *direct* abuse. It is perhaps not surprising that men who are violent towards women are also more likely to be violent towards children, and there are many research studies that confirm that this is the case. Hester et al. (2000: 30–2) summarize a number of these studies. One US study, for instance, found that in a sample of 775 mothers with violent partners, 70 per cent of the children were also physically abused (Bowker et al., 1988). Stark and Flitcraft (1985: 165) go as far as to argue that violence against women may be 'the single most important context for child abuse'.

In this chapter I have looked at definitions of the various kinds of abuse and at ways of recognizing that they are going on, drawing attention to the overlapping nature of the different forms of child maltreatment, and to the need to look not just at incidents in isolation, but at the context in which they occur. I have considered:

- physical abuse, noting the many different forms and contexts in which this can occur, and noting also the way that physical abuse lies on a continuum with the practice of smacking, which remains socially acceptable and is widely practised
- sexual abuse, drawing attention to the need to consider the power relationship between the alleged abuser and victim, as well as to the actual acts
- emotional abuse and neglect, noting that emotional abuse and neglect overlap in many respects, and that emotional abuse underlies all forms of abuse, and is again on a continuum with the kinds of negative behaviour which occur in any family
- what I have called 'indirect abuse', the abuse of one adult by another in the presence of a child, whose effects, as will be discussed in a later chapter, can be similar in kind and severity to those of actual direct abuse.

Having considered the problems involved in defining and recognizing abuse, and touched too on the problems of following it up and stopping it, in the next chapter I will consider the particular case of children with disabilities, and the special difficulties and challenges that arise in their case.

Disabled Children   5

In the previous chapter I looked at how to define and recognize child abuse and neglect in general. In this chapter, I will look at the specific case of disabled children and consider the particular issues that arise. I have chosen to make this the subject of a chapter of its own because it seems to me that disabled children are sometimes neglected in the child protection literature, even though for a variety of reasons they are a particularly vulnerable group.

A lack of attention to this group of children in the literature may at times reflect a lack of attention in actual practice. Laura Middleton (1992: 99) refers to 'a common, compartmentalized view that child abuse is one thing, and disability another'. Thinking on abuse of disabled children has moved forward a great deal over the past 10 years, but the way that social work services are typically organized can lead to a similar compartmentalization. On the one hand, child protection social workers may often not be particularly experienced in the needs of disabled children, while on the other, social workers specializing in work with disabled children may take a service provision approach in which child protection may not be the primary focus, because they see their task as the provision of support to families whose children are in need because of their disability. Indeed Middleton (1999: 80) argues that this polarization is maintained by both groups 'seeking to preserve their own status as experts', and also by fear – a fear of disability on the part of child protection workers, and a fear of dealing with abusers on the part of disability workers – leaving disabled children unprotected 'in the middle'.

If this is so, we need to try and rectify it, because there are a number of reasons why disabled children may be *more* vulnerable to abuse than other children. These I'll now consider. Many of the ideas which I will discuss in this chapter, however, are applicable too to children who do not have disabilities.

Vulnerability of disabled children

The evidence is that disabled children are more vulnerable to abuse and neglect than other children. In an American study, Cross et al. (1993), found that disabled children were nearly twice as likely to be abused as other children. In the UK, Jenny Morris (1999) reports that disabled children only made up 2 per cent of the population aged 0–17 in one county, but accounted for 10 per cent of the children on the child protection register there. *Working Together* confirms that 'The available UK evidence on the extent of abuse among disabled children suggests that disabled children are at increased risk of abuse, and that the presence of multiple disabilities appears to increase the risk both of abuse and neglect' (Department of Health, 1999: 69). *Working Together* suggests that this is because some disabled children:

- have fewer outside contacts than other children;
- receive intimate personal care, possibly from a number of carers, which may both increase the risk of exposure to abusive behaviour, and make it more difficult to set and maintain physical boundaries;
- have an impaired capacity to resist or avoid abuse;
- have communication difficulties which may make it more difficult to tell others what is happening;
- be inhibited about complaining because of fear of losing services;
- be especially vulnerable to bullying and intimidation; *and/or*
- be more vulnerable than other children to abuse by their peers. (Para 6.27, Department of Health, 1999: 69)

The caveat '*some* disabled children' is important, because, of course, disabled children are not an homogenous group. The issues that arise for a highly intelligent mobile child with a hearing impairment are very different from those that arise for a child who has profound learning impairments and mobility problems as a result of brain damage, and these are different again for those that arise for a child with Down syndrome or one with autism. And of course, just as much as everyone else, disabled children will also differ in terms of their own individual characteristics and circumstances, ethnic background and so on. But subject to the same caveat, I would add to the list above the following family and social factors that may also make abuse more likely to happen, and less likely to be detected and/or defined as abuse.

Family factors

The birth of a child with an impairment is a difficult thing for most parents to come to terms with – and some do not succeed in doing so. One does not have to go along entirely with the proposal of Solnit and Stark (1961) that the event is a kind of bereavement to recognize that an element of grief is commonly involved. (Solnit and Stark's suggestion was that the parent grieves the loss of the non-disabled child that they had hoped for.) With grief, typically, comes anger and some of this anger may be directed at the child herself. If this is not resolved, there may be long-lasting ambivalence on the part of the parents towards the child, if not outright rejection. I am not implying that this is *necessarily* the case for all parents of disabled children, of course, and it is worth noting here that ambivalence and outright rejection can be experienced by non-disabled children too. (It can occur, for example, in some situations where a child is the result of an unplanned and unwanted pregnancy, or is the result of a failed relationship, or the product of a rape, or is not the gender that was wanted – and indeed for many other reasons.) But the birth of a child with a disability is another factor that can sometimes bring this about. And ambivalent feelings, angry feelings or a secret longing to be rid of a child, can precipitate abuse and neglect. It is interesting that Morris (1999) found a 'different pattern of types of abuse' for disabled children: they were more likely to be placed on the child protection register under emotional abuse and neglect than non-disabled children.

Exercise 5.1

Harriet Davis is 13 and is learning disabled. Her language skills are limited, perhaps similar to those of a three-year-old non-disabled child. She attends a special school. One day she confides to a teacher there that she is upset with her brother, Greg, who is 16 (and is not learning disabled). He has been touching her in the genital area, and she does not like it. The teacher reports this to the social services and, after discussion with other agencies, a social worker follows it up by arranging to interview Harriet and talking to her parents.

When the social worker visits Mr and Mrs Davis, they tell her that they are convinced that Harriet has made the whole story up to get attention and sympathy, and to get Greg into trouble. Greg is an intelligent boy who could have a bright future ahead of him, they say. He puts up with a great deal from Harriet and it is grossly unfair that these allegations against him should now be taken seriously. When the social worker insists that the allegations made by Harriet do need to be taken seriously by the professional system, and that there will be a need for further follow-up, Mrs Davis becomes very angry.

'We are just fed up with all the things we have to do for that girl. All the problems she's caused for our family – meetings, special schools, doctors – and now *this*! She doesn't care or think about anyone except herself.'

What are your thoughts about Harriet's place in this family?

Comments on Exercise 5.1

As ever with these case examples, I would caution against drawing any firm conclusion on the basis of the limited information that I have presented. There could be other information, not yet come to light, that would completely alter your initial impression, and invalidate some or all of the points I am about to make.

However, initial impressions are important too, and you will probably agree that it is striking how Mr and Mrs Davis seem to view the meetings which they have had to attend on account of Harriet's disability as an imposition, by Harriet, on the rest of the family. The disability is seen as something that Harriet is inflicting on them (as opposed, say, to something which they and Harriet are dealing with together). Harriet's allegations about Greg seem to have been immediately placed in the same category: simply a further nuisance caused by Harriet.

It is worrying that the possibility that what Harriet alleges is true seems to be dismissed out of hand. What we know about sexual abuse suggests that the harm it does is likely to be compounded by the failure of others to believe in it. In fact the negative, dismissive attitude of Mr and Mrs Davis towards Harriet, if it is the normal pattern, could be seen as emotionally abusive in its own right. One might also speculate about the extent to which this family attitude might have allowed Greg to feel that it was somehow alright to abuse his sister.

I do not say that what Harriet says about Greg is necessarily true (though this would seem likely), but it is important that it is taken seriously. If it were not true, after all, there would still need to be serious thought given as to why Harriet would have made such a thing up.

Assuming that there has been sexual abuse of Harriet by Greg, the challenge in planning an intervention is the need to find a way to (a) support Harriet, in ensuring that abuse from Greg does not continue, (b) find ways of deflecting Greg from a pattern of abusive behaviour, while at the same time (c) not causing Harriet being cast even more as a sort of family 'scapegoat'.

Once again I am speculating, but this latter pattern may be linked to Mr and Mrs Davis's grief and disappointment at some much earlier stage on discovering that their daughter had a learning impairment: grief and disappointment which they have not been able to put behind them. It seems to me that this grief needs to be recognized, and their efforts and struggles acknowledged, if they are going to be able to hear the message that they need to take seriously what they are being told about the abuse of their daughter by their son. The primary goal of an intervention may be to protect Harriet, but this requires that the needs and viewpoints of other family members are properly addressed. Among the commonest mistakes that are made in child protection are attempts to 'rescue' children, which end up achieving nothing except to further isolate them.

In all this, it is equally important to bear in mind that Harriet has limited communication skills, and that time and effort needs to be set aside to hear her point of view, if this is not to be swamped by the views of more articulate family members.

Even for the most unreservedly loving of families there can be no doubt that a child with disabilities can be a source of additional stress, since any disability will place at least some additional demands on the carers – and some disabled children need an enormous amount of extra time and attention compared to other children. And, while parents of non-disabled children can expect the initial heavy demands to reduce as time goes on – a small baby may wake her parents several times every night, but they can look forward to a day when this will no longer occur – parents of some disabled children cannot necessarily look forward to a reduction in the demands upon them in the same way.

The additional stresses that caring for disabled children places on families is illustrated, for example, by the higher incidence of divorce that has been found among parents of children with Down syndrome

(Gath, 1977), and among parents of children with visual impairments. In the latter case, Hodapp and Krasner (1995) found the incidence of divorce to be 25 per cent, as against 15.3 per cent in a control sample whose children were not visually impaired. Since we know that stress is a factor in child maltreatment, it is therefore only to be expected that incidence of child abuse and neglect would also be higher for these groups of children.

Having said this, though, I do not wish to imply that child abuse or neglect – or indeed family breakdown – is in any sense an inevitable consequence of the presence of a child with a disability. Families may be strengthened too by the challenges and rewards of supporting a child with a disability. I am simply saying that the presence of a child's disability is a stressor, and hence an additional risk factor (as, for example, is poverty).

Exercise 5.2

Billy Thomas, aged eight, has been diagnosed as having an autistic spectrum disorder. Adults caring for him have always found his behaviour extremely challenging. It is difficult to get his attention, or to get him to retain information. He is restless all day and will not settle in his bed easily at night, coming downstairs again and again until midnight or later, and then waking very early the next morning. He is unsafe in the street, and, if not closely watched, is liable to run out across the road, or just wander off. In particular he is prone to getting into repetitive cycles of behaviour, which he may repeat over and over again, ignoring attempts to stop him or deflect him into other activities.

One day he becomes obsessed with pulling his little sister's hair. His father reprimands him and tells him to stop, but Billy then immediately goes and does the same thing again and again, without any apparent malice, but hard enough to hurt. When his sister leaves the room, he simply follows her and carries on. Billy's sister is distressed. Mr Thomas, Billy's father, is angry and upset. Mr Thomas cannot understand Billy's behaviour, which seems entirely pointless, and he cannot understand Billy's indifference to his sister's distress. Eventually Mr Thomas takes Billy by the arms, shaking him and shouting into his face to stop.

The next day, at school, Billy is found to have pronounced finger bruises, and some broken skin, on both his upper arms. In fact it is not the first time bruising has been noticed on his upper arms, and there have been several previous occasions when his teacher had wondered whether there might be some sort of physical abuse going on, but the

---

school decided to take no action. On this occasion, though, it is very clear and the school makes a referral to the local social services child protection team.

The school does this with some reluctance, as Mr Thomas (a single parent as the result of his wife's death two years previously) is a strong supporter of the school, and is seen by teachers there as a good and caring man who has had a great deal to cope with, what with Billy's exasperating behaviour and Mrs Thomas's death. He never complains, is always cheerful and never asks for help – indeed he is always willing to help others. This is the general perception.

What do you notice about this case, and what thoughts do you have about how it should be taken up?

Comments on Exercise 5.2

You may well agree with the school that behaviour such as Billy's would be extremely wearing for most people, and that it is understandable that Mr Thomas should have lost his temper. It may well be true that Mr Thomas is indeed a 'good and caring man' who is doing his best.

However it is dangerous to get too set in viewing any one situation in one way, without re-examining your assumptions. It seems that the school staff may have fallen into this trap, allowing their faith in and liking for Mr Thomas to prevent them from viewing repeated instances of suspicious bruising as physical abuse.

The fact that abuse 'is understandable', or that the person who inflicted it is basically well-meaning, does not alter the fact that it should not happen. Probably it is relatively easy for any adult to identify with Mr Thomas, because it is easy to see that Billy's stubbornly persistent behaviour must be maddening. The danger lies in the fact that it may be much harder to identify with Billy, whose behaviour and outlook is alien to most people's experience, and that therefore Billy's own needs may go unnoticed.

It would appear likely that this was not an isolated incident. It may also be a problem that is getting worse, seeing as the current bruising is the most serious to date. This is therefore a problem that needs to be addressed.

This does not require that a punitive attitude is taken towards Mr Thomas, but it does require that his behaviour is challenged and explored. It may be that, following initial investigation, an appropriate intervention would simply be to provide more practical help and support to the family, and perhaps make arrangements that allow Mr Thomas and Billy some time away from each other, or allow Mr Thomas to spend time with his children separately. (Mr Thomas's self-reliance and resistance to outside help might need to be challenged.)

These are things that need to be considered further down the line. It is possible that the relationship between Mr Thomas and Billy will, on further enquiry, turn out to be less benign than the school believes. Or it may turn out that there were other explanations for the other bruises, and that this may indeed have been an isolated incident.

Obtaining information from Billy may prove difficult, because people with autistic spectrum disorders do not typically communicate like other people, and may not be able to carry on what would normally be understood as a conversation. It would therefore be essential to have advice from someone with some specialist knowledge of this area and who is comfortable working with children like Billy.

Social factors

Families exist in a wider social context. The stress experienced by parents will be dependent in large part on the practical and emotional support that is available to them, and the messages they have received and internalized about the nature of disability. *All* of the factors cited by *Working Together*, which I listed above, are really just as much to do with social context as with the specific impairments that children may have. Indeed, disability itself is a matter of social context. Thus, for instance, the extent to which communication difficulties 'make it more difficult to tell others what is happening' may be dependent on the amount of skilled help with communication that is available. The fact that some disabled children 'have fewer outside contacts than other children' is not an inevitable consequence of having an impairment so much as a reflection of the opportunities that a particular society offers. Margaret Kennedy (2002: 149) argues that the dependent position which children who are disabled are placed in, and the messages and training they are given or not given, amounts to 'a situation in which children who are disabled have been taught to be good "victims"' of sexual abuse.

Widely held assumptions about disabled children may also increase the risk of abuse happening and/or failing to be detected. Several commentators even suggest that an unspoken view exists that disabled children are less important than other children, or that abusing them does less harm than to other children, or simply does not matter as much. Middleton (1992: 99) suggests that there has been an almost wilful failure of the child protection system to take seriously the problem of abuse of disabled children, given that research going back at least to the 1960s shows links between disability and abuse. 'Social work, it appears, does not WANT to know,' she comments. Kennedy (2002: 148, 149) quotes the comment of a counsellor to the mother of a disabled child who had been abused: 'well it would have been worse if it had been one of your other [non-disabled] children,' and the comment of a man with cerebral palsy about his childhood abuse: 'why bugger up a normal child when I am defective already?'

Sympathy for parents of children with disabilities, who are seen to be trying to cope with enormously difficult challenges, may also (as can sympathy for parents in other areas of child protection work) prevent professionals from thinking about the perspective of the child – and encourage them to overlook or collude in behaviour that might be seen as neglectful or abusive in other circumstances. As Jenny Morris writes:

> Ironically, the philosophy of working in partnership with parents is more advanced in work with parents of disabled children than it is with parents of non-disabled children, but this in itself is sometimes associated with a failure to focus on the child's needs and experiences. (Morris, 1999: 99)

A number of writers (Westcott and Cross, 1996, for example) have also identified a widespread 'myth' that no one would abuse a disabled child: 'handicapped children are sacrosanct, not to be touched. Other children perhaps, but not the disabled' (Watson, 1989: 113). It is odd that this view should exist in parallel with the opposite view that abuse of disabled children is *less* serious than abuse of other children, but both do seem to exist and both have the effect of reducing the likelihood that abuse will be detected and taken seriously. Burke and Cigno (2000: 99) observe that 'many people find it difficult to believe that disabled children may be the targets of abusers', and that this of course makes them 'ideal targets'. Failure of professionals to recognize the possibility of abuse will increase the likelihood that adults will attribute signs and symptoms of abuse to the child's impairment.

> It is important when we see bedwetting, fear of the dark or withdrawn behaviour also to consider the possibility that the child is being abused. Many workers with disabled children have not had child protection training (as it is believed that disabled children are not abused, and therefore that training is not necessary). So when any signs of possible abuse occur, workers do not know how to make sense of them and attribute them automatically to behaviour stemming from impairment. (Kennedy, 2002: 159–60)

But, of course, we should be aware too of the opposite possibility: that apparent symptoms of abuse may indeed be the consequence of impairments. And we should also be mindful that 'when alleged "neglect" is an aspect of abuse, difficult questions arise concerning the balance between parental protectiveness and the acceptance of the child's needs to take risks' (Burke and Cigno, 2000: 105). The same difficult balance must of course also be struck by the parents of non-disabled children, as I discussed in the previous chapter, but in the case of disabled children, overprotectiveness can sometimes amount to a sweeping denial of personal autonomy. In the long run such overprotectiveness can be counterproductive, because if we are prevented from having any exposure to risk-taking, we are denied the opportunity to learn to deal with risky situations. And indeed such restrictions may themselves do long-term harm. Howells (1997) argues that this contributes to the high incidence of mental health problems among adults with learning disabilities.

Different professional systems

I have already alluded to the different systems that characteristically deal with 'children with disabilities' as one category, and 'child protection' as another. 'Children with disabilities' services tend to operate by trying to provide a variety of services, including respite care, to help families to cope – and no doubt help to prevent a great many families reaching the sort of breaking point where abuse might occur. But one downside of this is that arranging for children to be looked after elsewhere can be used as a way of sweeping family problems under the carpet. (This can occur with children who do not have disabilities, incidentally, but more rarely, since respite care is not generally offered.) Jenny Morris gives the example of a young woman, 'Suba', who 'had been rejected by her mother at birth and experienced emotional and physical abuse throughout her childhood'. Suba was sent away to boarding school, and as an adult 'feels angry that the professionals who were in contact with her did not confront the abuse she experienced, but instead saw sending her away to school as a solution', to the point that

> when it became clear that she continued to experience . . . abuse during the holidays, various arrangements were made so that she did not go home but stayed at school or in adult residential establishments, or went on special holidays organized for disabled children. (Morris, 1999: 98)

I think it is much less likely that such an arrangement would have been seen as a 'solution' for a non-disabled child. It may have prevented Suba from being exposed to abuse from her mother, but it denied her the possibility of any sort of secure family life, either with her mother *or* with a substitute family. And this, in its own way, is also a kind of abuse.

Working with disabled children

In one sense, the issues involved in doing child protection work with disabled children are exactly the same as those involved in work with any other child. As with any child, the child protection worker must find an appropriate way of communicating that will allow the child to convey what she needs to say and the worker to provide the child with the information she needs to have. As with any child, the worker must be sensitive to issues of power, divided loyalties, and so on.

For disabled children, however, the power issues may be much more acute than they are for other children. Some disabled children may be dependent on adults to meet even their most basic needs, and options that are available to non-disabled children simply are not practicable. Kennedy (2002: 157) makes the point that the advice offered in pre-ventative programmes designed for non-disabled children may be irrelevant for disabled children, because of the different options that are available. A child with a visual or motor impairment cannot simply run away from a situation that she finds threatening or uncomfortable, for instance. On the other hand, advice that disabled children particularly do need may be absent. Children who are necessarily subject to invasive medical procedures, or who require intimate personal care, for example, may need particular help on the distinction between appropriate and inappropriate touching.

Communication with disabled children may involve a range of very specific skills, over and above the skills that are required in any case to work effectively with children. Morris found that, in one of the areas she studied, 'Only 27% of the children on the caseload of the Children with Disabilities team . . . used speech to communicate, while another 25% used limited speech' (1999: 100). Children who are unable to speak as a result of motor impairments may use a variety of techno-logical aids. Children with learning difficulties may communicate using sign systems such as Makaton. The first language of deaf children may be British Sign Language – or American Sign Language in North America – and these sign languages are not, as some hearing people mistakenly believe, visual representations of English, but different languages with their own grammatical systems. This means that, as Kennedy (2002: 153) points out, even if deaf children can write in English, the English they use may be a second language.

Attempting an investigative interview, or therapeutic work, without being familiar with the child's preferred means of communication, is equivalent to trying to work with a French child without being able to speak French. Child protection social workers whose brief includes disabled children either need to be familiar with the relevant communication systems, or need to develop close working relationships with other professionals who do have the necessary skills and are able to act as interpreters.

The communication challenge does not end there. Working with people from other countries requires more of us than just a way round the language difference, but also an understanding of the cultural differences. In the same way, effective communication with a child with disabilities requires not just a familiarity with the particular communication system she uses, but also a familiarity with the particular circumstances of the lifestyle of the child, who may attend a different kind of school, use different services and have different experiences of adult professionals than other children.

Exercise 5.3

Rodney French is a boy of 13 with Down syndrome. He lives with his mother and older sister. He occasionally visits his father, who is separated from his mother. Rodney has minimal language, consisting solely of single word utterances. These utterances are also very hard for others to understand, as he is barely able to articulate consonantal sounds at all. ('Mum' would therefore be something like 'Uh'. 'Dad' would be something like 'Ah'. His sister Holly is 'Oyee'.) He is receiving assistance from a speech therapist, with whom he has a very good relationship according to both his family and his school. Attempts are being made to help him to supplement his spoken language with Makaton signs, but so far he has made little progress with this.

Mrs French, Rodney's mother, is very protective of him, and anxious about his safety. For example, she is anxious about Rodney's contact visits with his father, as she feels that his father's flat is not a safe environment, and that his father does not supervise him closely enough.

Towards the end of the summer holiday, Mrs French reports the following to a duty social worker. Rodney seemed distressed and agitated at the prospect of returning to school, even though in the past he has always looked forward to school. Trying to establish why, Mrs French asked him to make a drawing, at which Rodney produced a picture of two figures (circles with lines sticking out of them), one of which she says represented Rodney and the other Mr Fleet, who is a learning support assistant at the school, a single, openly gay man of 55. She says that Rodney told her the picture represented Mr Fleet putting his finger into Rodney's anus. Mrs French says that she cannot allow Rodney to go back to school while Mr Fleet is there.

With Mrs French's permission, the duty social worker speaks to the headmistress of Rodney's school, Mrs Teal. Mrs Teal says that she is extremely sceptical about this allegation because (a) Mrs French has always been antagonistic to Mr Fleet's appointment and opposed his appointment because she believes it is not appropriate for a homosexual man to work with children (*although in actual fact there is no reason to suppose that homosexual men pose any more threat to children than hetero-sexual ones*). Mr Fleet is in fact very popular with the children, including Rodney; (b) Rodney is not capable of drawing a recognizable object or person, and (c) Rodney is not capable of making an allegation of this kind verbally, except by being asked a series of yes/no questions – and he is prone to respond in whatever way he thinks will meet approval.

If you were responsible for following this up, how would you proceed?

Comments on Activity 5.3

There are several different initial 'gut reactions' that one might have to the information so far presented. You might wonder, for example, whether the whole thing is really a manifestation of Mrs French's anxiety about separation from Rodney and of her homophobia – and that she is simply projecting these feelings onto her son. This seems to be the view of Mrs Teal. But whatever your initial reactions, these are serious allegations that are being made, which need to be looked into. It is important not to use the difficulty of communicating with Rodney – and the existence of a half-way plausible alternative explanation for the allegation – as a pretext for not trying to establish what Rodney himself has to say.

It might have occurred to you that one way forward would be to obtain the collaboration of Rodney's speech therapist, whom Rodney apparently knows and likes, and would seem to have some expertise in communicating with him. The speech therapist may not have much experience in child protection matters, however, so that any interview with Rodney would need to be planned collaboratively. Some care will need to be given to the questions that are put to Rodney, so that he is not led into either confirming or denying that Mr Fleet abused him. Thought should also be given to the venue and context in which he is interviewed, so as far as possible Rodney would feel comfortable and able to say whatever he wants. (The inter-agency strategy discussion, discussed in Chapter 2, is intended precisely for the purpose of thinking through these types of issues.)

Naturally one hopes that, by planning the interview carefully, and ensuring that it is conducted by someone with the appropriate communication skills and a good relationship with Rodney, it will be possible to determine whether there is any basis for believing that Rodney may have been sexually abused by Mr Fleet (or indeed by someone else). However there is a real possibility that, even after such an exercise, it may still not be clear whether there is a basis for the allegations or not. It is a fact of life in child protection work that some investigations are inconclusive, and this is true of investigations involving non-disabled children as well as disabled ones. This would leave very difficult questions to be decided by the inter-professional system and by the family. But careful planning of the investigation, and appropriate expert help, should at least ensure that the chances of obtaining useful information are maximized.

Opinions on this allegation are rather polarized between Mrs French, who is convinced that Mr Fleet has abused Rodney, and the school, who are convinced that this is a figment of Mrs French's imagination. The views of others – Rodney's father, the family doctor, the speech therapist – may help to give a more rounded picture.

Assessing families

In Part III of this book I will discuss why some parents mistreat or neglect their children. I look in Chapter 7 at how stressors of one kind or another can precipitate abuse and/or preoccupy parents and carers to the point where they neglect their children. And I will argue that families are most vulnerable when stress factors in the here and now ('horizontal stressors') touch on areas which a family finds difficult for reasons connected with its own history ('vertical stressors'), or the history of its particular community or society.

All the stressors – horizontal and vertical – that can occur in families whose children are not disabled, can, of course, equally well occur in the families of disabled children. But the presence of disabled children is itself commonly a stressor, (a) because the child's impairments commonly present the rest of the family with additional challenges, but sometimes also (b) for more complex reasons to do with hopes and expectations, which I discussed earlier. The cultural context, as well as the family history and the history of its individual members, will all influence the ability of the family to cope with the challenges facing them in the here and now.

In any assessment of a family where there are child protection concerns, it is important to try and get a sense of the relationships between the child and her family. In the case of disabled children, we perhaps also need to look at the relationship between the family *and the disability*. One starting point for this might be Minnes's (1988) categorization of factors affecting a family's ability to cope with disability into:

1. The child's own characteristics.
2. The 'internal resources' of the family.
3. The 'external resources' of the family.
4. The family's perception of the child.

Minnes was looking specifically at the families of children with *learning* disabilities, but these categories seem to me to be valid for the families of other disabled children too (and indeed they could be applied to the families of non-disabled children).

The child's own characteristics

Different children present very different challenges. For example, the families of children with Down syndrome seem to cope better – on measures of stress and depression – than those with children with some other kinds of intellectual impairment (Hodapp, 1996). This is probably due in part to the fact that Down children tend, on average, to be affectionate and sociable, and to be less prone to difficult and challenging behaviour patterns than some other learning impaired children. But it is perhaps also because the syndrome is relatively common and well known, and there are well-developed support networks.

Some physical disabilities may make very large demands on families in terms of physical care. Children with autistic spectrum diagnoses (as in Exercise 5.2) may be incapable of the normal give and take of human communication and make exceptional demands on the patience of adult carers.

No child should be seen as being so difficult and demanding that abuse or rejection is inevitable, but any realistic assessment should consider the demands that are made by the child on her carers and on other family members.

The 'internal resources' of the family

This refers to the personal characteristics of the family members and of the family as a whole, and to the way they deal with challenges. In this area as in others coping strategies based on practical problem-solving seem to be more adaptive than 'emotion-focused' ones. 'In virtually every study, mothers who were focussed on actively solving problems seemed better off than those focussed primarily on their own emotional reactions' (Hodapp, 1998: 81). It is possible to learn new coping strategies, however, and in some cases this might be the focus for an 'intervention'.

The 'external resources' of the family

'External' resources include such things as the family's financial resources, accommodation, and the services and support networks available to them, so these are important factors in any assessment. An obvious method of intervention in cases where parents are in danger of not being able to cope, is to improve the support network by providing services, or assisting them in recruiting additional support. But, as discussed above, this kind of intervention poses the danger of simply 'plastering over' a deeper problem such as emotional rejection. This is one reason why any assessment should pay close attention also to the family's attitude towards the child.

The family's perception of the child

Abuse can simply be the result of stress brought about by a particular situation. This is as true in relation to children with disabilities as to those without. (Most parents will admit to having, at some time or another, taken out angry feelings on their children, even if this has only taken the form of unnecessarily harsh words.) If an abusive incident is the result of a problem of this kind, then helping to alleviate the stress may well be a solution.

However if the abusive incident is part of a long-standing pattern of abusive behaviour, or reflects long-standing negativity or ambivalence towards a child, then the picture is rather different. Sending a child away for more respite, for example, may in these circumstances only confirm a child's feelings of rejection and abandonment. Any assessment should therefore explore the feelings of parents and other family members towards a child, and the child's towards them. Are the feelings predominantly positive or negative? Is the child's presence welcomed or resented? If the feelings are predominantly negative is this temporary, or is it the long-term view?

We all tell ourselves different 'stories' to give some sort of meaning to our lives. Parents of disabled children, and disabled children themselves, will come up with different narratives with which to deal with the question of 'Why us?' or 'Why me?' Some might view it is a special responsibility placed upon them, or a kind of challenge. Others might view the additional demands of a disability as being 'unfair', a burden, a distraction from the real business of their life. Some might view it as a punishment. (There may be cultural differences here: Westcott and Cross, 1996: 2–3, suggest that many religious traditions include the idea that disability is a punishment for the past actions of the parents.)

Some parents may end up viewing the disability as an affliction placed upon them by the child (the parents in Exercise 5.1, perhaps). Others may view it as something that they align themselves with the child against, battling on behalf of the child to overcome the obstacles that the world places in the way of those who have impairments. Some may be so preoccupied with overcoming the disability that they forget the child herself. There are many possibilities. The point I am making is that we need to understand the context in which abuse or neglect takes place, to understand its severity and meaning. It is always with these nuances, as much as the actual practical facts, that any child protection assessment (whether with disabled or non-disabled children) needs to grapple. Exercise 5.4 concludes this chapter by looking at this dimension.

Exercise 5.4

Looking at the previous three exercises in this chapter, how would you describe and contrast the attitudes of Mr and Mrs Davis, parents of Harriet (Exercise 5.1), Mr Thomas, father of Billy (5.2), and Mrs French, mother of Rodney (5.3), to being the parents of a disabled child?

Comments on Exercise 5.4

Of course, it would in reality be a serious mistake to make any judgement on how a family operates on the basis of the small amount of information contained in these exercises. But this is an exercise, not reality, and subject to that proviso you may agree with me that these three examples seem to illustrate three different attitudes. Mr and Mrs Davis seemed, on first impressions, to be frankly rejecting of Harriet and to resent her for making their lives more difficult. Mr Thomas was seen by others as struggling heroically with the demands of being a single parent of a disabled child, but perhaps his need to be seen to be coping may have resulted in his hiding (and perhaps denying even to himself) the real difficulties he was having, and the violent outbursts he was failing to contain. Mrs French was very protective and anxious about her child, to the point where, at least in the view of Mrs Teal, the headmistress, she was actually imagining dangers which did not exist. Whether or not Mrs Teal is right in this case, there is certainly a danger that parents of disabled children can become overprotective.

In this chapter I have looked at the special case of disabled children and considered:

- the particular vulnerability of disabled children to maltreatment for a variety of different reasons. I discussed in particular the role in this that is played by family factors, widely held assumptions about disabled children, and the fact that there may be different professional systems dealing with 'child protection' and 'disability'
- the particular issues that arise when working with children with disabilities, including issues of power and, in particular, issues to do with communication which arise for children with a variety of disabilities. I suggested that trying to interview a child without the relevant communication skills is akin to interviewing the speaker of a foreign language without an interpreter

- the need to assess the families of disabled children and how they deal with the disability, suggesting that for each family it is important to consider the characteristics of the child, the family's internal and external resources, and the family's attitude to the child.

The next chapter will return to children in general, rather than specifically disabled children, and will consider the long-term consequences of child maltreatment.

Harm 6

Preventing or minimizing harm to children is the purpose of child protection work. At the core of a child protection investigation is establishing whether or not a child is suffering, or likely to suffer, harm. The purpose of any subsequent work is to stop harmful things continuing to happen to the child, or at any rate to reduce the chances of them happening, and to reverse or mitigate whatever harm has already been done.

Not surprisingly, therefore, the concept of 'harm' is central in the legal systems under which child protection work is carried out. Thus, the law of the American state of Massachusetts, for example, permits state intervention in family life where there is 'a child under the age of eighteen years who is suffering physical or emotional injury resulting from abuse inflicted on him which causes *harm or substantial risk of harm* to the child's health or welfare' (NCCANI, 2002: 56, my italics).

In England and Wales, under the 1989 Children Act, local authorities have a duty to investigate when they have reasonable cause to suspect that a child in their area 'is suffering, or is likely to suffer, significant harm' (Children Act, section 47 (1)(b)). An emergency protection order (EPO) can be made only if the court concerned is satisfied that 'there is reasonable cause to believe that the child is likely to suffer significant harm'. And courts can only make a care or supervision order when 'the child concerned is suffering or is likely to suffer, significant harm' and the harm is caused by 'the care given to the child, or likely to be given to him if the order were not made, not being what it would be reasonable to expect a parent to give to him' or 'the child's being beyond parental control' (Children Act, section 31 (2)). (Children and families who are not subject to child protection proceedings, incidentally, are entitled to services, under section 17 of the Act, if they are 'in need'. The definition of need includes 'health or development . . . likely to be significantly impaired, or further impaired, without the provision . . . of such services'. So the idea of 'harm' is implicit too in the idea of 'need'.)

The difficulty lies in determining the seriousness of the harm that is likely to be caused in any given situation. In order to do this we need some ideas both about the *nature* of the harm that can be caused by child maltreatment, and also about the *ways* in which child maltreatment is harmful. This last point is important because just recognizing harm, or risk, is not enough. We must also have some idea about *how* the behaviour of a child's carers is linked to the harm done to a child, and about what would need to happen for this to change.

In many cases, there are dangers which are immediate and acute: a child may be in danger of sexual or violent assault. And in some cases children suffer, or are at risk of suffering, death or irreversible physical harm. In the majority of cases, however, the harm that is done by child maltreatment is in the main psychological and emotional: not acute, not immediately visible, but potentially devastating in its effects on the rest of a person's life.

Before going on to discuss the harm that can be done by abuse and neglect, it is important to note that the kinds of intervention that social workers carry out *can, in themselves, do harm*, a topic I will return to in Chapter 11. To give a simple example: to remove a child of nine from a family where he is being beaten and place him in a foster-home may prevent the beating from happening, but may be harmful in many other ways. He may be frightened. He may grieve for his own family. He may feel uncomfortable and out of place in an alien environment. He may behave in ways that result in the foster-parents being unable to cope with him, so that he has to experience rejection. He may even be abused in the foster-home. It's therefore important in decision making to try and balance the severity and likelihood of the harm that would be done by not intervening with any negative consequences that might follow from the intervention itself.

Physical harm

Death and serious injury

The most extreme physical consequence of child abuse and neglect, though fortunately also a very rare one, is of course death. Death occurs as a consequence of violent assaults such as punching, hitting, and (in the case of small children in particular) shaking, but it is important to be aware that parental neglect may be almost as common a cause of death as actual physical assault. In very rare, extreme cases neglect can be fatal if it results in children dying from starvation, or cold. More commonly, neglect kills by resulting in fatal accidents such as drowning, falling, burns and road accidents. One 50-state survey in America, for example, found that out of all child deaths resulting from maltreatment in a given year, 43 per cent were the consequence of neglect rather than physical abuse (Wang and Daro, 1998).

Both physical abuse and neglect can also lead to permanent physical damage. Brain damage, paralysis, blindness and permanent, profound intellectual impairment can result, for instance, from shaking a baby. Head injuries inflicted by hitting can have similarly long-term consequences, as can accidents resulting from parental neglect.

The following exercise looks at a possible instance:

Exercise 6.1

Simon, aged five, suffered extensive, disfiguring facial burns when he attempted to cook chips for himself and for his younger brother, aged three, and ended up pulling up the hot chip-pan over himself. This occurred at about 11 a.m. and it would seem that Simon's parents were upstairs in bed at the time.

Is this a case of neglect?

Comments on Exercise 6.1

It is important not to jump to conclusions about such cases. You will probably agree that for the children to be unsupervised until so late in the morning does sound negligent. If I added, though, that both parents had flu at the time, that the father had got up earlier and given the children some cereal, and that when the incident happened he had just got back into bed with his wife to drink a cup of tea with her, having left both of the children downstairs apparently engrossed in TV, it might seem less so.

On the other hand, if I added that the children had been the subject of repeated complaints and referrals to police and social services because they were regularly seen by neighbours playing unsupervised next to a busy road – and if Simon's school had been concerned that Simon often arrived late to school wearing inappropriate clothes, and that he often seemed to have had no breakfast, a very different picture emerges.

Context, as ever, is crucial.

Failure to thrive

Failure to thrive (FTT) can be seen in children who have grown up in institutional environments where they have suffered extreme deprivation, which may include both psychological/emotional elements and physical ones such as poor nutrition. A comparatively recent study of the long-term effects of early life in such environments is provided by Michael Rutter and the Romanian Orphans Study Team (Rutter et al., 1998). Such children may show marked delay in physical growth and a range of abnormal behaviours. The Rutter study found that early psychological privation appeared to be a more important predictor of long-term developmental problems than poor nutrition.

FTT does not only occur in an institutional context however. Sometimes babies fail to put on weight, or even lose weight, without any apparent organic cause. This has in the past been identified as a symptom of emotional abuse or neglect, but it is not an assumption which we should make too readily. It would now appear that the main cause of non-organic FTT is due to inadequate intake of food, and this may be due to a variety of causes: some babies are extremely resistant to feeding, for example, in spite of their parents' best efforts. Batchelor (1999: 35–6), discussing recent research in this area, concludes that 'a small number of children with an inborn constitutional predisposition will, in the face of stress or neglect, develop growth hormone deficiency which results in stunted growth. However, this is a very rare condition which affects perhaps three to five children per 10,000.'

Physical consequences of sexual abuse

Although sexual abuse can result in physical injury – and although it frequently has profound and long-lasting psychological consequences – it is unusual for sexual abuse to result in permanent physical damage. But one long-lasting and sometimes fatal consequence of sexual abuse is infection with sexually transmitted diseases, including HIV. Another consequence can, of course, be pregnancy.

Psychological harm

There is plenty of evidence that children who have been abused or neglected suffer long-term psychological harm, which may include some or all of the following:

- low self-esteem
- depression and suicidal impulses
- difficulties in relating to others
- difficulties as parents – including, in some cases, becoming abusers themselves
- mental health problems
- low educational attainment
- restlessness and difficulty in concentrating.

These consequences do not occur inevitably. A proportion of the victims, even of very serious abuse, appear to emerge relatively unscathed. Summarizing 26 studies of college students, Bagley and Thurston come to the conclusion that 'about half of those who experienced long-term intrusive abuse by a trusted family member or authority figure do not have psychologically abnormal outcomes as a young adult' (1995: 140).

But although every individual may not suffer long-term consequences to the same degree, nevertheless the likelihood of all these outcomes is certainly increased by abuse and neglect in childhood. All the consequences listed above can follow on from all the different varieties of maltreatment, and it would seem that the harm done by abuse may be related not so much to the precise form of abuse itself, as to the nature of the abusive relationship in which the abuse occurred. Thus, while I will discuss the different categories of abuse in turn, you will see common themes running though all of them. One of these is that abuse or neglect is much more harmful when it is chronic and long-lasting, and that isolated incidents – however distressing at the time – do not on the whole result in long-term harm (Rutter and Rutter, 1993).

Why is it that abuse and neglect can result in long-term psychological and emotional harm? Why, if no long-term physical harm has been done, are the mental consequences often still apparent, and still suffered, long after the abuse or neglect itself has stopped? There are a number of different types of explanation – not necessarily mutually exclusive – which may account for this.

Critical periods

In this view there are certain periods in development during which certain psychological structures are 'laid down'. If normal development is interfered with in those periods, then irreversible harm may occur which cannot fully be put right at a later stage. We know this to be the case, for example, in the development of vision. There is a certain critical period during which the visual cortex of the brain develops, and if a developing animal is deprived of visual stimulation during this period, it may never acquire normal vision (Rutter and Rutter, 1993: 12). The question is, are there similar critical periods in emotional development? Are some kinds of psychological harm irreversible if they occur at particularly sensitive stages of development? There is certainly evidence that various kinds of psychological harm resulting from deprivation at specific periods of development are difficult to completely undo.

For example, the study I mentioned above of children from Romanian institutions adopted in Britain (Rutter et al., 1998) found that children entering Britain from Romania at under six months, having previously been cared for in institutions, appear to have caught up cognitively with their peers by age four. Children entering Britain when *over* six months of age also showed substantial cognitive catch-up, but were nevertheless delayed compared to children who had not experienced an institutional upbringing. The differences between the children who were removed from the institutional environment at under six months, and those who were removed at an older age, suggest that there may be a critical period at which psychological/emotional privation has long-term consequences.

We should be careful not to follow this line of thinking to the point that we assume that all psychological harm from childhood is irreversible, and I personally would suggest that the quite common practice of referring to children and adults as 'emotionally damaged' is something to be avoided. Clarke and Clarke (2000) present a range of arguments against seeing early childhood as more of a 'critical period' than any other time of life.

Internalized working models

Another way of looking at the harm that is done as a result of abuse or neglect in childhood, is to look at it as 'bad information'. The term 'working models' comes from John Bowlby (1980), the originator of attachment theory, though it is an idea that has much in common with other psychodynamic models. In essence the idea is that during early childhood, we each construct a working model of the world and our position in it. The elements of this model will include ideas about our own value relative to other people, and ideas about what we can expect from other people and how best to relate to them.

Bowlby's idea was that when a child is in an abusive or neglectful situation – or indeed in any situation where for some reason the child's needs are not being met – it may be that she simply cannot bear to face the full reality of a frightening situation that she may be powerless to alter. She will therefore cope by constructing a 'faulty working model' of the world, which does not accurately reflect the reality of the situation, but helps in some way to reduce the anxiety. This may include using various strategies such as 'splitting', to separate off the abusive aspects of the situation, or to persuade herself that these aspects are somehow alright. (One way of doing the latter may be for a child to persuade herself that the abuse is something that she deserves.) The faulty working model is then maintained by what Bowlby called 'defensive exclusion' (Freud would have called it 'denial' or 'repression'), in which contrary information is simply excluded from consciousness.

As a result of defensive exclusion, faulty working models are very resistant to change, and indeed may be impossible to change unless the person concerned can be made aware of the distorted nature of her own thinking and the defences that she has put in place. The long-term emotional harm – low self-esteem, difficulty in relating to others – that we can often see in people who have been abused or neglected as children, is thus the result of faulty working models of the world which that person is continuing to apply to her relationships with other people and with the world in general, long after the original reason for it no longer applies.

The following exercise is an illustration of this process.

Exercise 6.2

William, aged four, lives with his mother. There is no one else in the family and William has very little contact with anyone else. William's mother is subject to extreme mood swings which are sudden and unpredictable. Sometimes she treats him kindly, but at other times she flies into frightening rages and threatens to abandon him, or kill herself, and tells him that it would all be his fault. On occasion she has followed up such threats by cutting herself with a knife. On other occasions she has gone out and left him alone in the flat, sometimes for hours on end.

At the age of four, William cannot deal with this situation as an adult could. He has no way of knowing, for example, that his mother's behaviour is abnormal and no life experience to tell him that it is unreasonable of her to blame him for her distress. He is probably not aware of any possible outside source of help. He cannot remove himself from the situation or find someone else to live with.

His mother may be terrifying, but she is also his only source of comfort, nourishment and safety. In many ways, she is his world.

How would William try to cope with this?

Comments on Exercise 6.2

It seems to me that William cannot defend himself in any real way from what is happening, so all that is open to him is to resort to various psychological defences.

One psychological defence that we all use when faced with an unavoidable fact which we find intolerable (such as the news of a bereavement, for example) is to tell ourselves: 'This isn't really happening', 'This isn't real'. In short, we 'go into denial' – or 'defensively exclude' – the thing that we can't cope with. This is a normal and necessary response to a shocking new event, but in most cases it is followed by a period of adjustment to the new reality, a gradual coming to terms with what has happened.

For a child in William's situation, however, there can be no coming to terms with something that cannot be consigned to the past but will recur over and over again. He can't really afford to come out of denial and is therefore likely to attempt a whole series of psychological manoeuvres to hold reality at bay.

He could tell himself that the mum who mistreats him is a different person from the mum who is kind to him – and that the kind one is his real mum – or he may even split his idea of himself into two, so that when things are relatively calm, he can dissociate himself from the memory of the bad times by seeing them as things that happened to someone else.

He could agree with his mother that he is a very bad boy, and that he deserves the treatment that he gets from her. Although this does not sound a very comfortable position to take, it may well be less frightening to think of himself as bad, than to think of the adult who controls his whole world as being capricious and dangerous.

He could tell himself that he doesn't really need his mother anyway.

He might find means of comforting himself, rather like the baby monkeys in the cruel experiments conducted in the 1950s and 1960s by Harlow and his collaborators (Harlow, 1963), which showed that monkeys deprived of the comfort of their mothers, would cling to crudely made monkey dolls covered in terry cloth.

And perhaps these patterns and habits of thought – and these means of self-comfort – may become so entrenched over time that even when he has grown up and left home, William will still use the same strategies to deal with the world: excluding what is painful from consciousness, holding contradictory stories in his mind at the same time, blaming himself for things that are not his fault (or perhaps being unable to distinguish between the things that are his fault and the things that are not).

Meanwhile, under the surface, would still be all the feelings that he has tried so hard to deny – anger, fear, longing – ready to erupt unpredictably at moments when the effort of containing them becomes too great.

Post-traumatic stress

In the above discussion, I have already made a connection between the effects of abuse and the known psychological effects on people, of all ages, of traumatic events. The fact that abusive incidents are clearly traumatic events has led some commentators to suggest that the characteristic response of human beings to trauma – a group of observable behaviours referred to collectively as post-traumatic stress (PTS) – is an appropriate way of looking at the effects of abuse. I will return to this below in the discussion of the effects of sexual abuse.

Continuing abusive/neglectful patterns

A point made by Ann and Alan Clarke (2000), in making the case against early experience being uniquely important, is that for most people, early experience, whether good or bad, is followed by more of the same. The apparent long-term effects of abusive incidents in early childhood may occur because, in fact, many children remain living in the environment in which the abuse took place. Even if the actual incidents themselves did not recur, it is likely that aspects of the parent–child relationship in which the abuse occurred, still continue. This is a subject I will return to in my discussion of the consequences of physical abuse.

Feedback loops/transactional factors

It is also possible that the effects of maltreatment become entrenched not because they are, so to speak, permanently 'hardwired' into the brains of victims, but because the victim's initial response to maltreatment causes her to behave in a way that has a tendency to provoke further negative responses from others, which in turn makes the victim generate more of the same behaviour – and so on. This would be an example of a 'feedback loop' – a pattern that is often found in biological systems that try to maintain a steady state in relation to their environment. Often feedback loops are beneficial, as in mutually satisfactory parent–child relationships in which both parties reward each other for their attention, but they can also be 'vicious circles', which lock all of those involved in a dysfunctional relationship.

It is certainly a commonly observed phenomenon that children from abusive or neglectful backgrounds who are placed in foster-homes, will often behave in ways that seem calculated to provoke rejection or hostility from their new carers. The following account of a 10-year-old victim of neglect, now in a long-term foster-home, illustrates this point:

> Bobby always set himself up for rejection. He inevitably asked for attention when the foster mother was tied up with someone else. For example, if someone was injured or crying, Bobby would demand her focus when she was busy bandaging or cuddling. On the other side, whenever she attempted to give Bobby positive attention, he rebuffed her. Bobby, whose history showed him to be sorely neglected, compulsively re-enacted that history within the foster home. (Delaney, 1991: 50)

In a way, this idea of a 'vicious circle' is really a development of what I said earlier under the heading of 'internalized working models'. Many of the psychological effects of maltreatment – such as low self-esteem, lack of trust in others and so on – are qualities that tend to be 'self-fulfilling prophesies'. A person whose fear of rejection makes her very withdrawn and uncommunicative, for example, may well find that people avoid her company.

It is therefore very important to remember that to break the vicious circle it is necessary not only to stop the abuse or neglect from happening, but to address the patterns of thought and behaviour which the abuse has established – patterns which may not only distort the thinking of the abused person, but may also provoke negative responses from others.

This is a point which is very often forgotten. Many people might assume, for example, that by removing a child from an abusive situation and placing him in a caring one, or by changing the abusive situation *into* a caring one, the effects of abuse and neglect can be undone. In fact, children who have been maltreated often can't respond to any amount of caring unless they are also given specialist help aimed at addressing the 'faulty working models' that they have internalized while living in the abusive and neglectful situation.

Emotional abuse and neglect

Although neglect and emotional abuse are, on the whole, less dramatic than other forms of abuse, their effects are just as severe, or even more so in some respects. Citing six different pieces of prospective and retrospective research, Gaudin (1999: 100) concludes that neglect results in cognitive and academic deficits in older school-age victims, and that 'These negative developmental effects have been found to be *far more enduring for neglect than for any other kind of maltreatment.*' (My italics.) Thus, for example, Eckenrode et al. (1993), found that neglected children had more school absences and lower standards of academic performance than either non-maltreated children *or* physically abused children.

One difficulty that such studies have is separating out the effects of neglect from those of poverty and social disadvantage. But a study which specifically controlled for socioeconomic status (that is to say, compared children who had been matched for socioeconomic status) still found that 'negative, uninvolved, neglecting parenting at the pre-school age has a negative impact on social competence at school age' (Herrenkohl et al., 1991: 73).

In another study, Erickson et al. (1989) explored the relative effects of different kinds of abuse on children and compared four 'abused' groups of children over the first six years of their lives – children who were physically abused, children whose parents were hostile and verbally abusive, children who were neglected and children whose parents were psychologically unavailable (the last being seen as emotionally abused). A further 'control' group of children who had not experienced mal-treatment was also studied. Not surprisingly, children in all four 'abused' groups scored lower on self-confidence and self-esteem than those in the 'control' group. At age four, of the four abused groups, it was the neglected and emotionally abused children who were faring the worst, intellectually and socially, *particularly the emotionally abused children*. At age six, however, this group was doing about the same as other 'abused' children, and it was the *neglected children* who were having the most problems, being very low achievers in school.

Another finding on the same lines was that of Oates et al. (1985), who found that neglected children seemed to be lower in self-esteem than children who had been physically abused.

The discussion below of physical, and even sexual, abuse also suggests that much of what is most harmful about those kinds of abuse is the emotional abuse, and/or neglect of a child's needs, that is inherent in all kinds of abuse, rather than simply the abusive incidents themselves.

Physical abuse

'We have certainly not found any evidence that physical abuse *of itself* (except in the most severe cases) causes long-term harm' was the perhaps surprising conclusion of one large British study of the long-term effects of physical abuse (Gibbons et al., 1995: 53). I will now consider this study and its findings in more detail in order to consider the implications of this statement, which I think are important. I should emphasize that the authors of this study were not implying that we need not be concerned about physical abuse.

Gibbons et al. looked at a group of 170 children who'd been put on a child protection register 10 years previously under the category of physical abuse. The children had been aged 0–5 at time of registration.

The study tried to control for other factors such as social deprivation by selecting a 'Comparison group' of children who were matched to the 'Index group' by age, gender, social class, and by the fact that they lived in the same neighbourhood and attended the same schools. The interviewers who talked to children and their parents did so 'blind', which meant that they did not know whether the children and parents they were assigned to interview were in the Index group (the children who had been on the register) or the Comparison group (the children who had not been on the register). The people who scored the interviews likewise worked 'blind'.

Various developmental measures were used to assess the children as they were, 10 years on from the time when the Index group children had been on the register. The measures used included:

- Growth – height, weight, head circumference.
- Behaviour – using standard questionnaires filled in both by teachers and parents.
- Emotions – these were assessed using the child's own self-reports. Children were interviewed on their current circumstances and these interviews included questions to do with *fears* and *depression*. The interview transcripts were rated 'blind' and given high or low scores for 'fears' and for 'depression'.
- Problems with peers – again using the children's own self-reports on issues such as friends, bullying and social isolation.
- Cognitive ability – using standard tests.

The researchers then looked at whether there was any significant relationship between these developmental measures and whether children were in the Index group or the Comparison group. In other words: were their scores on these developmental measures affected by whether they had been on the register for physical abuse 10 years previously?

The researchers also compared these measures with other factors, some of which related to the original abuse episode, some of which related to family history, and some of which related to current circumstances.

The main significant differences between the groups were in the areas of behaviour and problems with peers. Reports from both teachers and parents were more likely to say, for instance, that Index children were 'not much liked', 'often disobedient', that they 'often tell lies', that they could not settle 'for more than a few minutes' and that they were 'squirmy/fidgety' as compared to children in the Comparison group. Index children reported significantly more problems with peers than comparison children, an effect which was more marked for girls than it was for boys.

All these differences, however, though statistically significant, were not large, and there was a large overlap between the two groups.

A statistician, 'blind' to whether the children were in the Index or Comparison groups, sorted all the children into three outcome categories:

- Poor outcome (in terms both of behavioural and emotional problems and of school performance).
- Good outcome (in terms both of behavioural and emotional problems and of school performance).
- Low performance (good outcome in terms of behavioural and emotional problems, but low in terms of school performance).

Of the Index children, 42 per cent turned out to be in the poor outcome group, as compared to 19 per cent of the Comparison children, while in the good outcome group were 22 per cent of the Index children and 48 per cent of the Comparison children. In other words, about one-fifth of the Index children seemed not to show any long-term developmental problems, while about one-fifth of the Comparison children *did* display such problems. These differences could still be found when factors like economic disadvantage and household type were adjusted for.

Having sorted the children into these 'outcome' groups, it was then possible to use statistical analysis to see whether, and to what extent, these outcomes were linked to a variety of different factors.

One factor looked at was severity of injury. In the Index group, about 16 per cent of the injuries leading to registration were classified as serious: i.e., fractures, head injuries, internal injuries, severe burns, poisoning. Others had more minor injuries or had been registered because they were thought to be at risk of injury. But severity of injury had no significant link with outcomes, except in four cases where permanent physical damage had been done. Nor did whether or not there was subsequent physical abuse (after the incident leading to registration) have any impact on outcomes.

But, while severity of injury did not turn out to have a statistically significant link to outcome, a range of factors associated with registration did have a statistical link. Thus when neglect, as well as physical injury, had been an issue at time of registration, this was found to have a significant link with poorer outcomes in terms of behaviour at school, and depression. Higher depression scores were also associated with marital violence having been an issue at the time of registration. Children who'd been registered because of risk of injury, rather than actual injury, were also associated with higher depression scores than the other Index children. For professionals to identify a risk of physical injury, they would have to have picked up a strong sense of threat in the home. My suggestion would be that this atmosphere of threat, which would also, of course, be picked up by children in the family, is more harmful than actual incidents of violence.

The flavour of these findings was further corroborated in this study by the discovery of a number of statistically significant associations between children's reports of current parental style and outcomes:

- Difficulty in peer relationships was associated with a punitive style and use of physical punishment.
- Behaviour problems at school were associated with parental criticism and a punitive style.
- Cognitive attainment related positively with parental strictness and good relationships between parent and child, and negatively with parental criticism.
- Depression was linked to a child's rating of parental relationships.
- Problems with peers were associated with parental criticism and with punitive style and recent physical punishment.
- Poor outcomes were associated with parents reported by their children as being unpredictable or prone to shouting, making threats, smacking or hitting.
- Poor outcomes were associated with children who reported few shared activities with their mothers and who enjoyed activities with their mothers less.
- Poor outcomes were associated with children who disagreed with the statement that their mother usually kept her promises (57 per cent of the poor outcome group, as against 91 per cent of the good outcome group. For fathers the respective figures were 71 per cent and 84 per cent)

Poor outcomes were also more likely for children exposed to marital problems and domestic violence, and for children whose carers reported themselves to be lacking in support from the wider community.

What I take from studies like this, and from my own experience, is that physical abuse should be regarded as one of the *indicators* of an abusive parent–child *relationship*. It is the abusive *relationship* that causes long-term psychological harm. In order to minimize that harm, therefore, it is necessary not just to prevent incidents of physical abuse from occurring, but also to change the relationship which underlies those incidents.

To attempt a medical analogy: imagine a harmful disease which was commonly, but not always, accompanied by a distinctive skin rash. The presence of the rash would certainly indicate that someone had the disease, but the absence of it would not necessarily mean that they did not have it.

Sexual abuse

> Stephanie was in continuous psychiatric care for 25 years, including 3 years in closed wards following a psychotic break and suicide attempt at age 16. She kept trying to appease the devil who shouted inside her head to voice judgement and demand punishment for her stupidity. (Summit, 1988: 52–3)

Long-term effects of sexual abuse include self-destructive behaviour, anxiety, feelings of isolation and stigma, poor self-esteem, substance abuse, eating disorders, sexual problems and mental illness ('It is now well-established that up to a half of both men and women who experience long-term sexual abuse in childhood will have chronic mental health problems in adulthood,' according to Bagley and Thurston, 1995: 148).

The emotional and psychological effects of sexual abuse seem to be likely to be especially severe when the abuse is by the father or a close family member (see, for example, Beitchman et al., 1992), when it involves genital contact and when it involves the use of force. Long-term psychological effects are also related to the response received by the victim when the abuse came to light, for example whether she is believed and supported.

Among the various attempts that have been made to conceptualize the nature of the emotional and psychological damage that is done by sexual abuse, it has been suggested that it is an instance of so-called post-traumatic stress disorder (PTSD), which is experienced also by survivors of disasters and violent incidents. Post-traumatic stress typically occurs when people find themselves helpless in very dangerous and frightening situations (which would certainly be true of children facing abuse from much more powerful adults), and its classic symptoms include nightmares, frightening mental images, numbness and social withdrawal.

David Finkelhor, however (1988: 61ff) suggests that while PTSD might be a good model to apply to the effects of one-off abuse by strangers, it fits less well with abuse within the family, for two reasons. First, abuse within the family does not typically involve a single incident. It is 'less an "event" than a "relationship" or "situation".' Second, it does not adequately describe all the typical psychological consequences of sexual abuse, which may include cognitive disturbances such as 'distorted beliefs about self and others, self-blame, sexual misinformation and sexual confusions'.

Finkelhor proposes four 'Traumagenic [i.e. trauma-*causing*] dynamics' that are at work in sexual abuse, which I will now list. All but the first of these four dynamics are applicable also to physical abuse, emotional abuse and neglect.

Traumatic sexualization

Sexual abuse occurs under conditions which shape the sexuality of a child in inappropriate and dysfunctional ways:

- Children are often rewarded by abusers for sexual behaviour that is inappropriate for their age and as a result they can learn to use sexual behaviour as a strategy for manipulating others. In fact, sexually provocative behaviour by children is one of the ways in which it comes to light that they have been, or are being, sexually abused.
- Children also learn to give a distorted amount of importance to sexual parts of their bodies. Sexually abused children may become highly preoccupied with their genitals.
- Sexually abused children are commonly given highly inaccurate information by abusers about sexual behaviour and what is normal and appropriate.
- Sexually abused children may commonly learn to associate sex with frightening and disturbing memories. For example they may learn to associate sex with violence or threats.

Here, then, is an instance of a child developing a 'faulty working model' which includes ideas about the role of sex in human relationships that in the long run are likely to be harmful. The long-term implications of the distorted thinking and behaviour that may result from traumatic sexualization might include some of the following:

- A preoccupation with sex and compulsive sexual behaviours, or, on the other hand, an aversion to sex, reflected in avoidant or phobic behaviour.
- Involvement in prostitution. One American study found that 60 per cent of a sample of San Francisco prostitutes had been sexually abused (Silbert and Pines, 1981).
- 'Revictimization'. One study (Russell, 1986) found that women survivors of sexual abuse were nearly twice as likely as other women to be victims of rape or attempted rape, and more than twice as likely to have been subjected to physical violence from husbands or partners.
- Sexual performance problems.
- Difficulties as parents. Survivors of sexual abuse may inappropriately sexualize their children, and may themselves become involved in sexual abuse of children.

Betrayal

Sexual abuse – and, in different ways, all kinds of abuse – involve a betrayal. Someone on whom the child relies for protection becomes a source of distress and fear. Someone on whom the child relies to look after her interests is found to place his own gratification before her most basic needs. Even family members who are not involved in the abuse may be seen to some extent to have betrayed the child, by failing to notice the abuse, or failing to prevent it, or in some cases by actively tolerating it.

The effects of this dynamic might include a number of problems connected with difficulties in trusting others or in accurately judging the trustworthiness of others. Difficulties might include clinginess or isolation, marital and relationship problems, vulnerability to abuse and exploitation, failure of the survivor to recognize threats of abuse to her own children, or failure to protect them. (It may at first sight be surprising that some survivors of abuse are not good at protecting their own children from abuse. One might expect them to be exceptionally vigilant, as indeed many are. But we must remember that among the survival mechanisms of victims of abuse are 'dissociation' and 'defensive exclusion'. Thus a victim of abuse may become very skilled at blocking out the evidence of abuse.)

Stigmatization

Victims of sexual abuse (and victims also of violence) tend to report feelings of worthlessness, shame and guilt. As Finkelhor writes, children pick up these messages about themselves in a variety of ways:

> Abusers say it directly when they blame the victim . . . or denigrate the victim . . . They also say it indirectly through their furtiveness and pressures for secrecy. But much of the stigmatization comes from the attitudes the victims hear or the moral judgements they infer from those around them . . . [S]imply the fact of having been a victim is likely to impel the child to search for attributions to explain 'why it happened to me'. (Finkelhor, 1998: 70)

As I noted earlier, in the discussion of internalized working models, it may in some circumstances be easier for a victim to blame abuse on herself rather than face the alternative possibility that an adult, or adults, on whom she relies, cannot be relied upon at all.

The implications of stigmatization for adult life might include isolation, drug or alcohol abuse, depression, suicide and self-harm.

Powerlessness

Utter powerlessness and helplessness in a frightening situation is the stuff of nightmares. In sexual abuse (and again, in various ways, in other forms of abuse also), the sense of being invaded and of being powerless to resist it occurs at the most basic of levels. In some instances it is quite literally the child's own body that is being invaded. In all instances it is her privacy, her status as a child, her expectations of protection, that are violated.

In some forms of sexual abuse another kind of powerlessness is added in the form of violence or threats of violence, even of threats to life. While this is a major feature of much sexual abuse, it is present in physical abuse too, and in some kinds of emotional abuse. For a small child to be repeatedly threatened with abandonment, for example, may be extremely traumatic. Repeated traumatic events of this magnitude may simply be too much to bear, so that the victim has to resort to the psychological defences discussed earlier in this chapter, such as 'splitting' (also sometimes called 'dissociation') whereby she tells herself, in effect, that 'this is not happening to me'. It is worth noting in passing that these kinds of psychological mechanisms are also present in *abusers*, who are able to split off their abusive activity from the rest of their lives.

Long-terms effects of this dynamic of powerlessness might include things like nightmares, phobias, eating disorders, depression and revictimization, or various behaviours which are to do with trying to regain a sense of power, such as manipulative behaviour or even abusing others.

Finkelhor suggests that powerlessness may be exacerbated by experiences of attempting to escape from abuse but failing. He also makes the following very important point, which should be carefully noted by social workers and other child protection professionals:

> children often experience an enormous, unexpected, and devastating increase in powerlessness in the aftermath of abuse, when they find themselves unable to control the decisions of the adult world that may visit upon them many unwanted events – separation from family, prosecutions, police investigations – in addition to the termination of abuse. (Finkelhor, 1998: 72)

The following exercise is very loosely based on a real-life scenario in which this was, indeed, an issue:

Exercise 6.3

Suzanne, aged 14, lived with her mother, step-father and younger sister (aged 10). She had been showing signs of unhappiness for some time in school (weeping, poor concentration, isolation, truancy) and a particular teacher, Miss D, had spent a lot of time with her trying to establish a relationship with her and to encourage her to talk about whatever was on her mind.

Then, in one of her sessions with Miss D, Suzanne burst into tears and said something bad was going on, but she couldn't tell Miss D for fear of the consequences. Miss D tried to reassure her, and eventually Suzanne said that she would tell Miss D if Miss D could assure her that she would keep it secret.

Miss D said that she would tell no-one. Suzanne then told her that over the past few months, her step-father had been coming into her room, feeling her under her bedclothes and masturbating. He had told her to keep it secret, that her mother would never believe her, and that if she told her mother, she would be put into care.

Having been told this story, Miss D became very anxious. She had promised to respect Suzanne's wish that this be kept secret, yet unless

---

she took some action, the abuse would continue, and indeed not only Suzanne but also her little sister would continue to be at risk. Miss D discussed this with her head of year, who told her to go back to Suzanne and tell her that this would have to be reported to the social services.

Suzanne was angry and distressed, but Miss D went ahead and phoned social services who, in turn, contacted the police. A joint investigation was carried out. Suzanne reluctantly repeated her allegations. Her sister was also interviewed but did not make any allegations. The step-father was arrested and put on bail with a condition that he should move out of the family home.

The next day, Suzanne's mother contacted the police and said that Suzanne wanted to make a further statement. At the police station, Suzanne made a statement retracting all of her previous allegation and stating that she had made it all up to get back at her step-father after a disagreement.

There was no evidence other than Suzanne's now retracted original statement (no medical evidence, no witnesses, no corroborating evidence of any kind). The police could take no further action. The family indicated they wanted no involvement from social services. No further action was taken, even though Miss D was firmly convinced that Suzanne had told the truth about abuse and had retracted because she saw the situation getting out of her control and having outcomes that she did not want.

What went wrong here? What could have been done differently?

Comments on Exerise 6.3

You probably observed that it was a mistake on Miss D's part to promise to keep Suzanne's secret (although one can understand why she did it). If she had been clear that she couldn't guarantee to keep a secret, it is possible that Suzanne would not have told her what was going on. But Miss D probably could have guessed what kind of thing might be going on, and would have been able to discuss possible scenarios and to consider what might happen if Suzanne decided to talk.

If Suzanne had a chance to think through in advance what might happen, who would be involved and how she would have handled it, then perhaps, when and if she did decide to make an allegation, she would have been more likely to go through with it. If she had thought in advance about the implications and made her own decision as to when to take the next step, then she would not feel so powerless in the face of the professional system and would not have to feel that the professional system (in the person of Miss D) had betrayed her or lied to her.

It could be objected that this approach might have resulted in delay, or in Suzanne never making an allegation: so that she (and perhaps in the future her sister) would have gone on being abused. This might be so, but you need to bear in mind that what in fact happened also resulted in the professional system being unable to protect these children.

Indirect abuse

Children who are exposed to violence between adults in their family (usually male violence directed towards women, though violence by women towards men is not insignificant: see Cleaver et al., 1999: 31–2) are at an increased risk of violence themselves. But, as I noted in Chapter 4, children exposed to adult violence can suffer long-term effects, *even if they are not themselves the victims of actual violence*, which may be similar in kind and severity to those suffered by children who are direct victims of abuse. This is the reason that it seems appropriate to describe exposure to violence at home as 'indirect abuse'. It is striking, for example, that the study by Gibbons et al. (1995) which, as I discussed earlier, failed to find evidence that 'physical abuse *of itself* (except in the most severe cases) caused long-term harm,' *did*, however, find that exposure to marital violence was significantly correlated with poorer long-term outcomes.

In this chapter I have discussed the ways in which abuse directly towards children may do long-term psychological harm, and in fact, many of the same factors apply in the case of children in families where there is adult violence. The word 'trauma' surely applies to this situation, as do 'betrayal', 'stigmatization' and (perhaps particularly) 'powerlessness', and these were all words that I discussed in relation to the experience of direct sexual abuse. Children in violent households may live with intense and chronic fear of further violent incidents, including perhaps the fear that violence will at some point be directed at them. It is difficult to see how a family where there is regular adult violence could be experienced as a 'secure base'. Children may experience feelings of shame and isolation. They may feel guilt at being unable to intervene, or being too frightened to do so, or even at feeling obliged to collude with the abuse in some way. They will have to deal with excruciating conflicts of very powerful emotions towards their adult carers. Again these are all features that are characteristic of children who are the victims of direct abuse.

It is perhaps not surprising, therefore, that research into this form of indirect abuse have identified a wide range of effects that can persist into adult life (see for example, Henning et al., 1996; Silvern et al., 1995; Straus, 1992). These include low self-esteem, depression, drug/alcohol abuse and violent behaviour.

In this chapter I have looked at the nature of the harm that is done to children – and to the adults they become – as a result of child abuse and neglect.

- I discussed the physical harm that can occur as a result of physical abuse, neglect and sexual abuse.
- I then considered the psychological harm that commonly occurs as a result of maltreatment in children, and considered the ways in which such harm may come about.
- I looked then at problems in childhood that are associated with emotional abuse and neglect.
- I discussed the impact of physical abuse.
- I discussed different ways of conceptualizing the often devastating psychological impact of sexual abuse.
- Finally I considered the effects of indirect abuse – the witnessing of abuse towards others – which in form and severity seem to closely parallel the effects of direct abuse.

This chapter concludes Part II of this book. In Part III I will move on to consider the reasons that abuse and neglect occur, beginning in Chapter 7 with an overview of the causes and contexts of child maltreatment.

Part III

The Causes and Contexts
of Child Maltreatment

Causes and Contexts 7

Having considered the signs and consequences of abuse and neglect in the previous three chapters, I will now consider, in Part III of this book, the question of when and why abuse and neglect occurs. In this chapter I will consider the range of factors that may be implicated when parents and carers abuse or neglect children, and consider what is meant when we speak of 'risk factors' or 'predictors'. I will then consider the ways – the mechanisms – whereby certain factors may result in child maltreatment. In the next two chapters I will look more closely at two specific contexts which, in my experience, are increasingly coming to the attention of the child protection system: situations where one or both carers misuse drugs and alcohol (Chapter 8), and situations where parents have a learning disability (Chapter 9).

Just as we must have some understanding of how maltreatment affects a child's development if we are to know how to intervene and change things for the better, so we need some understanding of what factors may make it more likely that parents and other adults will maltreat children, and what factors will make it less likely, if we are to be able to make the right decisions about how to respond to particular situations, and how to go about trying to prevent abuse or neglect from occurring or re-occurring.

'Predictors' of abuse

One way of approaching these sorts of questions is to look at real families where abuse or neglect has occurred and to compare the characteristics of these families with those of other families where there has been no concern about maltreatment. It is then possible to identify 'risk factors' or 'predictors', characteristics that occur more frequently in situations where maltreatment occurs than they do in other situations. In order to ensure that such findings are valid a sufficiently large sample needs to be used, as well as a methodology which ensures that the characteristics are objectively measured in a way that will not allow the preconceptions of the researchers to creep in. The latter can be achieved by arranging that the measurement of various characteristics is done 'blind', by researchers who do not know whether the families they are scoring are in the 'control' group or not. (An example of a study that used this sort of methodology is that of Gibbons et al., 1995, which I described in the previous chapter, although the aim of their study was not to produce a list of predictors, but rather to look at the long-term consequences of physical abuse.)

Cyril Greenland (1987) produced a list of risk indicators based on studies of 107 actual child deaths in the UK and Canada. The risk factors which Greenland came up with are listed over the page in Table 7.1. Exercise 7.1, below, invites you to consider their implications.

Exercise 7.1

In the inquiry report into the death of Jasmine Beckford (London Borough of Brent, 1985) it is suggested that such tragedies might be avoided by using findings such as those of Greenland as an assessment tool to identify high risk families. Look through the list in Table 7.1. What difficulties can you see in using it in such a way?

Comments on Exercise 7.1

What probably struck you is the broadness of the categories. For example, being a single parent is one of the nine characteristics of parents, but obviously most single parents do not abuse or neglect their children. Their presence on this list merely reflects the fact that there were a higher

Table 7.1: Indicators associated with increased likelihood of child death through non-accidental injury

Characteristics of Parent
Themselves abused or neglected as a child
Aged 20 or less at the birth of their first child
Single parent/separated; partner not biological parent of child
History of abuse/neglect or deprivation
Socially isolated; frequent moves; poor housing
Poverty; unemployed/unskilled worker; inadequate education
Abuses alcohol and/or drugs
History of violent behaviour and/or suicide attempts
Pregnant, or post partum [i.e. has recently given birth]; or chronic illness

Characteristics of Child
Previously abused/neglected
Under five years old at the time of abuse or neglect
Premature or low birth weight
Birth defect; chronic illness; developmental lag
Prolonged separation from mother
Cries frequently; difficult to comfort
Difficulties in feeding/elimination
Adopted, foster or step-child

Source: Greenland, 1987

proportion of single parents among the parents of the 107 children in Greenland's sample of child death cases than there are in the general population. Likewise, not all premature or adoptive babies are abused, and their presence in the list simply reflects the fact there were higher proportions of premature babies and of adoptive babies among the 107 than there are in the population in general. Lists like this may tell us something, in a purely statistical sense, about the different characteristics of abusive families, but they are very little use in predicting abuse in any given individual instance, since clearly it would not make any sense to treat every single parent, or every parent who was under 20 when her first child was born, or every parent of a premature child, as a high risk case.

The factors identified by Greenland are predictive of abuse, only in a rather specialized, statistical sense and not in the sense that the word 'predictive' is normally used. If a number of these factors were present in a single case the situation would certainly look more risky than the average family. For instance, if a mother of 17, who had been physically abused herself as a child, was a heroin user and had convictions for violent offences, was caring on her own for a premature baby who was ill and cried a lot, then this would certainly be a situation in which there was a well above average risk of abuse or neglect of some kind occurring. But any one of these factors taken on its own cannot be said to *predict* that abuse or neglect will happen, and even in the situation I have just described we should not, and cannot, assume that abuse or neglect is a *certainty*.

The type of methodology used in studies such as Greenland's is known as *actuarial*, because it is essentially the same as that used by actuaries, the people employed by insurance companies who calculate the statistical likelihood of different kinds of accidents for different groups of the population. Actuaries, for example, have worked out that young men are more likely to have car accidents than older men or women, and as a result young men have to pay higher car insurance premiums. In this sense, being a young man is a 'predictor' of traffic accidents – or a risk factor – but this does not mean (a), that most young men will have traffic accidents, or (b), that other people will not have traffic accidents, or (c), that being a young man is, of itself, a *cause* of traffic accidents.

In relation to child protection work, there is a lot of muddled thinking about this sort of thing, which leads to many people having quite unrealistic ideas about the ability of professional agencies to predict abuse. I will return to this in Chapter 12. For the moment I will just draw your attention to the following points:

- There is no assessment tool that will tell you for certain which situations are dangerous and which are not.
- Risk factors or predictors such as those listed by Greenland do help to suggest in a general way what kinds of situations *may* result in abuse, but none of them should be seen as an inevitable (or even necessarily a probable) *cause* of abuse.
- Subject to these provisos, it is worth noting that two of Greenland's factors refer to situations that may be brought about by social work intervention: separation of mother and child, and adoption and fostering. This is a reminder that social work intervention itself carries its own risks.

The factors listed by Greenland relate specifically to abuse resulting in child death. The profile would be different for other forms of abuse. Child sexual abuse does not have the same link with socioeconomic status as exists in the case of physical abuse and neglect. 'A growing number of studies have reported weak or no association between measures of family socioeconomic status and risks of CSA' (Fergusson and Mullen, 1999: 37–8), though there are statistical links with marital dysfunction, the presence of step-parents in the family, parental alcoholism and parental criminality. The victims of sexual abuse are more likely to be female than male – the risk for girls being 'two to three times higher than the risk for males' according to Fergusson and Mullen (1999: 36). By combining the findings of a variety of studies, these authors also arrive at the following 'weighted average' figures:

- Abusers of girls are 97.5 per cent male, while abusers of boys are 78.7 per cent male.
- 10.4 per cent of child sexual abuse involved close family members, including parents, step-parents and siblings.
- 'The most frequently reported perpetrators were acquaintances of the victim.' On average 47.8 per cent of perpetrators were described as acquaintances.
- 'CSA perpetrated by parent figures is relatively uncommon . . . with the weighted average estimate suggesting 3.3 per cent of CSA incidents were perpetrated by natural fathers.'
- The weighted average for step-parents was 2.7 per cent, but 'the fact that rates of perpetration by stepparents are similar to rates of perpetration by natural parents, suggests that stepparents are more likely to commit CSA, since there are far fewer stepparents in the population than natural parents.' Anderson et al. (1993) suggested that step-parents were roughly ten times more likely to sexually abuse than parents.

(List compiled from Fergusson and Mullen, 1999: 45, 47. These weighted average figures should be treated with some caution, since the studies they are compiled from often came up with widely divergent findings.)

Patterns of maltreatment

Another way of approaching the question of what causes some parents to abuse or neglect their children is one that, in a medical context, would be described as 'clinical'. A clinical approach is based, not on actuarial calculations, but on observation of actual cases and of patterns that recur, and on a process of learning what helps and what does not, which allows tentative models to be developed as to what is going on in abusive situations. Adopting more of a 'clinical' than an 'actuarial' approach, I would suggest that we could divide up child maltreatment into three types of pattern:

1. *Premeditated abuse*: in which the abuser is drawn towards some sort of abusive behaviour in order to meet some need or desire of his or her own, and in which the abuse is deliberate, planned – and fantasized about – in advance. The main instance of this sort of abuse is sexual abuse, but it could also be said to apply to deliberate, planned cruelty, such as so horrifically occurred in England recently in the case of Victoria Climbié. This kind of behaviour is difficult to understand for those who are outside of it (most adults probably cannot imagine *wanting* to sexually abuse a child, let alone acting on it) so that, of the different patterns it is the least amenable to a 'commonsense' approach.
2. *Stress-related abuse and neglect*: a good deal of abuse and neglect is linked to stresses of one kind or another, to which different individuals are more or less vulnerable, depending on their own history, circumstances, temperament and so on. This kind of maltreatment is probably the easiest for most people to understand. Any parent who has ever snapped at her children after a difficult day at work has, in a small way, 'been there'.
3. *Competence-related abuse and neglect*: some maltreatment of children is related to ignorance about children's needs. In most cases this sort of problem should not come under the umbrella of child protection at all, but it sometimes does, especially when issues of competence overlap with stress-related issues.

Reality is always more complicated than any attempt to classify it. These three categories do in fact shade one into another, but they seem to me to be a convenient way of dividing the subject up for the following discussion – and of highlighting the fact that child abuse and neglect can occur in very different ways and for very different reasons. I will now look at each of these three categories in more detail.

Premeditated abuse

What makes an adult deliberately want to set out to abuse a child? Why do some adults become sexually preoccupied with children? It seems to me that discussion around these questions remains quite speculative. In respect of sexual abusers, one factor that is common to a significant proportion is that they themselves were sexually abused as children: 'estimates of the percentage of CSA perpetrators who report being sexually abused in childhood typically range from 20% to 30%,' according to Fergusson and Mullen (1999: 49). But these figures still mean that the majority of sexual abuse perpetrators are not themselves victims of sexual abuse. Similarly, most victims of abuse do not become perpetrators.

However, if you look back at the discussion on the psychological effects of sexual abuse in the last chapter, you can see how some of these effects – such as 'traumatic sexualization' and the habit of 'dissociation' – might result in some individuals (a) learning to view children and childhood as 'sexual', (b) coming to view closeness, intimacy and power in extremely sexual terms, (c) being able to 'dissociate' from normal inhibitions and taboos, (d) developing difficulties with forming normal relationships and finding closeness and intimacy in that way, and (e) developing a sense of powerlessness and a need to compensate for this by obtaining power over others (see, for example, Finkelhor and Browne, 1986; Erooga and Masson, 1999). But clearly sexual abuse in childhood is not the only, or even the main, developmental route by which children can become primary objects of sexual interest, or inhibitions can be overcome. Emotional immaturity, fear of adult relationships, a preoccupation with power and control and fear of rejection are all overlapping factors which may lead an individual down this pathway. They *can* arise as the result of sexual abuse, but they can also arise for other reasons.

We can look at the origins of sexually abusive behaviour historically; that is, in terms of the factors that may have brought about the behaviour in the first place. Alternatively we can look at it as a behaviour that sustains itself in the present and ask what is it about this behaviour that is so powerfully self-reinforcing. Wolf (1984) proposed that offenders typically get into a cycle whereby individuals with low self-esteem isolate themselves, and retreat into sexual fantasy and masturbation to make themselves feel better and obtain an illusion of being in control. Fantasy then leads to planning and carrying out actual abuse. Dawn Fisher summarizes the rest of Wolf's cycle as follows:

> Once they have committed the offence, itself a highly reinforcing event, the diminished sexual excitement following ejaculation (either as part of the abuse or subsequently through masturbation), is followed by a period of transitory guilt. . . . In seeking to reconstitute his self-image the offender typically uses further distorted thinking to alleviate his guilt and anxiety, by minimising or justifying the abuse and promising himself that he will not do the same again. However, underlying this he is left with the

knowledge that he has committed a sexual offence, resulting in further damage to his self-esteem, bringing him back to the feelings he had at the start of the cycle. (Fisher, 1994: 19–20)

The following account gives some idea of how this cycle might feel like from the point of view of an abuser:

> One father who had abused his daughter for 4 years described how he would feel a physical tension rising in his body when he was under stress. It would make him feel like bursting, and he knew that he would sexually abuse his daughter and he created the circumstances accordingly. He was tense and driven and felt as if in a cloud of mist around him. He then abused his daughter. Afterwards he felt guilty, but avoided facing what he had done. (Furniss, 1991: 33–4)

Sexual obsessions are highly addictive, so that once on the pathway of sexual abuse it is very difficult to get off it. There are many parallels between the behaviour and thinking of sexual offenders with that of other kinds of addict. Characteristic of addictions of all kinds is distorted thinking, which allows the addict to carry on doing something which he knows to be wrong by somehow denying to himself what he is doing. Interestingly this quite closely resembles some of the defence mechanisms by which *victims* of abuse cope psychologically, by telling themselves 'this isn't happening to me', and it is worth noting that a significant proportion not only of sex offenders, as I've already mentioned, but also of alcoholics and drug addicts, are themselves victims of childhood abuse.

Sexual abusers of children, like other addicts, become extremely skilled at minimizing and rationalizing their conduct. They get very good at concealing from themselves and others the extent of their problem and at releasing themselves from responsibility for their own behaviour by blaming others and/or by a kind of mental compartmentalization. And, as the lives of other kinds of addict can become increasingly organized by their habit – the day of a drug addict, for example, may be largely taken up with obtaining funds in order to pay for drugs by whatever means possible – so also can the lives of sexual abusers of children become organized around finding opportunities for more abusive behaviour. Interactions with others can then become essentially manipulative, not pursued for their own sake, but aimed at making new opportunities for abuse. Sexual abusers become highly skilled at manipulation, at identifying vulnerable children (typically children who are short of adult attention, and are perhaps already the victims of neglect or abuse), and 'grooming' them for abuse. They may also become adept at identifying vulnerable adults who will give them access to children and manipulating adult relationships to this end, for example by moving in with a single mother with the aim of abusing her children. (The novel *Lolita*, by Vladimir Nabokov, is a famous fictional instance.)

These skills of manipulation, deception and self-deception, built up by constant practice, can make sexual abusers highly plausible. *It is not safe or sensible to make judgements about the dangers posed by such people, or their responsiveness to treatment, unless you have specialist training and have a sufficiently specialized role to allow you to accumulate a lot of experience in this area.* I would make the same comment about other forms of premeditated abuse, such as planned and deliberately inflicted cruelty. Indeed I wonder whether these may in fact involve even *more* distorted thinking than that which is involved in sexual abuse, since the child's suffering is not, as it were, a by-product of the abuse, but its actual primary aim.

Although the parallels between the behaviour of sexual abusers and other kinds of addicts is, I think, striking (and I will return to them in the next chapter when I discuss parents who are drug addicts), there are of course also differences. There is, for one thing, a moral difference, in that drug addiction does not involve making another human being into an object of gratification in the way that sexual offenders do, even though it can often result in the needs of others being unnoticed or disregarded. Another thing that is common to sexual offenders, but for which there is no exact parallel in the case of other addictions, is the way in which fantasy and masturbation (and often pornography) become part of the cycle, fuelling the sexual obsession and allowing the offender to not only 'groom' his victim for abuse but also, as it were, to *groom himself* for further offending.

Implications for assessment and intervention

Protecting children who have been sexually abused is generally a matter of ensuring that they have carers who are capable of preventing the abuser (or abusers) from being given further opportunities to abuse them. This often entails assessing, and trying to support and strengthen, the ability of other adults around the child to stand up to the abuser, and to recognize and resist his attempts at manipulation.

Of course, where the abuser is an important figure to the child, the ideal intervention entails helping the abuser to give up abusive behaviour, but the treatment of sexual offenders – and assessment of the risks that they continue to pose – is a difficult and complex area, and is not something that should be undertaken by professionals who do not have specialist knowledge and experience. In the absence of clear and compelling evidence to the contrary from an authoritative source, child protection plans need to be based on the assumption that a sexual abuser continues to present a high risk indefinitely if he is allowed unsupervised contact with a child.

Stress-related abuse and neglect

In order to think about the ways in which different kinds of stress may push adults towards physical abuse, emotional abuse or neglect, I find it helpful to draw upon the notion of *horizontal stressors, vertical stressors* and *system levels,* which I take from Betty Carter and Monica McGoldrick (1989), and have discussed previously (Beckett, 2002a). Horizontal stressors refer to events that occur as we move through life, some of which are predictable, some of which are not. An illness, for example, would be a horizontal stressor, as would a car accident, or the birth of a child, or a school examination. Vertical stressors are areas of difficulty that we carry from the past. Life becomes particularly stressful when horizontal and vertical stressors intersect. For example, a difficult exam is moderately stressful for most people, but would be far more stressful for a person of limited ability who comes from a background that puts a very high store by academic achievement. (Indeed this particular combination of vertical and horizontal stressors has been a regular cause of suicide in university towns.) *System levels* refer to the fact that both horizontal and vertical stressors operate at a range of different levels. Each individual encounters her own unique challenges and carries her own unique legacy from the past, but so does each family, community, or even nation.

Taking this simple model back into the arena of child abuse and neglect, you will see that some of the risk factors identified by Greenland (1987) could be seen as horizontal stressors – a child who is sick or cries a lot, for instance, or a parent's own illness. A parent's history of having been abused or neglected herself as a child, on the other hand, would be a vertical stressor. As in the example I gave in the previous paragraph, danger points are likely to arise when horizontal and vertical stressors interact. Thus a screaming child is a stressor for any parent, but if the parent was himself habitually ignored or shouted at when he was in distress as a child, he may well find a screaming child much more difficult to cope with than would a parent whose own parents consistently responded to his distress. For the father whose own screams of distress were ignored, the sound of a screaming child may bring up powerful – even overwhelming – feelings of loneliness, impotence and rage. It is not difficult to see how such feelings may sometimes translate themselves into physical abuse.

We can also see how the risk factors in Greenland's list describe stressors that operate at several different system levels. Each individual carries her own unique history. But stressors such as poverty, poor housing and unemployment may affect whole communities. And whole communities, too, may carry vertical stressors (such as, for instance, an awareness that the area where they live is seen by the rest of the town as a 'sink estate'). It is a very serious limitation of social work as a method of protecting children – and of the interprofessional child protection system in general – that they are largely powerless to address factors such as poverty, poor housing and unemployment, even though these clearly and demonstrably have a very direct impact on the ability of parents to cope. (I will return to this topic in Chapter 10.)

But one system level, other than the individual one, that it is possible to address at the casework level is that of the family. It is important to remember that vertical stressors can be carried and reproduced by families over many generations, and that changing the way an individual operates may require changes to be made by those around her too, and for the whole family to operate in a different way.

Exercise 7.2

The following case is an instance of neglect, though I suspect that the British professional system would deal with the case as a 'child in need' rather than a 'child protection' case. What vertical and horizontal stressors are present in this situation?

Robert, aged 14, is picked up by the police at 2 a.m. with some friends in a disused lock-up garage, where they have been drinking and inhaling solvents and seem to intend to spend the rest of the night. It transpires that Robert has been away from home for two days, although his mother, Janice, a single parent, has not reported him missing.

Janice says he does what he likes and when she tries to stop him going out he shouts abuse at her and pushes her out of the way. He is taller and heavier than she is. He regularly stays out all night, and misses school nearly 50 per cent of the time. He also helps himself to money from his mother's purse. Janice is resigned and seemingly indifferent to this. Asked why she does not report him missing, she shrugs and says 'What's the point? Even if the police do find him he'll only go out again the next night.' She says he should be in care, because she can't do anything with him.

Janice is 42. Her own father walked out of the family home when Janice was six and did not maintain contact. Her mother remarried and Janice was abused by her step-father, sexually and physically, until her mother and her step-father separated when she was 12. Her mother could not cope with her, and at the age of 13 she entered the care system, after which her mother only had intermittent contact with her. She had several moves within the care system and suffered further abuse there at the hands of a male residential social worker.

The family live on state benefits. She has a younger son, John, aged 10, by a different father. John attends school and is presenting no difficult behaviour problems for Janice, or his school, as yet, though she says he is starting to copy Robert.

Comments on Exercise 7.2

The most obvious current – 'horizontal' – stressor in this situation is surely adolescence and the challenging behaviour associated with adolescence. Most parents find this difficult to cope with at times: it typically involves having to insist on certain boundaries against constant pressure to drop them. (Janice seems to have abandoned any attempt to hold this line, and as a result her son is putting himself in some danger, apart from creating problems for himself in the future.) Coping with this task alone as a single parent is probably harder than doing so with the support and reassurance of another parent, so being alone is another horizontal pressure. Another is poverty and its practical consequences.

Among the vertical (historic) stressors are, I suggest, the following:

- Janice's history of abuse by men, and therefore her experience of powerlessness in relation to men. This must make it harder to stand up to a son who is now, physically, a young man.
- The fact that Janice's own mother felt unable to parent her after the age of 13. This must make it feel harder to parent a child who is older than that age.
- Janice's rejection by her own parents. This will make her vulnerable to feelings of rejection and prone to employ various psychological defences

to ward off the anxiety and pain that rejection evokes. I suggest that Robert's angry defiance of her will feel like rejection and that a common defensive strategy would be to (a) give way to him to avoid his anger, and (b) shut down her own positive feelings for him so as to make his rejection of her less hurtful.

You will see that the three examples of vertical stressors that I have suggested are, in the current situation, interacting with the horizontal stressor of Robert's adolescent transition, making it far harder to cope with than it would be for another parent who was not carrying the same baggage from the past.

I would suggest that an approach to this case that is based simply on demanding that Janice takes more responsibility for her son, is not likely to work, because she already has her answer: 'Take him away. I can't cope.' But taking Robert into care is unlikely to work either. To really address the difficulty would require addressing the patterns of behaviour and emotional response which they have got into as a result of their particular family history.

Parenting children is a stressful activity at times for all parents, but most parents manage to get through it without lapsing into seriously abusive behaviour. (I do not think that many parents could claim *never* to have behaved in an abusive or neglectful way.) My suggestion is that abusive or neglectful behaviour becomes more likely when the stresses of parenting are combined with other horizontal stressors from other sources, and/or with vertical stressors that are the legacy of the past.

Implications for assessment
_____

Looking at the problem in this way, assessment becomes a matter of trying to identify the horizontal and vertical stressors, at various levels, that are contributing to the abusive or neglectful behaviour. The more difficult part of this is identifying the vertical stressors, which are of course invisible, and which individuals and families may not themselves be consciously aware of. But the sort of patterns which might suggest the presence of powerful vertical stressors might include:

- Extreme distress/anger caused by a child crying or making demands.
- A preoccupation with order, tidiness or control, within which childish behaviour becomes a nuisance and a threat.

- A preoccupation with academic achievement. In my experience this is a not uncommon cause of abusive behaviour when children fail to meet parents' expectations. It may be more common in middle-class families, and more common in some cultures than others.
- An inability to say no to a child, or to set boundaries, resulting in a child becoming more and more demanding. This may result from feelings of powerlessness on the part of the parent which may well date back to childhood experience.
- Very negative and rejecting messages directed towards a child. Sometimes these simply reflect the fact that the child was never wanted.
- Particular children being singled out either for positive or negative attention as against other children in the family.
- Children being strongly identified with a particular parent, or with particular grandparents or other family members, suggesting that feelings about that family member are also being projected onto the child.

One could go on compiling such a list indefinitely, because every individual and family has a unique history.

Implications for intervention

In a minority of cases, the conclusion of such an assessment may be that a parent simply does not have the emotional resources to cope adequately and safely with the demands of a child on top of the other things – both in the present, and from the past – that she has to deal with. More commonly though, such an assessment will identify stressors in the present and from the past which have contributed to abusive or neglectful behaviour. Sometimes a child protection plan may be able to actually reduce or remove some of the present (horizontal) stressors. If part of the problem is that child and parent never get a break from each other, for instance, it may be possible to arrange for the child to have some day care. If part of the problem is overcrowded housing, then it may be possible to negotiate a move to a bigger place. Or if a problem is that the parent has a disability or illness which makes practical tasks more difficult and time-consuming, then it may be possible to arrange for help in the home. Other horizontal stressors – lack of money for instance – may not be within the scope of social workers to tackle, and a child protection plan may be able to offer no more than opportunities for parents to discuss different strategies to deal with stressful situations.

In the case of vertical stressors, the approach to be taken varies from individual to individual and family to family. Some people find it helpful to develop a clearer understanding of 'where they are coming from' and why they are distressed by particular things. Some may need help to move on from painful events in the past, which they have never acknowledged or grieved, and which therefore have become volcano-like sources of unpredictable distress. Some may respond better to a more pragmatic approach, aimed less at understanding the past and more at finding different ways of behaving in the future, which will allow them to leave past patterns behind them. Opportunities to talk, reflect and be listened to are important for any of these approaches.

But work on such matters is crossing over into the realm of what would be called 'therapy', and child protection social workers need to consider, in consultation with service users, whether they are the best placed people to do it. Do they possess the necessary skills and experience, or the time? Would family members not find it easier to work with someone who was not also involved in the policing and administrative aspects of child protection work?

Professional intervention as a stressor

For most families intervention by child protection agencies is a considerable source of stress in its own right. In many cases it will interact with, and activate, vertical stressors. For poor families, social work intervention may be yet one more instance of humiliation at the hands of the state. A parent who was herself in the care of social services as a child, and who was unhappy there – or even abused there, as in the example given in Exercise 7.2 – might find the intervention of a social worker into her family life particularly difficult. If an intervention has the effect simply of adding to the stressors on a family, then it is likely to actually *increase* rather than decrease the risk of child maltreatment.

The implications of this are that, first, as I discussed in Chapter 2, it is sensible as far as possible not to use the 'child protection' route as a way of helping children, if there are other, less intimidating ways of providing help. Second, if the child protection route must be followed, it is essential that something is actually offered *to* the family, and that their difficulties and their efforts to cope are acknowledged.

Competence-related abuse and neglect

It sometimes happens that behaviour appears at first sight to be neglectful or abusive but seems to be the result neither of deliberate premeditated intent, nor a reaction to circumstances, but of genuine ignorance about the needs of a child or the role of a parent. Some adults may have lacked appropriate role models while growing up; some are very isolated and have little access to sources of advice, and to the mutual comparing of notes that most new parents use to widen their knowledge and build their confidence. Some parents have extremely unrealistic expectations of what a child should be capable of at a given stage of development, or to be unaware of what children need in terms of diet, or physical care, or stimulation, or to have no idea how to set boundaries. Occasionally cases of sexual abuse involving perpetrators who are young or who have learning disabilities may have a competence component, if they seem to partly result from a genuine lack of understanding about appropriate sexual behaviour.

When there seems to be a lack of knowledge or of parenting skills, an appropriate form of intervention is educational: the provision of advice, information, instruction or role models. In Britain this kind of role was traditionally taken on by health visitors (specialist, community-based nurses) in relation to parents of younger children, but social work agencies have also taken on an educational role in this sense. In British social services departments, 'family centres' typically have a partly educational brief, as do 'family aides', who visit families at home. Voluntary agencies also operate family centres and home visiting schemes.

In my experience, it is seldom the case that apparent abuse or neglect is *purely* competence based, however. If a parent was consistently dressing a child in ways which were inappropriate to the weather, I would be hesitant to conclude that this was the result of simple ignorance, since observation alone would indicate that a child was too cold or too hot. Failure to notice the child's discomfort would therefore seem to me to indicate that the parent was not very 'switched onto' their child's needs, perhaps because of the existence of other stressors which were taking away a great deal of the parent's attention. (Some instances of this kind of thing will be discussed in Chapter 8, which looks at problems experienced in some families where the parents misuse drugs or alcohol.) Some parents who themselves grew up in abusive environments, will have learnt the survival skill of shutting out much of the outside world.

Another reason why a parent might not pick up on a child's needs is lack not of competence but of *confidence*. Some people have learnt not to trust their own judgement or commonsense, perhaps as the result of consistently receiving negative messages. A purely educational approach, aimed at imparting factual information about child-rearing, may be counterproductive in such cases, since it may have the effect of further 'de-skilling' the parent: confirming that they do not know what to do and cannot trust their own judgement. (Rather in the way that overly detailed prescriptions for social work practice can sometimes make social workers lose faith in their own judgement.) And sometimes an overly didactic, 'educational' approach can 'infantilize' parents by making them feel that they are back in school again. It is therefore important that an 'educational' approach to issues of competence is carefully handled, so as not to humiliate adults and so as to acknowledge and build on strengths and on their status as adults and parents. As Tucker and Johnson (1989) put it, support offered to parents should be 'competence promoting' rather than 'competence inhibiting'.

Although this point is applicable to all situations where there are issues of competence, Tucker and Johnson's comments were addressed in particular to those working with mothers with learning difficulties. In families where parents have learning difficulties, issues of competence are particularly relevant, and often contentious, and I will separately discuss the issues involved in Chapter 9.

Mental health and competence

Issues of competence of a particular kind may also arise where parents have mental health problems. (Amy Weir and Anthony Douglas, 1999, offer a collection of writings from various perspectives on this topic. See also Cleaver et al., 1999). Mental health problems may operate as a stressor in families in the kinds of way that I discussed earlier, but acute mental health problems may also distort a parent's judgement to the point where she is no longer competent to make decisions about a child's needs. In rare cases, a parent's delusional ideas resulting from mental illness may place a child in very direct risk, and may even have fatal consequences. This is another area in which a 'commonsense' approach is not at all adequate, and where a child protection social worker, both in carrying out an assessment and in planning an intervention, must enlist the help of professionals with specialist knowledge and experience.

Exercise 7.3

Mr and Mrs Thomas, both of whom have a history of psychiatric illness, bring their daughter Jane to the family doctor to ask him to examine her for signs of sexual abuse. They say that they have reason to believe that Jane is being abused at night by evil spirits. They also say they are concerned that Jane's young brother Bill (aged six months) has been 'invaded by spirits at the atomic level' and is now the conduit through which spirits are entering the house to abuse Jane. They wonder whether it may be necessary for Bill to be 'destroyed' in order to stop the abuse of Jane.

What would be your thoughts on how to respond to this if you received such a referral from the doctor?

Comments on Exercise 7.3

I have several times in this book referred to the difficulty in predicting abuse in advance with any level of certainty. This is an instance, though, of a situation where there can be little doubt of the real danger of fatal abuse if the children are left in it. We actually have a statement from the parents that suggests that killing their son is a possibility they are seriously considering. Living within a delusional system that is so frightening and so seriously dislocated from reality will, in any case, certainly in the long run have serious implications for the development of these children. Since both parents are similarly deluded there is no adult reference point that a child could use in this family to gain a grip of reality.

So (at least on the basis of the information which I have so far given) this is a situation in which actual removal of the children from the family is indicated, until the parents' mental state can be assessed and, hopefully, treated. But there is no doubt that any intervention requires the involvement from the outset of professionals with experience and expertise in working with people who are suffering these kinds of mental health problems, because their reaction to an intervention from the outset is hard to predict, and could in itself be dangerous to the children.

Abuse by children

Mary, 11, told how the next door neighbour, a teenager, has kissed and felt her since she was 6. Now he asked to lick her and asked her to go to his bed. She described being terrified but didn't know who to tell.

A 12-year-old girl called frightened and uncomfortable. An older girl was following her into the toilet and touching her vagina. She wanted it to stop.

A mother called to talk about her 7-year-old son, who complained of an older friend 'sucking his penis'. The same child had been touching a little girl in a similar way and both mothers had shared concern, but didn't know what to do next. (Howarth, *Foreword* to Erooga and Masson, 1999: xvi)

These examples, quoted by Valerie Howarth, Director of the British charity Childline, are a reminder that child abuse can be perpetrated by children and teenagers as well as adults. In the case of sexual abuse, in fact, abuse by children and young people constitutes a very substantial proportion of all detected abuse. Looking at criminal statistics for England and Wales, Erooga and Masson (1999: 1–2) found that 'children and young people aged between 10 and 21 years accounted for 47 per cent of all cautions for sexual offence; and 13.5 per cent of findings of guilt as a result of a court process'. Erooga and Masson review the available literature and conclude that between about 25 and 33 per cent of all alleged sexual abuse involves young (mainly adolescent) perpetrators.

In fact adolescence, perhaps not surprisingly, is the time when a large proportion of adult offenders report having started out on their abusive careers: as many as 50 per cent, according to Abel et al. (1985). This means that identifying cases of abuse by children is important not only for the sake of the current victims but also, potentially, as a means of 'nipping in the bud' abusive careers in which perhaps hundreds of children might subsequently be abused by a single, persistent offender.

Working with children and young people who abuse is a complex subject, which again requires the involvement of professionals who have the space to obtain the appropriate knowledge, skills and experience. I will not discuss it in detail here. (See Erooga and Masson, 1999, or Calder, 1997, for example.) As with other kinds of abuse there is no 'blueprint' that will allow us to recognize in advance those individuals who will go on to become abusers, but among the factors associated with sexually abusive behaviour by children and young people, are the following:

- Abnormal sexual environments, including families where sexual boundaries were too rigid or too relaxed.
- Sexualized models of compensation, where sex is seen as a comfort in difficult times.
- A parental history of sexual or physical abuse.
- History of drug or alcohol use in the family.

- Parental loss.
- Social isolation, lack of confidence, lack of social skills and mal-adaptive coping skills. (Summarized from Calder, 1997: 51.)

This chapter has looked at the reasons that child maltreatment happens – the when and why of child maltreatment – including the psychological origins of abusive behaviour. I have looked at:

- 'risk factors' or 'predictors' of abuse, what they are, and what their limitations are in predicting specific instances of abuse
- different ways in which abuse or neglect can arise – I divided these into 'premeditated abuse', 'stress-related abuse and neglect' and 'competence-related abuse and neglect'
- 'premeditated abuse' and sexual abuse in particular; its possible origins, both in terms of the past experience of abusers, and in terms of the ways that abusive behaviour reinforces and maintains itself in the present
- the ways in which stress, both in the 'here and now' and from the past, can be a factor in abuse
- the extent to which some forms of neglect and abuse may arise from lack of competence
- abuse by children and adolescents.

In the next chapter I will move on to look at a *particular* context where abuse and neglect occur more frequently than in the general population: families where one or more parents abuses alcohol or drugs.

Parents, Drugs and Alcohol   8

In my own experience, the number of child protection cases involving parental drug use – and particularly heroin addiction – has risen steadily over the past two decades from a time when it was a factor in only a fairly small percentage of cases to the point where use of illegal drugs is a factor in 50 per cent of cases, or even more.

As far as I am aware, there are no British national figures on the incidence of drug use among parents in child protection cases against which to compare my own impressions. But there is evidence from the USA of an increasing percentage of child protection cases having a drug-related component. For example, over the four years from 1994 to 1998, the percentage of families reported for maltreatment where substance abuse was identified as one of the two main problems, rose from 76 per cent in 1994, to 85 per cent in 1998 (Wang and Harding, 1999).

In Britain there is evidence of drug use *in general* being on the increase. Not only has illegal drug use in the UK reached unprecedented levels, but an increasing proportion of illegal drug users are girls and women – nearly 50 per cent among young people – there is an increasing incidence of mixed alcohol and drug use; drug use is also starting at an earlier age (SCODA, 1997). There is also British evidence of an increasing percentage of crime being drug related. One Home Office survey published in 2000 found that in some areas the percentage of arrested offenders who tested positive for drugs had doubled over the three year period 1997–1999 (Bennett and Sibbitt, 2000). And I will quote below studies from various parts of the country that show high proportions of child protection cases where parental drug use is an issue.

So my subjective impression of an increasing percentage of child abuse and neglect cases being related to drug use does seem to have some foundation, even though we do need to be aware that some of these statistics may partly reflect increasing *awareness* of drug problems, as well as an actual increase.

Indeed it seems to me that the real size of the impact of increased illegal drug use on children is something that those who write and think about child protection social work have still only begun to take on board. In the USA, a huge increase in the demand for foster-care in the 1990s was attributed to problems caused by increasing drug misuse (see Alison, 2000). It seems possible that the increasing drug problem was a factor, too, in the steadily increasing number of care proceedings in the UK over the same period. (The number of care orders made nationally nearly tripled between 1992 and 2000 – see Beckett, 2001a.) However, at time of writing, Harbin and Murphy (2000), is the only British book that I am aware of that exclusively addresses the link between substance misuse and child maltreatment. (Another British book, Cleaver et al., 1999, looks at substance misuse alongside parental illness and domestic violence as a factor affecting parenting capacity.)

Drugs and alcohol

Most of the same issues that apply to the use of illegal drugs, and particularly the issues that arise in relation to highly addictive drugs such as opiates, apply also to alcohol use. Both in the case of alcohol and of illegal drugs there is a distinction to be made between controlled use for recreational purpose, and problem use. In the latter case the user has developed a physical addiction or psychological dependency on the substance, and it is affecting day-to-day functioning. Alcohol, along with opiates and cocaine, can, as we'll see, have harmful consequences on a child if used during pregnancy (so too, though, can cigarette smoking). And most of the other parenting problems that I will discuss in this chapter relate to alcohol use as well as to use of illegal drugs. Summarizing research on the effects on children of problem drinking by their parents, Velleman (2001) concludes that 'many children experience very negative childhoods, often experiencing high levels of both violence and inconsistency', and that:

many children show very negative effects of these experiences, having problems in a variety of areas, showing higher levels of behavioural disturbance and anti-social behaviour, or emotional difficulties, of school problems, and a more difficult transition from childhood than do children who have not had this upbringing. These effects are frequently worse if both parents have alcohol problems, or if the problem drinking occurs at home. (Velleman, 2001: 36)

Additionally, use of illegal drugs and drinking are linked in that there is an increasing tendency to mix illegal drug use and alcohol use. There is also evidence that drug users who become drug free are significantly at risk of developing alcohol problems (Department of Health, 1997).

Researchers have found that different substances are related to different types of child maltreatment. Alcohol is particularly associated with physical abuse. Incidence of sexual abuse is higher in cases of crack cocaine use than it is with other substances (Alison, 2000: 10). Velleman (2001: 39) adds that 'children of drug-misusing parents seem less likely to be abused than children of alcohol-misusing parents (although slightly more likely than controls); but they seem just as likely to be neglected as children with alcohol misusing parents, and far more likely than controls'.

Substance abuse as a 'risk factor'

I don't want to imply in this chapter that all adults who use illegal drugs, or who are alcoholics, are necessarily poor parents. It is important *not* to make this assumption. The vast majority of parents in this country use alcohol, a very substantial number use illegal drugs recreationally, and a large number who have a dependency either on alcohol or on illegal drugs still manage to act as caring and responsible parents. Labelling all drug users or drug addicts or alcoholics as 'bad parents' not only does an injustice to all of these people and their children, but also discourages people with substance misuse problems from seeking help, for fear that their children will be taken from them. An American study of cases coming to court (Murphy et al., 1991) found that drug-misusing parents were half again as likely to have their children permanently taken away from them by the courts as alcohol-misusing parents, and that drug-misusing parents were less likely to take up services offered to them than alcohol misusers. Discussing this finding, Velleman comments that there are 'major implications here for care services . . . with the obvious point needing to be re-made very often: that the issue is whether or not parenting ability and actual behaviour is satisfactory, not whether one or more parents use or misuse hard drugs' (2001: 39).

On the other hand, it *is* the case that a wide range of studies, in the USA, Britain and Europe, show a strong statistical association between drug use and child maltreatment, and especially child neglect. If parents use drugs it does not automatically mean they are bad parents, but people with drug and alcohol problems are considerably more *likely* to have parenting problems than the population at large. Drug use is therefore undoubtedly a risk factor, in the same way that poverty or growing up in care are also 'risk factors' in the sense that I discussed in the last chapter. They do not result in child maltreatment in a simple deterministic way, but are associated with an increased likelihood of child maltreatment.

Thus, in America, Chaffin et al. (1996) found that when parental substance use was a factor in cases of reported child maltreatment, it was a strong predictor of further maltreatment incidents – in fact, the chances of further incidents being reported were three times higher than in cases where parental substance misuse was not identified as a factor. And Guterman (2001: 118) cites a variety of research studies that have 'consistently found impaired attachment patterns in substance-abusing mothers and their infants, including decreased maternal responsivity and disturbances in infants' attachment behaviours', while other studies suggest that 'substance-abusing parents often employ ineffective and inconsistent discipline'.

In Britain, Forrester (2000) found that substance misuse was strongly related to neglect, and cases where substance misuse was a factor were twice as likely to become subject to care proceedings. Harbin and Murphy (2000) found in 1995 that 50 per cent of children on the child protection register in Bolton came from households where substance abuse was an issue. SCODA (1997) reported that: 'Child and adolescent mental health services also report that long standing drug and alcohol misuse in a parent is a substantial risk factor for child and adolescent mental health.' And Alison and Wyatt (1999), comparing drug-using mothers in Sheffield with a control group matched by postcode and on other measures, found that the control children were only half as likely to be subject to case conferencing as the children of the drug users, and were one-third as likely to be fostered.

But the relationship between drug abuse and child abuse is not a simple, one-way one. There are many ways in which parental drug use can result in harm to children, which I'll discuss shortly, but we should note that:

1. The relationship is a two-way one. Just as drug use may result in child abuse, child abuse may result in drug use. Cohen and Densen-Gerber (1982) for example, found that, of patients being treated for drug or alcohol addiction, 84 per cent reported having experienced physical abuse or neglect as children. As discussed in Chapter 6, alcohol and drug use are also found to be associated with witnessing partner violence as a child. Drug use may be seen as an attempt to 'self-medicate' in order to alleviate the anxiety and distress which may be the result of such experiences. It may also be seen as an attempt to establish a sort of control over one's environment.

2. Both substance abuse and neglectful/abusive parenting may be the consequence of other factors. In the last chapter we considered the way in which abusive and neglectful behaviour is linked in a complex way to a number of factors: social, individual, familial, 'horizontal' and 'vertical'. Drug and alcohol misuse is also linked to factors operating at the same mixture of levels – and indeed to many of the same factors. Both drug use and child maltreatment may be the result of poor childhood experiences. Poverty, a factor in child abuse, is also a factor in drug abuse:

> Put simply, addiction fills voids. These voids can be psychological, social, emotional, spiritual and temporal. Mass unemployment is a most efficient way of creating these voids and heroin addiction comes along to fill them. The symbiotic relationship between unemployment and heroin addiction in the UK started in the early 1980s and has been maintained to this day. (Gilman, 2000: 23)

We should be careful, therefore, not to read the association between drug use and child maltreatment as meaning that drug use 'causes' child maltreatment. But having said this, there are a number of ways in which drug use by parents can specifically result in harm to children.

How parental substance abuse impacts on children

Drug use by parents can impact on their children in a range of ways.

Prenatal effects of maternal drug use

The use of alcohol, heroin and other opiates and cocaine during pregnancy can result in impaired growth. Alcohol use, in particular, can result in permanent physical harm (Foetal Alcohol Syndrome).

A common result of the use of heroin during pregnancy is that babies become addicted to opiates *in utero* and display withdrawal symptoms at birth. Withdrawal symptoms can make babies extremely difficult to manage, even for experienced foster-carers: they may show chronic distress and seem impossible to settle or comfort. Neonatal Abstinence Syndrome, as this is called, can produce a range of effects including irritability, hyperactivity, abnormal sensitivity to touch, accelerated cardiac action, an increased respiratory rate, changes in the sleeping/waking rhythm, wild sucking at fists, shrill and long phases of screaming tremors, shivering, sneezing, perspiration, fever, vomiting, diarrhoea, inhibited feeding and, in some cases, convulsions (Leopold and Steffan, 1997).

Apart from the distress caused to the child by these symptoms themselves, they may have longer-term developmental consequences on the child's development as a result of their effect on the interaction between child and carer. Coping with a baby suffering from withdrawal symptoms can place additional stress on already vulnerable parents.

Direct effects of drug use on parenting capacity

Specific behavioural changes resulting from drug use can affect the quality of the parent–child relationship. The use of amphetamines can result in anxiety, paranoia and even psychosis (SCODA, 1997: 12). Alcohol is a disinhibitor, which can reduce an individual's ability to control violent impulses.

More generally, the effects of the use of drugs and/or alcohol on the functioning of users can make parents less available to a child, both while actually intoxicated and also in between these times as a result of tiredness, oversleeping, poor concentration and lack of energy. This presumably is one of the reasons why use of illicit drugs is associated with things like accidents arising as a result of neglect, and failure to obtain medical help for children who are sick or hurt ('medical neglect'). It may also explain some of the attachment difficulties that can occur, since the healthy development of attachment requires parental responsivity to the needs of a child. If a child is demanding and hard to please as a result of Neonatal Abstinence Syndrome, and the parents are unresponsive, exhausted and limited in energy as a result of continuing drug use, these are hardly optimal conditions for the formation of a secure and comfortable attachment.

Exercise 8.1

At 3 p.m. on a Thursday afternoon, Simon, aged just 20 months, very narrowly escapes serious injury when he wanders out into a busy road into the path of a taxi. Luckily the taxi driver is just able to stop in time. Simon is wearing a disposable nappy (full) and a dirty tee-shirt. His face is very dirty and encrusted with dried mucus. There is no sign of any adult in charge of Simon, but when the taxi driver makes enquiries at a nearby block of flats he is directed to a first-floor flat. The front door of the flat has been left open and, since no one responds when he rings the bell, the taxi driver goes inside, calling 'Anyone at home?' He finds a very bleak environment in which litter, clothing and dirty crockery are scattered over floors which are stained with food, drink and what looks to the driver like dried vomit. There is a strong smell of urine. In the kitchen the sink is piled with dirty dishes. There are several dozen empty beer cans piled in one corner.

Simon's mother is in her bedroom and only wakes up when the taxi driver walks into the room. He has some difficulty getting her to understand what has happened. She clearly had no idea that the front door had been left open or that Simon had wandered out. Her speech is blurred, she appears confused and incoherent and she smells strongly of alcohol.

The taxi driver makes coffee for her and a drink of squash for Simon, and leaves Simon with her, making sure to shut the front door. He then phones social services to express his concern for Simon's well-being.

How would you react to this?

Comments on Exercise 8.1

Parental neglect results in nearly as many child deaths as actual physical assaults. Simon has had a close shave and is clearly acutely at risk if this sort of event is a regular occurrence, so the circumstances require urgent investigation.

It appears quite likely from the information so far presented, that Simon's mother may have a serious drinking problem. If this results in her regularly being completely unavailable to Simon, it will not only place him at physical risk, but could be emotionally devastating at a developmental stage when ready access to secure attachment figures is very important.

Of course it is possible that this may have been a single isolated 'binge', and that Simon's mother does not have a drink problem. If so, though, it would appear that there are other difficulties in her life. It sounds as if the poor state of the flat is something that has built up over some time.

Although you could not be sure on the information available that the problem here was primarily to do with substance abuse, the example does illustrate the way in which substance abuse can make a parent effectively unavailable to a child for long periods. If drinking does turn out to be a chronic problem in this case, then a child protection plan will need to address the drinking and the reasons for it.

Although it would be a mistake to assume on the basis of this one incident that Simon's mother had a drink problem, it would also be a mistake to assume that alcohol is the only substance at issue. Drinking is increasingly commonly associated with use of other (illegal) drugs.

Social effects

Problem use of illegal drugs and alcohol has a number of social consequences that can impact on family life. In particular, the cost of maintaining supplies of addictive drugs drains financial resources to the extent that daily life for the addict can be completely dominated by activity – including criminal activity – aimed at obtaining money to buy more. This can impact on the addict's children in a very direct way if insufficient money is left over for food, clothing, fuel and so on. It can also mean that a parent who is an addict is unavailable to the children for much of the time (even when not under the influence of drugs). Children may also be drawn into the business of obtaining drugs in various ways. They may have to accompany a parent trying to obtain supplies of drugs, or in some instances they may become more actively involved, acting as couriers, or becoming involved in crime aimed at funding the habit. The issues are slightly different in the case of alcohol, since alcohol is legal, easier to obtain and, relatively speaking, cheap compared with drugs such as opiates and cocaine. But alcohol use, too, may place an intolerable financial burden on a family.

The financial burden of substance abuse can undoubtedly result in standards of care that fall quite clearly into the categories of neglect and emotional abuse (even sometimes sexual abuse, in cases where children are prostituted to fund an adult's addiction). But it is worth noting here that this is a much more acute problem for *poor* families. The children of a rock star with a drug dependency are clearly not likely to go hungry as a result of their parent's habit, and are not likely to have their family lifestyle disrupted by the parent having constantly to find money for more drugs. I do not say that the children of a rock star drug addict might not suffer in other ways, but I am making the point that some of the problems I have been discussing are as much the result of social circumstances as of substance abuse itself. Here is another way in which poverty can increase the risk of neglect or child abuse.

The lifestyle of an addict also carries with it risks of imprisonment and/or hospitalization, with the resulting impact on children as the result of separations. Children may also be exposed to an environment in which drug use and/or drug dealing is normal. (This is presumably one of a number of reasons that 'Children of drug abusing parents may be at greater risk of developing drug or other substance misusing problems later in life', SCODA, 1997: 13.) They may also be exposed to frightening events, such as overdoses, police raids or bizarre behaviour. Normal daily routines may be impossible to maintain.

Exercise 8.2

There has been increasing concern in their school about Paul and Tracey Scott (aged 10 and 8). They are often late into school and in class they seem very tired, pale and with bags under their eyes. On one occasion Tracey nodded off in a corner of her classroom. They are behind in their schoolwork and do not socialize with other children. Their teachers have talked about this to their mother, Alice, who is a lone parent. She always seems concerned and anxious to cooperate, but can give no explanation for their tiredness other than to say that they both have been going through a phase where they can't settle at night. Teachers like Alice Scott and observe that she has a very close and warm relationship with both her children. The children are always well-dressed and are polite and helpful. Teachers have noticed though that Alice also seems very tired and sometimes quite 'dazed'.

At 3 a.m. one morning, Alice is stopped in her car by the police outside an international airport some seventy miles away from the family's home. The arrest is part of an extensive undercover operation taking place at the airport. Alice is found to have a substantial quantity of heroin in the car, and confesses to acting as a courier for a drug dealer in her home town in order to finance her own addiction. Both children are in the back of the car at the time of the arrest.

The police contact the emergency duty team at social services to arrange overnight accommodation for the children. It is likely that Alice will be charged and released on bail the following morning, though she is likely to face a custodial sentence in due course.

What are the child protection issues here?

Comments on Exercise 8.2

It seems likely that the explanation for the tiredness of these children is that they have been going regularly on these overnight trips to the airport with their mother. Here is an instance where not the drug use itself, but the need to fund the drug habit, is having a very direct impact on the children by depriving them of sleep, with the resultant impact on their education and their social interactions with other children. (They may also be being put at some physical risk by the car journeys with a driver who is herself short of sleep.) We can't tell from the information so far given what else the children may be exposed to, or the extent to which Alice's own drug use impacts directly on them. If Alice goes to prison, this will, of course, be a further instance of her lifestyle having a very direct effect on her ability to care for them.

On the positive side, though, we have reports of a warm relationship between Alice and her children. The children are reportedly well-dressed, which may perhaps be an indication that she is not allowing her habit to take priority over their material needs. Even the fact that she takes the children with her in the car to the airport, rather than leaving them on their own, may represent an attempt on her part to be responsible.

Having noted these positive points, I would add that it is important in child protection work not to be deflected by the fact that someone is 'likeable', first because it is possible to be a very nice person and still not to be a competent parent, and secondly because 'being likeable' is to some extent an acquired skill. I would also add a note of caution about necessarily interpreting a warm, close relationship as a happy or secure one. Children who are insecure in their attachments may be particularly loving towards and considerate of their carers, precisely because they are anxious about losing their attention – sometimes taking on a protective, almost parental role in relation to their own parents.

Health risks

There are health risks to which children of substance misusing parents may be exposed. They can be at risk of accidental overdosing if drugs are not safely stored. They may also be exposed to illnesses associated with drug use, including – in the case of users of intravenous drugs – HIV and hepatitis (40 per cent of injecting drug users have hepatitis A; 60 per cent have hepatitis B (SCODA, 1997: 34)). If much of the family income is being spent on a drug habit, children can suffer malnutrition.

Distorted thinking and addiction

One area that seems to be comparatively little addressed to date in the literature on the relationship between drug abuse and child maltreatment, is the kind of distorted thinking that is involved in drug addiction – and the impact that this in itself can have on parenting capacity.

Child protection social workers are probably more familiar with the concept of distorted thinking in relation to sexual abusers, as discussed in the last chapter. As I said before, I am not suggesting that there is necessarily a *moral* equivalence between drug addiction and sexual abuse, but it seems to me that there are clear psychological parallels. Drug addicts, like sexual abusers, may become adept at rationalizing behaviour that is harmful to themselves and others, at minimizing that behaviour, at 'splitting' themselves – for example, simultaneously sincerely believing that they are going to stop the habit while at the same time actively working on plans to obtain more drugs – and in presenting a plausible front to the world. Again, not unlike sexual abusers, they may become skilled at coopting others in support of their habit.

These mental manoeuvres can amount to a radical distortion of reality, in which feeding the habit, for example, becomes in practice more important than feeding the children, even while the addicted person insists and believes that the opposite is true.

Exercise 8.3

The following referral is made to a social work office by the police:

Tommy (four months old) is the child of Frank (21) and Wendy (29). The family are known to the social services department because of concerns on the part of health professionals at the time of Tommy's birth that Frank's heroin addiction might affect his parenting capacity, but the health professionals agreed to offer support and to refer back to social services if necessary – and up to now there have been no concerns about the standard of care offered to Tommy. According to the family doctor, Frank dotes on the baby, and says being a father is the best thing that has ever happened to him.

Last night, the police arrested Frank attempting to break into a shop. Frank then told the police that he was concerned for his son, who he had left at home on his own. The police went round to Frank's house, to find Tommy in a cot in front of an electric fire, very overheated and screaming. In the room around him were syringes and other signs of drug use. A piece of clothing hanging on the fireguard had started to singe and smoke. Frank told the police that Wendy had gone out to see a friend, leaving him in charge of Tommy. He says he knows he should not have gone out, but he was desperate to buy heroin and had no money to do so. A woman police officer had waited at the house for Wendy's return. She reported that Wendy seemed drunk or possibly under the influence of drugs on her return, but seemed to be capable of caring for Tommy. Wendy seemed annoyed at Frank for going out when he was supposed to be looking after Tommy but, in the opinion of this officer, she was not seriously upset about what had happened, and did not seem to see its seriousness.

Police records show that both Frank and Wendy have been charged before with minor drug-related offences, and other offences such as shoplifting. On one occasion a year ago, the police were called out to a domestic dispute. Wendy alleged that Frank had punched her and she had a black eye coming up, but when the police arrived she seemed to want to shrug it off and did not want to press charges.

If you were a duty social worker taking this call, what would your first actions be?

What child protection issues are raised by the information given so far?

Comments on Exercise 8.3

Tommy does not seem to be immediately at risk in the care of Wendy. No one is alleging that Wendy (or indeed Frank) has acted in a way that was deliberately intended to harm Tommy. Your immediate task is to gather information that may contribute to your understanding of the situation and help you to decide what other action should be taken. You would need to check your agency's own files for background on this family and identify and contact any other agencies which might have information. (In this case this would include the health visitor and GP – you would also need to check with probation and drug and alcohol services.) Do either Frank and Wendy have other children, and if so, what is their history?

If this incident formed part of a pattern, it would fall clearly into the category of neglect. In pursuit of his own needs, Frank has placed Tommy in physical danger (of fire, of overheating), and also neglected Tommy's emotional needs by leaving him in a frightening situation on his own.

Could this be a one-off incident (as Frank may possibly maintain)? Well, the evidence so far suggests that Frank's drug use, at any rate, is not simply a one-off. There is evidence of drug use in the flat; there are previous drug offences. But in particular the fact that he was apparently so desperate to get money to buy drugs there and then (not even able to wait until Wendy was back) seems to me to suggest that Frank may have difficulty in making even the physical safety of his child a higher priority than maintaining his drug habit.

But perhaps, now that she knows the risk of Frank abandoning him, Wendy may be relied upon to make sure that Tommy is not left alone again? Again, this is something to look at, but it does appear that such a conclusion should not be drawn too readily. We have the police officer's observation that she seemed not to grasp the seriousness of what happened. We have evidence that in the past she was resigned to accepting violence from Frank. There are also reasons to believe that she is also a drug user.

Addiction and family systems

An added layer of complexity occurs when we consider the possibility that drug addiction may serve a purpose for the functioning of a family as a whole:

> Frequently the addiction serves a purpose in maintaining family stability. Remove the addiction and the unmentioned fear of the family is that it will fall apart. . . . Therefore, while the family may protest loudly about the misery of addiction, giving up their roles in this and accepting a temporarily unbalanced and addiction-free family, while developing new roles, may be too difficult for them to deal with. This would result in family members having to address underlying issues that remain unresolved all the time that an addiction exists. (Watts, 2000: 98)

If addiction fills voids, it follows that breaking an addiction will leave a gap in the life of an individual, a feeling of emptiness. The feeling of emptiness is unpleasant and people feel a strong need to fill the gap somehow. This helps to explain, for instance, why recovered drug addicts may be at increased risk of becoming problem drinkers.

The point I am now making is that this gap may not only be experienced by the individual, but by a whole family, which may have effectively organized itself around the maintenance of an addictive pattern. The family's social networks, its daily routines, its dramas and excitements, its identity, may all have been constructed around obtaining and using drugs. Not only for an individual but also for a family, breaking an addiction may not be the 'solution' that it might seem to an outsider. It may present new and difficult problems.

Assessment and intervention

One of the challenges of working with drug-using families is that the work spans not just several agencies but two different multi-agency systems (in England and Wales, the Area Child Protection Committees and the Drug Action Teams), with different traditions, rules and priorities. Murphy and Harbin (2000: 3) suggest that the 'two different assessment processes, that would normally be completed by practitioners in both systems, need to come together as a three-stage process that measures both substance misuse and its subsequent impact on the child', and propose that the parts of an assessment should include:

1. The use of the substance.
2. The effect of substance use on parenting.
3. The child's needs.

They suggest that these things impact on one another. Drug use may impact on parenting, but difficulties in parenting and the demands of the child will, in turn, impact on the parents' drug use (Murphy and Harbin, 2000: 4). Drug abuse is certainly a substantial stressor on any family and yet it may arise from an attempt to *reduce* or escape from stress, and will increase – or become more difficult to resist – at stressful times.

Building on the areas suggested by Murphy and Harbin, and freely adapting them, I suggest the following need to be addressed in an assessment of a family where parental drug use seems to be affecting parenting.

The use of the substance

Addressing these questions will fall more in the area of expertise of the drug and alcohol service professionals, rather than the child protection professionals:

- What substances are being used, and what are their effects?
- The extent and context of drug/alcohol use. Is it recreational use only or an addiction?
- What are the cost implications of use, and what does this leave the family to spend on other things? How is the habit funded? (Drug dealing? Other crime? Prostitution?)
- What are the lifestyle implications of using, and maintaining supplies of, drugs/alcohol? (Who with? Where? When?)

The effect of substance use on parenting

These questions need to be addressed both by the drug service and child protection service professionals:

- What are the parents' own experiences of being parented, and what are their expectations of themselves as parents? (Bearing in mind that drug abuse is commonly associated with childhood neglect or abuse, which may also impact on parenting capacity.)
- How available are the parents to the children as a source of protection, care, support, attention and control – and to what extent is this availability affected by substance misuse?
- Do the parents protect the children from exposure to their drug/alcohol use?
- Do the parents involve the children in any way in the business of obtaining drugs, or obtaining funds for drugs (for example, by acting as couriers)?
- Do the parents place the children at physical risk from drug/alcohol use (for example, by leaving used needles where children might pick them up)?

- Are the parents able to prioritize the children's needs over drug/ alcohol use, and if so, at what level (needs for food, needs for physical safety, needs for attention)?
- Are the parents willing to stop or modify their drug/alcohol use, if this is necessary to improve their care of their children?

The child's needs

These questions would be addressed mainly by the child protection agencies, except for the last one, which requires an understanding of the drug use itself, and its relationship (for instance) to stress and anxiety:

- What are the child's current needs, taking into account his developmental stage and individual history?
- What other sources of support and help are available for the child?
- What sort of demands is the child making on the adults? (Has the child got a disability, or is the child presenting difficult behaviour problems?)
- Are the child's demands such as to impact on the parents' drug/ alcohol use?

If an assessment concludes that neglect or abuse is caused or exacerbated by drug and alcohol use, then part of the child protection plan would need to be that drug and alcohol use would have to be reduced or stopped, and that drug and alcohol use would need to be monitored in the future. The implementation of this part of the plan would need at least in part to be in the hands of drug and alcohol agencies. But both the drug and alcohol agencies and the child protection agencies need to be mindful of the difficulties for addicts themselves, and for their families, in the early stages of recovery from an addiction, and ensure that both individuals and families receive adequate emotional and practical support.

We should remember though, that in planning an intervention with a family where a parent is misusing drugs and/or alcohol, it is important not to *assume* that the substance misuse is the problem. No child protection plan should demand perfection of parents, or expect them to conform to some conventional standard of appropriate behaviour. Only if there is evidence that drug or alcohol use is impacting on the child, is it legitimate (or sensible) to insist on addressing the substance use in a child protection plan.

In this chapter I looked at what seems to be an increasingly common phenomenon: child protection cases where drug or alcohol abuse by parents is a factor. I have looked at:

- the relationships between illegal drug use and alcohol abuse
- substance abuse as a 'risk factor' in child protection cases, and what is meant by 'risk factor'
- a range of ways in which substance abuse by parents can impact on children
- issues to be considered in making an assessment and planning intervention in cases where a parent misuses drugs or alcohol.

In the next chapter I look at another group of child protection cases that has also become more common in recent years: that of families where parents have learning difficulties.

Parents with Learning Difficulties 9

Over the last twenty years or so it has become easier, and commoner, for British adults with learning difficulties to become parents. For most of the twentieth century, in Britain and elsewhere, adults with even only quite mild learning difficulties typically lived in large institutions where the sexes were segregated and relationships between them policed, and it was really only over the last two decades of the century that there was a major shift away from institutional care towards living 'in the community'. The increasing number of families where parents have learning difficulties has been reflected by an increasing number of such cases coming to the attention of the child protection system.

When people with learning difficulties become parents, they can of course encounter all of the same problems that anyone else encounters. The risk factors that increase the likelihood of parenting problems in the general population apply equally to those with learning difficulties: factors such as poverty and a history of childhood abuse. Indeed poverty and childhood abuse apply *more* frequently to adults with learning difficulties than to the general population – they are more likely to be poor and more likely to have experienced abuse as children (see Chapter 5).

But there are two other kinds of reasons why having learning difficulties may make parenting harder than it is for other people:

- Learning difficulties may present obstacles to acquiring parenting skills.
- The widespread *perception* that learning difficulties present these obstacles may result in society placing obstacles in the way of parents with learning difficulties.

There are some parallels here with the discussion in the previous chapter about parents using illegal drugs, for whom difficulties with parenting may reflect the real effects of the drug use itself, but may also reflect the perceptions and assumptions of others.

Although terminology varies, I will use the words 'learning difficulty' or 'learning impairment' interchangeably to refer to actual deficits in intellectual functioning, relative to the general population. The extent to which a learning impairment is *disabling* depends on the social context as well as on the impairment itself, in the same way that partial sight is an *impairment*, but the extent to which it is a *disability* depends on such things as the availability of spectacles, large print books and so on. So in this chapter I will reserve the term 'learning disability' to describe the difficulties faced by learning impaired people in a *specific social environment*. Not all the sources I quote use the words in the same way, however. Many use 'learning disability' synonymously with 'learning difficulty', and some authors still refer to 'mental retardation'.

Two viewpoints

Another parallel between working with parents with learning difficulties and working with substance-misusing parents, is that in both these cases the parents may be entitled to services in their own right, and not just as parents. (The same can apply too to parents with mental health problems and parents with physical disabilities.) I discussed in the last chapter the way in which drug-using families may be receiving a service both from drug and alcohol services and from services for children and families, and the need for these two separate systems to find ways of working together. This applies too to parents with learning difficulties, who may be simultaneously receiving support in their own right from learning disability agencies and from agencies whose primary brief is the welfare of children.

When there are concerns that children are being neglected or abused by parents with learning impairments, these two types of agencies may find themselves approaching the problem from very different angles. Learning disability agencies generally see themselves as operating on behalf of the person with learning difficulties, and attempting to remove or mitigate the obstacles between that person and a normal life: that is, the life that is led by non-disabled persons. They may see themselves as advocates on behalf of people with learning impairments, and may view their task in terms of fighting for the rights of a group of people who have historically been oppressed and denied human dignity. Those rights might include access to social and leisure facilities, to work, to housing, to political representation and to services which will enable them to off-set their learning difficulties. Historically, people with learning impairments have often been characterized as permanent children ('He is fifty but he has a mental age of five'), so that fighting for the rights of people with learning difficulties can be seen as fighting for their right to be treated as adults. Over the past few decades, the right to be parents has come to be seen as an important part of this. If parents with learning difficulties cannot cope adequately on their own as parents, it is argued that society has a responsibility to provide sufficient services to make it possible.

By contrast, while child protection workers may see themselves as working for the whole family, their primary responsibility is not towards the parents, but towards the child (the tone is set in England and Wales by section 1 of the 1989 Children Act, which states that 'the child's welfare shall be the paramount consideration' for courts making decisions about children). All parents who maltreat their children have reasons of one kind or another why they find it difficult to be protective parents, and many of those reasons may be just as much outside of the individual's control as are learning difficulties. There is no absolute right to be allowed to continue to parent, and parenting should only be bolstered up with supportive services if such an arrangement is in the best interests of the child. The needs of the child, rather than the rights of the parents, should be the yardstick for planning an intervention.

Examples of the 'right to parenthood' perspective are provided by the many publications of Tim and Wendy Booth (for example Booth and Booth, 1994; 1998), who strongly advocate for the rights of people with learning difficulties to be parents. They believe that parents with learning difficulties 'too often receive rough justice from the child protection system' (Booth and Booth, 1996: 81). Challenges and obstacles are placed in their way and the professional system then ends up 'blaming the victim by putting all the problems parents may be having down to their learning difficulties' (1996: 85).

On the other hand, Gillian Schofield considers that 'the approach which Booth and Booth appear to pursue fails to consider the welfare of the child or to see children in themselves as significant actors in the family situations in which they live' (Schofield, 1996: 87) . She agrees that there are 'some cases which are inappropriately accelerated through the system because the parents have learning difficulties,' but suggests that 'there are also situations where children of parents with learning difficulties are remaining at home and suffering significant harm because it was felt that the mother had learning difficulties and therefore could not be held responsible'. She cautions that:

> care needs to be taken about the ways in which parents with learning difficulties are treated as a special case. It cannot be disputed that the fundamental developmental needs of children are going to be the same whether parents have learning difficulties or not. (Schofield, 1996: 91)

These kinds of differences in perspective can, in my experience, lead to quite sharp disagreements between learning disability professionals and child protection professionals about the handling of particular cases. To some extent such disagreements are useful – a 'creative tension', which challenges the assumptions of all parties and promotes fresh thinking. But these disagreements can also result in a kind of gridlock, effectively paralysing decision making. And when this happens both children and parents are ultimately the losers, since the result is a protracted limbo in which no one can feel secure and settled and no one can get on with their lives.

Perhaps we might reduce this tendency to take up polarized positions if all parties kept in mind that what is at stake in these situations is not, in fact, a question of absolute principle, but one of *degree*. No one (as far as I am aware) is arguing that being of below average intelligence means that you cannot be a good parent. Equally, no one could really dispute that there are some people whose learning impairments are so severe that they could not act as parents in any meaningful sense. (Some people are so severely learning impaired, after all, that they cannot acquire language, or even the *concept* of parenthood, and require assistance with meeting their own most basic needs.) The potential area of disagreement, therefore, is not really about whether people with learning difficulties have some absolute right to parent – no one, after all, has such a right – but about the level of learning impairment that is compatible with being able to act as a parent, the importance of learning impairment as a factor in any given case, and the kinds of help that should be offered.

What do we mean by 'learning difficulties'?

The debate about parents with learning difficulties is not helped by a frequent lack of clarity in the literature about what is meant by 'learning difficulties', and about what level of learning difficulty is being discussed. McGaw and Sturmey (1993: 104) note that some programmes which 'claim to be addressing the needs of parents who have learning disabilities' turn out to be actually aimed at adults whose IQ is above the threshold that is generally recognized as defining a learning difficulty. Obviously it would be a mistake to generalize about the needs of people with learning difficulties on the basis of such programmes.

Indeed, it is a mistake to generalize about people with learning difficulties in any case. Intellectual ability, like height or shoe size, is something which varies widely across the population, with the largest number of people being of average ability, and increasingly small numbers towards the two extremes. At the above-average end of the spectrum there are people who are recognized as being sufficiently distinctive from the norm that we sometimes apply terms to them like 'genius' or 'exceptionally gifted'. There are a similar number of people at the below-average end of the spectrum and, below a certain point, they too are recognized as being sufficiently distinctive from the norm as to acquire special terms to describe them. Words like 'mental retardation' and 'mental handicap' were used in the past, but are now widely felt to be derogatory so they have been replaced with terms like 'learning difficulty'. But, whatever words we use, the fact is that where we draw the line between 'not very bright' and 'having a learning difficulty' is, in the end, arbitrary, just as it is arbitrary where we draw the line between 'very bright' and 'exceptionally gifted'. These things lie on a continuum.

Wherever we choose to draw the line that defines 'having learning difficulties', the group that falls within that line will still include a huge range of abilities. People with learning difficulties are not at all a homogeneous group in terms of ability (let alone in terms of other qualities, in which they are just as diverse as the rest of the population). At one end of the ability range they include individuals who lack the cognitive skills to develop language or to use a knife and fork, while at the other end of the range they include individuals who can read and write, cook, keep house, manage money and go out to work. 'Learning difficulties' is a very wide band indeed on the still wider continuum of human intellectual ability, and we cannot generalize about the capabilities of people with learning difficulties as if they were all a single group.

The traditional measure of intellectual ability is the IQ test, in which average intelligence is given a score of 100. There are a lot of problems with using a uni-dimensional measure of this kind to capture something as complex as intellectual ability (even measures of shoe size, after all, have two dimensions!) but I will not go into these here. If we accept the concept of IQ for the purposes of the present discussion, a working definition of learning impairment, given by Anthea Sperlinger, includes the following: 'significantly sub-average intellectual functioning (i.e. a composite score of two standard deviations below the mean on an accepted assessment of intellectual functioning) . . . a score of, or below, IQ 74 for the UK population'. Her definition of *severe* learning disability includes a 'score below IQ 50 on standardised tests of intelligence' (Sperlinger, 1997: 4–5), and she writes that approximately '20 people per 1,000 in the UK have learning disabilities. Within this group, some 3–4 per 1,000 of the general population have severe or profound learning disabilities' (Sperlinger, 1997: 5). (These statistics do not include people who developed an intellectual impairment after the age of 18 as a result of brain injury or diseases such as Alzheimer's, or people with specific learning problems such as dyslexia.)

The arbitrary nature of these categories, though, is illustrated by the fact that Dowdney and Skuse (1993: 26) define 'mental retardation' as an IQ of below 70, *mild* learning difficulties as an IQ of 55–70 and *severe* learning difficulties as below 40.

Intelligence and parenting

It seems rather misleading to assert, as Tim and Wendy Booth do, that 'there is no clear relationship between parental competency and intelligence' (Booth and Booth, 1993a: 463) since at the low end of the intelligence spectrum there are people who lack the cognitive ability to meet their own basic needs, let alone the needs of others, and could not conceivably be competent parents. More realistic, surely, is Fiona Painz's comment that 'few would disagree that people with quite severe learning disability have limitations preventing them from becoming adequate parents: what is at issue are people with a more moderate and mild learning disability' (Painz, 1993: 18).

What research does seem to show – and what I imagine Booth and Booth's comment refers to – is that, *above a certain minimum level,* parenting competence is not related to IQ. In other words, a minimum level of intellectual ability seems to be required to carry out the tasks of parenthood, but above that level, increased intelligence does not result in better parenting. Tymchuk and Andron (1994) suggest that there is no clear correlation between parenting competence and IQ until it falls below 60. And Dowdney and Skuse write that:

> There is general agreement that IQ does not relate in any systematic way to parenting competence until it falls below 55–60. . . . Below this level, less competent parenting has been reported . . . above it successive increments within the retarded range are not associated with increased parenting competence. (Dowdney and Skuse, 1993: 33)

A decision about a person's capacity to parent should *never* be made on the basis of an IQ measurement, of course, but what these findings suggest is that it is only as we approach the more 'severe' end of the very broad spectrum of abilities encompassed by the term 'learning difficulties' that intellectual ability *per se* begins to present difficulties for adequate parenting.

Doing the job of a parent may not be 'rocket science', but it does require some basic skills in reasoning. As Glaun and Brown put it,

> it would be simplistic to assume that competent parenting depends primarily on love. It also involves cognitive abilities, such as exercising judgement by weighing up situations or options, anticipating the consequences of actions, using forward planning and organisational skills, remembering routines, understanding the developmental capabilities and limitations of the child, and demonstrating flexibility of thinking. (Glaun and Brown, 1999: 102)

These authors go on to say that intellectual functioning is 'mediated by emotional status', reminding us that parents of average, or above-average intellectual abilities can also have difficulty with weighing up options, forward planning and so on, if they are preoccupied with other things, or they are under stress, or their thinking has been distorted in some way by their own experiences or circumstances, as I discussed in Chapter 7. But it seems clear that adults below a certain level of intellectual ability, even under optimum conditions, may have difficulty with these tasks. It seems clear too, however, that this is not going to be the case for parents at the 'mild' end of the learning disability spectrum.

Society, parenting and learning *disability*

Although many parents with 'mild' learning difficulties do have difficulties in providing adequate care for their children, this is probably the result of other factors such as poverty, social isolation and childhood deprivation, rather than of the learning difficulties in themselves (Tymchuk, 1992; Dowdney and Skuse, 1993). These sort of difficulties are faced by other parents too, of course, but, as I've already mentioned, there are particular obstacles in the way of parents with learning difficulties which are not the result of their learning difficulties as such, but are placed there by the rest of society. In other words, having a learning *disability* may be a problem, even when having a learning *difficulty* is not. Parents with learning difficulties may have the task of parenting made unnecessarily hard for them by *unwarranted assumptions*, and by *inappropriate help*.

Unwarranted assumptions

Booth and Booth's view is that a presumption that people with learning difficulties cannot adequately parent can lead to their children being removed from them in circumstances where other parents would not have had their children taken from them. The presumption is then in danger of becoming self-perpetuating because statistics about the high percentage of children of learning-impaired parents taken into care may then be used as evidence that such parents cannot cope (Booth and Booth, 1994: 41). As I've already noted, not everyone agrees with them about this, but I think we must recognize at the least that they have identified a danger. They are right in asserting that 'Parenting behaviour rather than IQ should be the criterion by which parental competence is assessed' (Booth and Booth, 1993a: 463), in just the same way that substance-misusing parents, as I discussed in the last chapter, should be assessed on the way they function as parents, not on their substance misuse. I agree with them too that we should be cautious about using statistics of children taken into care as a measure of competence, because this does indeed run the risk of setting professional biases in stone.

Unwarranted assumptions about the unfitness of people with learning difficulties to parent can distort the perceptions of professionals. If we expect people to fail as parents, there is a danger that we will be on the look-out for failure, and will take any instance of less-than-perfect parenting, any problem that may occur, as confirmation of our view, even if we might tolerate the same parental behaviour in other families. Booth and Booth (1993b) quote the following comment from a Mr Derby, a father with learning difficulties. He had been concerned that his daughter might be being abused at a house which she and other girls were frequenting while truanting from school, and had expressed his fears to the family's social worker.

> You feel as though they're telling you you're inadequate as a parent. I mean there's about three or four girls involved with this sex thing, but how come our Ann always seems to be the one that's put into a home? The other girl she was with, she's still at home. We saw her the other day, she wasn't at school. (Booth and Booth, 1993b: 165)

This sort of selective perception on the part of professionals can occur not only in relation to parents with learning impairments but to other parents too who are 'labelled' or unusual in some way: parents with mental illness, drug users, people from ethnic minorities, gay and lesbian parents, even sometimes single fathers – and indeed *any* family who enters the child protection system, and is therefore labelled as 'having problems'. It is something to watch out for generally and child protection professionals need to keep asking themselves the following question: 'This parenting behaviour may not be ideal, but is it something that we would be concerned about in the same way if it happened in another family?' It is very important that struggling families are not expected to reach *higher* standards than other families, or different standards from those that are generally accepted as normal in the community in which they live.

What is particularly unfair about labelling families or expecting them to fail is that such expectations can become self-fulfilling prophesies. To be monitored and criticized – and to have the expectation of failure hanging over our heads – is a substantial stressor for any of us, which may actually prevent us from operating as well as we otherwise would have done.

Inappropriate help

Professionals 'must *never seek permanently to remove a child from home* for reasons of neglect, inadequate care or abuse by omission before every effort has been made to equip the parents with the skills they need to cope' (Booth and Booth, 1993a: 466). Again, this is applicable to all parents, and not just those with learning impairments, but particular issues arise in relation to learning-impaired people. A learning difficulty is not the same thing as an inability to learn. People with learning difficulties can acquire new skills, but may do so at a different rate than other people, and may require appropriately designed teaching techniques. This is an area in which a child protection worker needs to enlist the skills and knowledge of professionals with experience in working with people with learning difficulties. It is one of those areas in which it is not safe to rely on 'commonsense' and intuition, because those who do not having learning impairments do not have any experience of being learning impaired to draw upon.

'Help' which is not in fact helpful serves no purpose at all. As we would use interpreters in work with a family who did not speak English, so we should obtain help in translating the concerns of the child protection system into a form which learning disabled parents are able to understand and act upon. Before concluding that someone is incapable of acquiring the necessary skills to parent, we need to ensure that every effort has been made to find an appropriate way of helping them to do so.

Having said this, however, I should caution that 'every effort' should not be taken to mean going on forever. There has been a trend in recent years towards subjecting children and families to lengthy processes of assessment. (This is reflected in the increasing length of court proceedings: see Beckett, 2000; 2001b.) It is fine to offer a level of support to a family on a long-term or permanent basis, but it is abusive to all concerned to drag out indefinitely an assessment process intended to determine whether or not children should remain in their parents' care. Professionals in the child protection system, and the courts, owe it to families to make hard decisions in a reasonable timescale, and not keep putting them off again and again while yet another assessment is carried out.

Assessment

Susan McGaw and Peter Sturmey propose a model for the assessment of the parenting skills of parents with learning difficulties (McGaw and Sturmey, 1994) that considers what they call *primary* and *secondary* indicators. Primary indicators of good-enough parenting are:

1. the child's development
2. observable childcare skills of the parents, including physical care, affection, ability to provide security, taking responsibility, ability to offer guidance to a child and to take control.

Secondary indicators include:

1. life skills, such as reading, language skills, social skills, work skills and home care skills
2. family history, including such things as the adults' own experience of being parented (bearing in mind that adults with learning difficulties are more likely than others to have experienced institutional care during childhood)
3. resources and support available to the parents.

I would suggest that, where a child is health, happy and developing well, and the parents are able to demonstrate good parenting skills, then there is no reason why the 'secondary' questions above should be any business of a child protection agency. Where the 'secondary' indicators do become important to explore is where an assessment identifies primary indicators of weaknesses in parenting. It does then become important to be as clear as possible as to the reasons for those weaknesses. Are they the result of learning difficulties? Or are they the result of unhappy childhood experiences, or a childhood in institutional care with no parental role models? Or are they the result of social isolation or a lack of resources? In order to decide what action to take in any child protection case it is necessary not only to identify problems in parenting, but to have some understanding of the likely cause of those problems. In the case of parents with learning difficulties we need to be as clear as possible whether the problems with parenting are:

1. the direct result of the learning impairment on the acquisition of parenting skills
2. social factors resulting from having learning difficulties (social isolation, for instance)
3. the result of other factors that apply also to parents who do not have learning difficulties (marital issues, poverty, mental health problems, drug and alcohol abuse, poor childhood experiences).

If the answer is simply number 3, then it is important to be clear that the learning difficulties as such are not the problem, and to ensure that the family are not singled out for differential treatment on account of them.

Number 1 is, as I discussed above, unlikely to be applicable to parents who are only mildly learning impaired. But where there are some deficits in acquiring parenting skills resulting from the learning difficulty, these are likely to be amplified by numbers 2 and 3, for reasons that I discussed earlier.

Exercise 9.1

Annette King is two months old. Her mother Lucy (aged 23) has a moderate learning disability (her IQ has been assessed as 55–60). Lucy is supported by a health visitor and by the Community Learning Disability Team (CLDT), who support adults with learning difficulties living independently, and by a 'family aide' from the social services department, who visits daily to help with practical parenting skills.

Lucy is physically affectionate with Annette, though she is inclined to become agitated when Annette cries or is difficult to feed or settle. In the view of professionals working with her, Lucy finds it hard to plan ahead and deal with unexpected situations; she has difficulties with absorbing information; and she also finds it hard to see Annette's needs as distinct from her own. (For example, she will take Annette out with barely any covers on a cold day, even though she herself has put on a jumper and coat.) It is with these kinds of things that the family aide, the health visitor and the CLDT are trying to give support.

Annette's health visitor has been very concerned about the level of care offered by Lucy. The CLDT workers feel passionately that Lucy has a right to be a parent, and that it is up to the various agencies to provide a sufficiently comprehensive package of support to enable her to cope. The CLDT request that the children and families social work team provide such support.

A recent episode has, however, sounded alarm bells, and resulted in you – as a social worker – being allocated to look at child protection issues. What happened was that an acquaintance of Lucy's visited Lucy and asked to 'borrow' Annette for the night to show to her friends. (This acquaintance was a woman called Janet, who does not have a learning disability, but has a police record for drug offences and several violent offences against adults.) When Lucy's health visitor came the next morning she found that Lucy had no idea where Annette was, or where Janet lived, or how to get in touch with her. Annette was only found later that day when the police stopped a car speeding and crossing a red light, and Annette was found to be in the back seat with two of Janet's friends, aged 14 and 15.

The health visitor feels that this episode shows that, however much support Lucy has, she simply is not capable of being a parent to Annette. 'It's all very well the CLDT talking about Lucy's "right" to be a parent,' she says, 'but where are Annette's rights in all this?'

Background on Lucy King: Lucy lives in a flat on her own, but she requires support from the CLDT with tasks such as budgeting, planning meals and so on. She is the unplanned child of a brief relationship between her mother, who is white, and a black American serviceman, whom Lucy herself has never met. Her mother considered having a termination at the time. There were serious concerns for Lucy after her birth because her mother was depressed, very dismissive of Lucy and was unsupported by her own family, who referred to Lucy as 'that black baby'. When Lucy's mother and step-father (who is also white) had two more children together, it would appear that Lucy became something of a Cinderella figure in her family. There were several occasions when professional agencies were concerned that she was being subjected to neglect or emotional abuse. A teacher once observed that Lucy's half-siblings sometimes referred to her as 'blacky', in apparent reference to her African-American father. At 14 Lucy became pregnant and had a termination. Soon afterwards her mother and step-father insisted that she was accommodated in a foster-home and she lived in three different foster-homes for the remainder of her adolescent years.

She has (in the view of team members who know her) often been exploited by men because of her very trusting nature. She is not certain who is the father of Annette.

What issues would you want to consider in an assessment of this case?

Comments on Exercise 9.1

You will probably agree that a problem that emerges from the above account is that Lucy seems to find it difficult to see Annette as a person with needs of her own. Letting a friend 'borrow' her seems akin to treating Annette as a kind of doll. (Of course you would need to explore this incident with Lucy herself before coming to firm conclusions about what it meant. Many parents, after all, leave their children with friends at times.) Lucy's failing to realize that Annette will feel the cold, just as she does, sounds like another instance of the same kind of thing.

One of the things that you would look at in your assessment, then, would be the extent that Lucy is capable of recognizing Annette's needs, and/or the extent to which Lucy is capable of learning to do so.

But you would need to be careful not to assume that the cause of the problem is primarily Lucy's learning difficulties. People of average, or above-average intelligence, can also find it difficult to recognize or focus on their children's needs if their own unmet needs as adults are sufficiently pressing to preoccupy them. There is plenty of material in Lucy's history to suggest that she may indeed have many unmet emotional needs from her own childhood. It seems that she may have been made to feel unwanted through much of her childhood for a variety of reasons, and to have been made to feel an outsider in her own family. For one thing she was a mixed-race child in a family that was otherwise all white. Low self-esteem, and the need to please others and forestall rejection, may have been behind the Janet incident as much as any specific cognitive problem resulting from Lucy's learning difficulties.

In your assessment you would need to try and tease out these different factors because they make a difference to any subsequent work. You cannot really expect to be able to offer help unless you have a sense of where the difficulty lies. If Lucy's problems as a parent were mainly to do with her learning impairment, then you would want to look at the possibility of using appropriate educational techniques to try and improve her ability to think about Annette's needs. If, however, her problems are to do with her own childhood history and negative self-image, then you might want to look at ways of helping her to address these issues, though of course you would still need to do so in a way consistent with her level of understanding.

What you would need to hold in your mind, though, is that however sad Lucy's history is, your first priority as a child protection worker would be Annette. Lucy's mistake was not to think about Annette's needs. The professional system should be careful not to make the same mistake.

Appropriate intervention

In most cases where child protection issues arise in families where parents have learning difficulties, there probably will be a number of different causes for the problem, of which some will be the same sorts of thing that cause problems for other parents, but some relate specifically to the learning difficulty. A learning difficulty is, after all, exactly what its name suggests – a difficulty with learning – and people with learning difficulties may find it more difficult than others to absorb and apply information, to retain skills once learnt, and to use reasoning to anticipate difficulties and dangers and take evasive action. But *difficulty* is not necessarily the same thing as *impossibility*, and people with learning difficulties can and do learn, if offered help in appropriate ways.

This is one of those areas in which a child protection social worker should definitely seek the assistance of professionals with the relevant experience and training. Booth and Booth (1994: 18–19) offer 10 'training points' gleaned from the research literature. Among these are the following:

- 'The acquisition of new skills is more likely and training more effective where clearly specified, individualized goals are set and presented in small, discrete and concrete steps.'
- 'Training is less effective when parents are having to cope with external pressures in their lives.'
- 'The maintenance and generalization of new learning is assisted by teaching in real-life settings rather than in the classroom or clinic.' (A point also emphasized by Susan McGaw, 1996: 25, who maintains that 'home based visits have proven to be the most successful mode'.)
- 'Training must be geared to parental learning characteristics – for example, their slower rate of learning, inability to read, low self-esteem, difficulties in organizing, sequencing and sticking to time schedules.'
- 'Periodic and ongoing long-term "refresher" support is needed to maintain learned skills.'

This last point is also emphasized by Susan McGaw, who argues that there 'is a need to move from an assumption that our purpose is always to help a family achieve totally independent functioning' (1996: 25) she goes on to say that:

> the permanent disability of the parent requires that support for the family needs to be available on a continuing basis. Crisis-driven, short-term services often result in frustration, burn-out and blame on the part of the worker and mistrust, despair and cyclical crisis episodes for families. (McGaw, 1996: 27)

This is a point which is relevant to other families too, as well as those with learning difficulties. Certainly it can be demoralizing for all concerned when a family case is closed, only to come back to the attention of the child protection or family support services again and again when lack of support has resulted in family functioning deteriorating and crisis point being reached. There is certainly a case for some families –

and not only families whose parents have learning difficulties – being recognized as in need of long-term back-up by professional agencies, just as some individuals with chronic health problems require long-term support from doctors. Susan McGaw also says, in respect of parents with learning difficulties, that 'Some parents will always require instrumental assistance in areas such as money management, meal planning, or obtaining medical care' (McGaw, 1996: 25). In other words, there will be some parents who cannot acquire all the necessary skills themselves and will need the professional agencies to do some things *for*, or at least *with*, them.

This may be so. After all, everyone relies on others to perform some tasks for them. As a parent I take responsibility for putting a roof over my children's heads, but if the roof leaked, I would need to get a roofer in to replace the slates. But it seems to me that, after a certain point, 'instrumental assistance' offered to parents ceases to be merely assistance and begins to become doing the parenting *for* them. I would question whether it is necessarily in children's interests to stay in their parents' care if the only way that this can be safely sustained is for a whole team of professionals on a rotating basis to visit daily, plan the meals, take the children to school, see they are put to bed, and supervise every aspect of their parents' interactions with them. I would suggest that for parents to operate as parents in a real sense, they do need themselves to be capable of taking primary responsibility for their children, and of thinking about and generally meeting their needs.

When support is provided to parents it should be offered in a way that is appropriate to the parents' needs. But the level of support that is offered is a matter that should ultimately be determined by the needs of the children, rather than by the notion of some absolute 'right to parent'. I cannot agree, for example, with Susan McGaw (1996: 26) when she argues that it is wrong to set tight timescales for assessments to decide whether the children of parents with learning difficulties should remain in their care. 'A tension . . . exists,' she writes, 'between the "No Delay Principle" [in England and Wales this is enshrined in section 1 (2) of the 1989 Children Act] which stipulates that a delay in court proceedings is presumed to be prejudicial, and the rights of a parent which may be compromised by actions that lead to a swift termination of their parental responsibilities.'

However, delay in court proceedings *can* be harmful to children. It denies children security until the matter is settled, and it also closes off options for their future. For instance, a child of five, who has been waiting three years in foster-care for a court decision, will be much harder to find a substitute family for, *and* also much harder to settle successfully back in her own family if that is the eventual outcome, than would have been the case if the decision about her future could have been made, one way or the other, when she was two. This remains true whether or not her parents have learning difficulties, and should therefore be a matter of *equal concern* whether or not her parents have learning difficulties.

A similar sort of issue is illustrated by the example in the following exercise, with which I will conclude this chapter.

Exercise 9.2

Consider the following comment from Booth and Booth:

> several study families reported having been warned against smacking their children. Ever fearful of losing them . . . they did as they were told. However, generally lacking powers of verbal reasoning, they were left with no effective method of discipline and began to encounter problems of control. These problems were then cited by social workers as evidence of parenting deficits. (Booth and Booth, 1993a: 169).

What questions does this raise?

Comments on Exercise 9.2

There is a substantial body of opinion which believes that smacking *per se* is unacceptable and should be illegal (as it already is in some countries). From this point of view, smacking is a form of adult violence towards children and an abuse of power. It is wrong, this argument goes, that we should tolerate violence towards children when we would not tolerate similar violence towards adults and, by tolerating smacking, we are providing a pretext for more extreme forms of violence towards children.

Clearly if you subscribe to this point of view, then smacking will not suddenly become acceptable to you just because a parent has learning difficulties. If we lower the standard of parenting we are willing to accept to take account of the parents' limitations, then we are putting the parents' needs in front of the child's.

Having said this, though, the fact is that in the UK and elsewhere, smacking by parents is widely practised and widely regarded as normal and acceptable. It is not illegal and it is not treated as child abuse warranting the attention of the child protection system, unless it is exceptionally severe. It is therefore surely wrong to demand of parents who happen to be under the scrutiny of the professional child protection or family support systems – whether or not they have learning difficulties – that they give up a form of discipline which is widely, openly and quite legally practised by their neighbours.

While it is wrong to lower minimum standards in order to take account of a parent's limitations, it is certainly also wrong to expect struggling parents to conform to a higher standard than that which would normally be regarded as acceptable among the general population. The child protection system is, in my view, quite often guilty of this, and it is a kind of oppressive behaviour that sets parents up to fail and which we should be very careful to avoid. Booth and Booth have quite rightly made this important point many times.

What may have struck you, though, about the quotation given above was the assertion that lack of 'powers of verbal reasoning' means that parents with learning difficulties need to be able to use smacking. Whether or not you believe smacking is acceptable, you will probably agree with me that it cannot be used as a *substitute* for verbal reasoning and I would be seriously concerned about a parent for whom smacking was the only method of control. What will they do when smacking fails to have the desired effect? (Will they increase the severity of the smacking?) How will they maintain control when their children are teenagers and are as big, or bigger, than their parents? How will they cope when their children demand an explanation for a rule that seems to them to be unnecessary or unfair?

It seems to me that when considering a person's capacity to parent we do need to think about the situations that that person is going to encounter and is going to have to deal with, and think realistically about whether they are going to be able to cope or not. A capacity for verbal reasoning may not be so necessary when a child is 18 months old, but it is legitimate to think ahead and ask whether a parent will have the necessary skills to cope when the child is a little older. It is certainly doing no favours to a child to ignore predictable future problems because when the problems actually occur (for example, when the child becomes uncontrollable by adults), they may be much more difficult to put right. And it is doing no favours to parents either, because it is just another way of setting them up to fail.

In this chapter I have looked at some of the particular issues that arise in child protection work when there is a parent or parents with learning difficulties. I have discussed:

- the different perspectives of child protection professionals and of professionals who work to support adults with learning difficulties – and the potential for conflict between these two groups

- what 'learning difficulties' actually means and how it is defined; I also referred to other terms such as 'mental retardation', 'learning impairment' and 'learning disability'
- the relationship between intelligence and parenting ability
- the ways in which the attitudes of society at large can impact on parents who have learning difficulties; I mentioned unwarranted assumptions and inappropriate help as two particular problems
- what needs to be considered when carrying out a parenting assessment involving a parent who has a learning difficulty
- what is required to carry out an appropriate intervention where a parent has learning difficulties, including the specific training skills that are involved and some of the dilemmas that may arise.

This concludes Part III of this book. In Part IV I will look at some current issues and dilemmas faced by child protection work as a whole, beginning with the question of poverty and its relation to child maltreatment.

Part IV

Problems and Dilemmas for
Child Protection Work

Poverty 10

Outside the town of Centreville there is a large factory which manufactures salt cellars. The salt cellar factory pumps smoke into the atmosphere and, although this pollution does not seem to do any harm to the majority of the population, a rare and dangerous disease – 'hypotheticitis' – has increased since the factory was built to the point where one in twenty of those in the area immediately adjoining the factory now suffer from it. Elsewhere hypotheticitis only affects one in five hundred.

The mayor of Centreville calls a meeting to discuss the problem. Should the factory be closed down?

All kinds of reasons are advanced for not doing so. How can we be sure that the factory is responsible? After all hypotheticitis was not unknown before the factory came, and to this day 19 out of 20 of those who live beside the factory do so quite happily without any ill effect.

Swayed by these arguments, and by the political impracticality of closing the factory (which, in truth, is a major contributor to his campaign fund), the mayor sets up a Hypotheticitis Task Force, the HTF, whose job is to identify the factors that lead a minority of Centrevilleans to suffer from hypotheticitis while others do not – and to take steps accordingly to protect them.

The HTF sets to work. It identifies various things, such as lifestyle and diet, which may be predisposing factors, and uses them to try and pick out the Centrevilleans who may be at risk of developing hypotheticitis.

But a year on, Centrevilleans near the factory are still dying of hypotheticitis at a far higher rate than the national average. The mayor is furious. So are the local media. The HTF is clearly incompetent. It has failed the people of the city.

The director of the HTF is sacked. Some suggest that the owner of the salt cellar factory, with his proven track record as a successful businessman, should be invited to take over . . .

Real life is always much more complicated than any allegory, but in some respects, child protection social workers are in the same position as the 'HTF' in the story. In Britain and other English-speaking countries, the general public and its political representatives expect the child protection system – and child protection social workers in particular – to anticipate and prevent child abuse. Yet poverty and social exclusion are a major factor – perhaps even *the* major factor – in child maltreatment and they are things which, except in very marginal ways, social workers can do nothing about, just as the HTF in the story could do nothing about the factory that was the major cause of the problem they'd been charged to deal with.

A cynic might go as far as to argue that the real function of child protection social workers, like that of the HTF in the story, is not so much to solve the problem they've been given to address, as to provide someone to take the blame. I think that this would be too simplistic a view. But I do believe that it is important for child protection social workers to be aware of the difficulties faced by parents in poor communities. The fact that most poor people do not mistreat their children, and that child abuse does certainly also occur among the middle classes and the wealthy, should not blind us to the fact that poverty is a major stress factor, which can push people who otherwise would have coped quite adequately into abusive or neglectful parenting. For the remainder of the chapter I will consider the ways in which poverty and social exclusion are related to child maltreatment, and discuss the position of the child protection social worker in dealing with problems that are largely structural in origin.

This chapter is the first of three in Part IV of this book that will look at broader questions that relate to the future development of child protection work. Chapter 11 considers the ways in which child protection systems themselves can become abusive or neglectful. Chapter 12 looks at the limitations of an approach aimed at preventing abuse by identifying 'high risk' cases.

Poverty as a risk factor

It will soon become apparent, I think, to any child protection social worker starting work in any of the prosperous nations of the English-speaking world or Western Europe, that there are, even in these very wealthy countries, large numbers of families who are very clearly poor. They are poor in the sense that they live lives which the majority of the population would regard, in material terms, as intolerably bleak. A very large proportion of families on child protection caseloads are poor in this sense.

Poverty is a risk factor. Cyril Greenland (1987), whose work on predicting child abuse I discussed in Chapter 7, identified poor housing, poverty and unemployment among his predictors of abuse. Greenland's study was based on British and Canadian cases. In the USA, Neil Guterman (2001: 27), summarizing a number of different studies, writes that 'families reported to child protection services are more likely to be single mothers, have unemployed fathers, receive public assistance, and/or live in poor neighbourhoods. . . . Several sets of studies, as pointed out by the National Research Council [1993: 133] . . . have further found that child maltreatment is likely to be concentrated in the "poorest of the poor".' In Britain, Gibbons et al. (1995), for instance, found that, of their sample of children who had been on child protection registers, 57 per cent came from families without a wage earner.

As ever, we need to be careful about how we interpret such figures. For one thing, children on child protection registers, or children reported to child protection agencies, may not necessarily accurately represent the distribution of child maltreatment. It may well be that more prosperous, articulate and powerful parents are better able to conceal child maltreatment from the authorities than are poor people. As Guterman points out, the poor are typically subjected to 'greater scrutiny by public authorities' (2001: 27). One could also make out a case that forms of child maltreatment that might be more typical of well-to-do families are less likely to be defined as child abuse and neglect, though they may in fact be harmful. For instance, the practice of sending children as young as six away to boarding school still exists in some sections of the British middle and upper classes. Many would argue that it is likely to cause 'significant harm', but it does not result in intervention by child protection agencies.

Nor should we necessarily assume that a statistical correlation between poverty and child maltreatment necessarily means that poverty *causes* child maltreatment. In Chapter 8 I cautioned in a similar way against interpreting a statistical link between drug misuse and child maltreatment as meaning that drug misuse necessarily causes maltreatment, and the same sorts of arguments apply. For one thing, since most poor people do not maltreat their children, and since a significant number of better-off people do maltreat their children, we need to be clear that, even if poverty increases the likelihood of abuse and neglect, on its own it is not the automatic cause of such behaviour. We should also bear in mind that different kinds of child maltreatment have different causes, and that sexual abuse in particular is not as closely correlated with socioeconomic factors as physical abuse and neglect (see Chapter 8).

We should also consider the possibility of other kinds of causal relationships. A statistical correlation between child maltreatment and poverty could mean, not that poverty causes child maltreatment, but that both poverty and child maltreatment are associated with some other factor. For instance, people with certain personality characteristics may have difficulty both with finding and holding down a job and with being adequate parents, in which case these personality types would be associated both with poverty and with child maltreatment. Or there might be a causal relationship between poverty and child maltreatment, but in the other direction: child maltreatment may cause poverty. We know, for instance, that one of the consequences of chronic abuse and neglect on children is a deterioration in school work, and poor school performance results in lower qualifications and less opportunities for well-paid employment.

The question of causal relationships is a very complex one when we are considering social systems, and it is usually unrealistic to expect to find a primary cause of anything, rather in the way that it is impossible to say whether the chicken or the egg came first. But having acknowledged these complications, I do suggest that the application of a little imagination is all that is required to see that poverty must cause considerable stress to families. And since, as I discussed in Chapter 7, stress is a major factor in child abuse and neglect, it would be surprising indeed if we did not find that child abuse and neglect did not occur more frequently among those who are poor. Therefore, while there is doubtless a complex systemic relationship between poverty, child maltreatment and a number of other phenomena (such as intellectual ability, mental health, physical health and educational attainment), it would be perverse not to acknowledge that poverty is a major factor in the causation of child abuse, just as pollution caused by the salt cellar factory was a major factor in the causation of 'hypotheticitis' in the fictional example with which I began this chapter.

Poverty as a factor in stress-related child maltreatment is something that I will return to below, but first I would like to look at what we mean by poverty, and at what poverty means to those who experience it.

Poverty, social exclusion, unemployment and homelessness

What exactly do we mean by poverty? Clearly it is about not having things: a low material standard of living. But where do we draw the line between those who are simply not particularly well off, and those who are in poverty? Like the line defining 'having a learning difficulty', which I discussed in the last chapter, the precise level of the poverty line is to some extent arbitrary.

One distinction that is sometimes made is that between 'absolute poverty' and 'relative poverty'. A person might be described as living in absolute poverty when they are so poor as to be unable to gain reliable access to the things that they physically need to keep alive. A subsistence farmer in Africa, whose crop has failed and who has no other source of income or food other than his farm, could be said to be living in absolute poverty. Relative poverty is poverty relative to the standards of the society in which a person lives. For example, what might be considered to be very poor, inadequate accommodation in Britain, Western Europe or the USA – a house without an inside toilet, electricity, or hot and cold running water – might be considered adequate and normal in some countries. But a person forced to live in such accommodation in Britain would be generally recognized as being poor.

The difficulty with this concept of relative poverty, however, is that it carries a certain implication that relative poverty is distinct from *real* poverty. This is not so. Humans are social beings and to participate fully in a particular society, they need to be able to operate within the norms of that society. To a citizen, say, of Haiti, or Afghanistan – or Russia – a house with running water, separate bedrooms, a gas cooker and a TV set, might well not seem like the home of a poor family. But in the context of the UK, or the USA, or France, a family might have all these things and still be in a real sense poor. In a society in which the norm is to have holidays, to be able to travel, to be able to go out in the evening to a bar or the cinema, then people who cannot afford these things are poor. 'Poverty is not just about what is needed to stay alive, but also about the conditions that allow people to stay healthy and participate in society' (Blackburn, 1991: 152).

One measure of defining poverty that is commonly used in Britain is households living on less than half the national average income. On this measure something like a quarter of the population live in poverty, while the number of children living in poverty trebled over the last three decades of the twentieth century (Family Policy Studies Centre, 2000). There are difficulties with using this sort of measure, though. For instance, a drop in the average income could result in an apparent drop in the number of people below the poverty line, even if there had been no real change in living conditions for those people who had been below the line but were now above it. And, by defining poverty in such a broad way, attention may be drawn away from those at the very bottom of the economic pile.

But no method of measuring poverty will be free of drawbacks. I suggest that we need to be careful to prevent arguments about the precise nature of poverty from allowing us to see what is surely obvious to any child protection worker, which is that real poverty continues to be widespread in the twenty-first century in the world's most prosperous economies.

What *is* useful about standard measures, even if they are ultimately arbitrary, is that they allow comparisons to be made between different areas and different groups. Such comparisons show us that, for instance, members of ethnic minorities and one-parent families are far more likely to be poor than members of the majority ethnic group and two-parent families. Among the British statistics cited by the Family Policy Studies Centre are the following:

> Pakistanis and Bangladeshis are by far the poorest groups in Britain. Sixty per cent are living in households with less than half average income.

> The risk of poverty has increased for all children in all family types but the main risk now for children is living in a family where no adult works.

> The highest concentration of poverty is to be found around Merseyside where just over one-quarter of the population is living in poverty. (2000: 1)

The family type that is most vulnerable to poverty is the lone parent family, and this is a family type that has become much more common in Britain, tripling in number over the period 1971–1998. 'By 1998, a quarter of families with dependent children were headed by a lone parent, compared with only 8% in 1971' (Howard et al., 2001: 88), the great majority of lone parents being women. An indication of the relative poverty of lone parent families is that 55 per cent of lone parents in 1998/99 were dependent on income support, as compared with just 4 per cent of two-parent families. Lone parent families, which form a large part of the caseloads of child protection workers, are often uniquely trapped in poverty, because of the 'Catch-22' situation which makes a job or training impossible (or at any rate very difficult) without childcare, and childcare impossible to pay for without a job.

Howard et al. also report that a number of studies have found a strong correlation between lone parenthood and male unemployment – worse unemployment opportunities in a given area being 'associated with more childbearing outside marriage' – and between marriage breakdown and indicators of relative poverty such as living in rented accommodation or remaining in the parental home (Howard et al., 2001: 89). This is not a topic which I can pursue further here, but it suggests yet more strands in the complex web that links material deprivation with the way that families are formed and the way they function.

Environmental poverty

Poverty is not evenly distributed within a country. It is also not evenly distributed within any given town or area. If you live in a city, you are almost certainly aware of neighbourhoods that are seen locally as 'poor' or 'deprived' or 'rough' (and, even if you live in a village, you will probably be aware of a road, or a row of houses, which has this reputation). What is more, if you were to visit a city you have never visited before, you would have no difficulty in recognizing which were its 'deprived' areas, just by their physical appearance. In many cities, there are areas which are so obviously 'deprived' that outsiders are reluctant to enter them at all for fear of crime, and are even advised not to enter them in guidebooks. And this sense of danger is not just based on prejudice and not just confined to outsiders. People in such areas are proportionately much more likely to be victims of crime than people in other neighbourhoods. Pantazis and Gordon (1997) found that poor people were more likely than others to feel unsafe walking in their own neighbourhood or being alone at home.

Exercise 10.1

Suppose you were walking in a city which you had never visited before? What are the signs that would tell you that you were entering a 'poor area'? What would your likely reaction be?

Comments on Exercise 10.1

You will probably think of others, but perhaps among the visual signs that would suggest to you that you were in a 'poor area' are:

- A high proportion of public housing
- Buildings in a poor state of repair and/or cheaply constructed
- Parks and other public areas poorly maintained and perhaps vandalized
- Shops tending to be confined to small convenience stores; no banks or large chain stores
- Graffiti, boarded-up windows, uncleared litter and other rubbish
- Small children playing in the street.

I don't know what your reaction would be to finding yourself in such an area, but I would suggest that a common reaction for anyone not having any specific business in the area, would be to leave it as promptly as possible.

This exercise was intended to make the point that poverty is not just something that happens to certain individuals or certain families, but is often *an instantly recognizable characteristic of whole communities.* Poverty is not just something that happens to individuals or families in isolation. Part of the typical experience of being poor is living in a 'poor neighbourhood': a neighbourhood which other people might prefer to avoid even passing through, and perhaps a neighbourhood which not only *feels* dangerous, but actually is.

Péter Townsend (1979) introduced the idea of 'environmental poverty' to encapsulate that aspect of poverty which is not to do with an individual's or a family's income, but with the circumstances in which they live. Under the heading of environmental poverty we might include, 'lack of access to, gardens, parks, play space, shopping facilities and health centres, as well as taking account of pollution such as noise and dirt' (Blackburn, 1991: 93).

Social exclusion, unemployment and homelessness

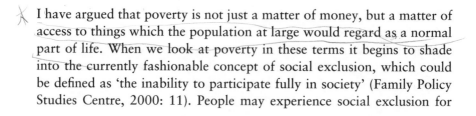

I have argued that poverty is not just a matter of money, but a matter of access to things which the population at large would regard as a normal part of life. When we look at poverty in these terms it begins to shade into the currently fashionable concept of social exclusion, which could be defined as 'the inability to participate fully in society' (Family Policy Studies Centre, 2000: 11). People may experience social exclusion for reasons other than poverty – as a result of disability, for instance, or of institutional racism – but poverty is certainly a major cause.

Social exclusion can take many forms. As we've seen, lack of money can result in people being effectively excluded from activities and services which most of us would regard as normal and from necessary sources of support, relaxation and social interaction, such as evenings out on the town, holidays, a convenient means of transport, childcare facilities. But families can also experience social exclusion as a result of not having a job, or a home of their own.

Chronic unemployment has been a feature of Western economies for many years. In the USA, as of April 2002, unemployment stood at 6 per cent. (Bureau of Labor Statistics, 2002). In Britain in spring 2002, 0.9 million people were unemployed (using the standard International Labor Organization definition of unemployment), which was 3.2 per cent of the total working/available-for-work population (Office of National Statistics, 2002). This is the lowest figure for some time, but remains a very large number of people. And when we also consider the large number of single-parent families where the parent is not seeking work, and is therefore not counted as unemployed, it is clear there is a very substantial number of children growing up in households where no one goes out to work. In spring 1999, in fact, 'almost one-fifth of children (2.2 million) lived in workless households' (Family Policy Studies Centre, 2000: 1). The other point to note is that the risk of unemployment is not evenly distributed throughout the population, but falls disproportionately on certain groups; there are areas where unemployment is the norm, and families for whom regular paid employment has not been an experience for several generations. A Danish study (Christofferson, 2000: 436) found that 'the 10% of parents hit hardest by unemployment account for 50% of the total unemployment figures'.

Homelessness is another problem which touches a very large number of people in Britain. 'Over one million households in England were homeless at some time during the ten years ending 1998/99,' according to Howard et al. (2001: 114). In 2000, '110,790 households were accepted as homeless', and of these 14 per cent were housed in bed-and-breakfast accommodation. Among those most at risk were lone parent families.

Psychological consequences

Anyone who contemplates for a moment the prospect of coping with children for any length of time in a cheap bed-and-breakfast establishment, where kitchen and bathroom facilities are shared with other residents, will surely not find it surprising that 'twice as many people in B & B experience psychological distress than in the general population' (Howard et al., 2001: 115). They are also 'more likely to have infections and skin conditions, and children have more accidents'.

People who are poor and/or unemployed and/or homeless have significantly worse mental and physical health than the population at large. Although we must again be careful about assuming that the causal link between health and social exclusion is necessarily all one-way, there are certainly a number of ways in which poverty and unemployment can impact on mental and physical health. First there is the very direct physical consequences of things such as poor nutrition and unhygienic or unsafe living conditions. Second, there are stresses resulting from lack of access to sources of support, relaxation and respite, due to insufficient finances or to 'environmental poverty'. Third, demoralization and low self-esteem resulting from the stigma of social exclusion may have a direct effect on psychological functioning and this, in turn, can impact on physical health.

How precisely the correlation between psychological or physical health and social exclusion works in any given instance is always a complex question, and open to debate, but the following examples give a flavour of the ways in which poverty impacts on those affected by it. The quotations from Beresford et al. (1999) that I have italicized are comments made by people with personal experience of poverty:

> Children in the bottom social class [in Britain] are five times more likely to die from an accident than those at the top. (Howard et al., 2001: 115)

> *. . . being poor is just so much work your whole life. You see people going into a shop. They buy what they want and they leave. But you're there, you're having to calculate how much money you've got as you go round, you're having to look at one brand and then another, and meanwhile the store detective is looking over your shoulder . . .* (Beresford et al., 1999: 94)

> For many women, caring for children is a twenty-four-hour physically and emotionally demanding job, with no pay, low status and poor work conditions. Whilst certain aspects of the job are common to all mothers, the conditions under which mothers care vary with income, and the research evidence suggests that conditions are poorest and most stressful for mothers in low income families. (Blackburn, 1991: 115)

> *Poverty strips your dignity. You can't have any dignity with poverty. Where I come from you've people, like they go to the supermarket, they haven't enough money to pay for what they need. And how does that*

person go home and say to the children that they haven't got enough food to feed them? (Beresford et al., 1999: 90)

Low-income families not only face more barriers to receiving support than other families, they are also more likely to face more barriers to giving material and social help than higher-income households . . . low-income households are less likely to have the material resources to offer service exchanges or help. (Blackburn, 1991: 115).

It's the boredom of poverty and the boredom is what wears you down and makes you despondent in the end. . . . It's deadly boring having to penny pinch all the time. (Beresford et al., 1999: 91)

The most useful information on income and mental health comes from the *Health and Lifestyles Survey*. This survey examined how various dimensions of health, including psycho-social health . . . are related to a number of socio-economic circumstances, individual characteristics, attitudes, belief and behaviour. Data from this survey indicated that at all ages, both men and women living in low-income households had poorer psycho-social health (and physical health) than the average population. Moreover, the data suggested that low income (independent of social class) increased the likelihood of poor psycho-social health. (Blackburn, 1991: 152, citing Cox et al., 1987)

Another survey published in 1997 found that one in 20 mothers sometimes went without food to meet the needs of their children, with lone mothers on income support 14 times more likely to go without than mothers in two-parent families not on benefit. (Howard et al., 2001: 109, referring to Ashworth and Braithwaite, 1997)

Christmas and birthdays is when you dread most because you know you haven't got the money. (Beresford et al., 1999: 91)

Looking specifically now at the impact of unemployment, Fryer (1992) reports that studies from the Great Depression of the 1930s found that unemployment was associated with 'hopelessness, low self-esteem, social isolation, anxiety, depression and impaired physical health', but also found that the effect was not homogeneous and that different individuals responded to unemployment in different ways. Studies in the 1980s found much the same things: 'groups of unemployed people . . . have poorer mental health than matched groups of employed people' and that 'depression . . . has been demonstrated to be higher in groups of unemployed people than in matched groups of employed people' (Fryer, 1992: 107), but again different individuals responded in different ways.

These effects may be the result of the poverty that is a usual consequence of unemployment. Warr and Jackson (1983), for instance, found that their unemployed respondents had an income of 35–50 per cent of what they were paid when employed. And Hutson and Jenkins point out that:

> A shortage of money does not just result in economic deprivation. . . . As a medium of exchange, money is also caught up in a culturally defined complex of notions about reciprocity, notions which are themselves concerned with a further set of ideas of honour, status and appropriate behaviour. Exchange relationships – whether we choose to view them as strictly 'economic' or not – are basic to social interaction and the production and reproduction of social groups, large or small. (Hutson and Jenkins, 1989: 41)

But not having a job can have negative effects in other ways, not necessarily to do with lack of money. For most of us, work is an important part of our identity. 'What do you do?' is, after all, one of the most commonly asked questions on first meeting someone. Work provides not only money but also 'opportunity for control; skill use; interpersonal contact; external goal and task demands; variety; environmental clarity; . . . physical security; and valued social position' (Fryer, 1992: 114). The loss of this sense of identity, position, purpose and structure, or its *absence* in the case of those who have never been employed, must surely be a factor in the poor mental and physical health of the unemployed relative to the rest of the population.

The humiliation of unemployment is added to by the stigma of having to claim benefits. 'Unemployed people still have grounds to complain about the ignominy of poor conditions, seat-shuffling, queuing and long waits' as Fryer observes (1992: 117), and by the inability to engage in 'conspicuous consumption' in a society where possessions are an important mark of status. The last point is an important one for child protection professionals to bear in mind before criticizing poor people for getting into debt by buying 'luxury' items such as state-of-the-art DVD players.

In the Danish study mentioned earlier, Christofferson suggests that unemployment can impact on the mental health of parents as a result of decreased social status, disruption of family roles and feelings of personal failure as well as of specifically financial problems, and that this in turn is likely to impact on children. Based on a statistical analysis of two birth cohorts of children, the study found that unemployment was associated with a rate of family break-up twice as great as for families where parents were employed, and that, for instance, '7% of children from families enduring long-term unemployment have experienced the suicide or attempted suicide of one parent [which is] three to four times the frequency for families having full-time employment' (Christofferson, 2000: 428).

Hypothesizing that unemployment is likely to make parents 'less supportive of, or sensitive to their children's needs', and that it might result in increased incidences of child abuse and neglect, Christofferson particularly considered the relationship between abuse incidents and a history of unemployment, and concluded that 'Although it is very seldom that children are hospitalized as a consequence of violence, a disproportionate number of such cases can be observed among the children of the long-term unemployed' (Christofferson, 2000: 431). Aware of the possibility that there could be other factors which caused both unemployment *and* child abuse – and could thus result in a statistical correlation between child abuse and unemployment but no actual causal link between the two – Christofferson adopted a methodology intended to tease out the effects of unemployment from those of other social factors, and concluded:

> the analyses revealed that the connection between unemployed parents and abuse of their children was still to be found even after taking account of parents' education and existing risk factors and adverse social circumstances. Some of these social factors may even be the result of unemployment. (Christofferson, 2000: 437).

In Chrisofferson's view, 'Parental unemployment [and especially *maternal* unemployment] . . . is one of several risk factors which may increase the risk for child abuse even in ordinarily stable families exposed to unemployment' (2000: 436).

Poverty as stressor

As Michael Rutter puts it: 'Good parenting requires certain permitting circumstances. There must be the necessary life opportunities and facilities. When these are lacking even the best parents may find it difficult to use their skills' (1974: 20).

I do not think that we should be surprised that researchers have found links between the experience of unemployment, poverty and homelessness with depression and poor health, along with a whole range of other phenomena such as marital breakdown, crime, drug abuse and suicide. By the same token, I do not think we should be surprised that they are also linked with an increased incidence of child abuse and neglect. This is not to say that poor people are worse parents than other people, or that they care less for their children, but simply to say that poverty and social exclusion in its various forms throws up many, many additional sources of stress – and cumulative stress is a factor that pushes parents towards abusive or neglectful behaviour, as any parent must surely know from his or her own experience.

Exercise 10.2

Elsie is a lone parent aged 22, living on state benefits with two children – Ben aged three years and Jack aged nine months – in a fourth-floor council flat. (She has never had paid employment and left school without any qualifications.) Elsie goes shopping for groceries several times a week, a trip which involves a walk of about three-quarters of a mile to a small supermarket in a small shopping precinct. Unless she can arrange for a neighbour to look after them, she takes both children with her in a double buggy.

Elsie is returning from the shops on a hot summer day, pushing the buggy laden with children and groceries. She has spent all her money until her next benefit payment in three days' time. Ben and Jack are hot, tired and bored, as is Elsie, who is rather overweight and has difficulty with the buggy, which has seen better days and now has the annoying habit of pulling constantly to the right. Jack has been crying the whole way home and Ben has been whining and demanding sweets.

In the building where they live, the lift is out of order, as it frequently is. It is impossible to carry buggy, children and groceries up the stairs. Elsie tells Ben to get out of the buggy and walk up stairs, while she herself carries Jack and one bag of groceries, leaving the buggy and the other groceries for her to come back and collect when the children are installed in the flat. This makes her very anxious because on one occasion she had all her groceries stolen when she left them downstairs like this, so she wants to get back down again as quickly as possible.

Ben is infuriatingly slow on the stairs, complaining all the way up and asking her to carry him too. When they finally reach the landing outside her flat, she puts down her groceries and Jack so as to get out her key. At this point, for some reason, Ben takes it into his head to pull a bottle of cooking oil out of the groceries, which he then drops onto the concrete floor of the landing, where it smashes, right next to where his baby brother is sitting.

Consider Elsie's likely reaction (or your likely reaction if you were in Elsie's shoes). Then consider the following different scenario. Elizabeth is a university teacher aged 35 who has temporarily given up work to be a full-time mother. She is married to a doctor and lives in a detached house with its own car-parking space right outside the front door. She has just returned from her monthly grocery shop at a large out-of-town supermarket. Coincidentally she also has a Ben aged three and a Jack aged nine months. In the car on the way back Ben has been listening to a story tape and Jack has gone to sleep. Elizabeth helps Ben out of his car seat and then picks up Jack, along with one of the ten bags of groceries. Outside the front door she puts down the groceries to take out her key and Ben, for some reason, takes out a bottle of olive oil, which he promptly drops on the doorstep where it smashes.

What differences do you notice between the two experiences?

Comments on Exercise 10.2

Obviously how Elsie and Elizabeth might react to their respective smashed bottles of cooking oil will depend on their own personalities, what is going on for them at the time, and their own personal histories. It might be that Elsie is the sort of person who can deal calmly with minor crises of this kind while Elizabeth is the sort of person who finds this sort of thing intolerably exasperating.

But other things being equal, I think you will agree that grocery shopping is far more stressful for Elsie than it is for Elizabeth. She has to do it far more often (and has to worry much more about how much she spends), she has to undertake an exhausting journey to do it and, at the end of it, she has the difficulty of getting everything up the stairs. Even the money wasted on the cooking oil is more serious for Elsie than Elizabeth. She has no money left to buy a replacement. Other things being equal, then, you will probably agree that, for the two women, the bottle-smashing incident is much more likely to be the final straw for Elsie than it is for Elizabeth and that – out of the two – Elsie is therefore the one who is more likely to react in an abusive way, perhaps hitting Ben, or screaming at him, or dragging him roughly into the flat.

The example in the exercise related to contrasting experiences of shopping trips, but I would suggest that if you contrast the experiences of middle-class or upper-working-class parents with those of the poorest parents, you would find a whole range of ways in which the experience of the latter is more stressful, and I would suggest that the cumulative impact of these differences must be enormous, although its effects will of course vary from one individual to another. If we add to these additional difficulties of parenting on a low income, the fact that poor parents are more likely to be victims of crime, more likely to suffer depression and poor health and be less likely to have a partner, then the observable association between poverty and the physical abuse and neglect of children hardly seems to require an explanation.

Intervention and oppression

But how should an awareness of the relationship between poverty and child maltreatment actually change the practice of child protection social workers? Social workers are not equipped or mandated to alleviate poverty or homelessness and unemployment, all of which have causes at the level of macroeconomics and of national and international politics. In some small ways it may be possible to mitigate the effects of poverty in particular situations – assisting with a claim for benefits, arranging for a grant to pay for some day care to allow parent and child a break from one another – and sometimes doing so can be the most effective form of intervention. But the material assistance that social workers can offer is extremely limited, and even what they *can* do comes, from a family's point of view, at a price. By becoming recipients of 'welfare', their status as poor and dependent on others is necessarily underlined and confirmed.

Social workers often have to deal, I believe, with parents who are failing to cope, but would have been able to do so adequately if it were not for the external stressors that they are up against. Of course, children cannot be left to suffer maltreatment just because we are sorry for their parents, or are aware of good reasons why their parents are struggling. But on the other hand, frequent intervention by child protection agencies into the lives of poor families in poor communities can add up to a very substantial additional source of stress for those communities as a whole, as well as for the families who are actually on the receiving end.

I have previously quoted (in Chapter 2) Neil Guterman's warning that, if intervention by child protection agencies 'engenders in parents deeper feelings of powerlessness and adds additional ecological challenges,' there is a possibility that it 'may even heighten the risk of child maltreatment – precisely the opposite of the stated purpose of the intervention' (Guterman, 2001: 49). I believe this is a real danger. Sadly some interventions do indeed have the effect of making things worse both for the parents *and* the child. But I would add the following. It seems to me a real possibility that a pattern of regular interventions could have the effect of making things more difficult for a whole neighbourhood, by increasing general feelings of powerlessness, threat and alienation, and that this may in the long run result in more harm being done to children in that neighbourhood, *even if those interventions in any given case were helpful to the children immediately involved.*

There are neighbourhoods within which the child protection system must feel at times like something akin to the surveillance system of a totalitarian state. Schools talk to social workers about children and their parents, social workers talk to doctors about their patients, schools and social workers hold liaison meetings with the police. A system that is justified on the grounds of protecting children can end up looking awfully like a system to oppress and spy on the poor. And though even an oppressive system may protect some children, there is a danger that, in the long run, this will only be at the expense of others.

Exercise 10.3

In Exercise 10.2, the three-year-old son of Elsie smashed a bottle of cooking oil on the concrete landing outside her flat. For the purposes of this exercise, let us suppose that the bottle incident does indeed feel to Elsie like the final straw and that she slaps Ben hard across the face. He is caught just above the eye by a heavy ring which she is wearing. The result of this is a large bruise and swelling on one cheek and a black eye.

Next day, a neighbour in the flat opposite, Mrs Rowe, sees the injuries and telephones the local Child Protection Team (CPT), reporting that she heard Elsie yelling at Ben on the landing the previous day, following a smashing noise, and heard Ben screaming in distress. She had also heard Jack screaming throughout the incident.

Mrs Rowe says she hears a lot of screaming and shouting coming from the flat, and has sometimes thought she had heard hitting before.

On checking its records, the CPT finds that there were several referrals from a different neighbour at a previous address, concerned about Elsie screaming at the children, although on those occasions the CPT had decided there was not a basis to take any further action other than talking to the local health visitor and to Elsie's GP, who had both reported that Elsie had a short fuse but that they had never seen evidence of physical injury to the children.

The CPT visits Elsie. During the course of this visit Elsie learns for the first time that there have been previous referrals about her to the CPT, that the CPT has had discussions about her with her GP and her health visitor, and holds a file on Ben and Jack. Elsie at first attempts to deny that she hit Ben and suggests that he may have fallen and hit his face on a toy car. Taking his cue from his mother, Ben tells the CPT worker that he fell over.

At the insistence of the CPT Ben and Jack are taken to a paediatrician, who says the injury has clearly been caused by a blow with the hand across the face. The paediatrician also notes some older bruising on Jack's shoulder, but is unable to suggest a cause for it.

As a result of this investigation, a child protection conference is called and Ben and Jack's names are placed on the child protection register. A protection plan is agreed between the CPT, the other professionals and (because she feels she has little choice) Elsie. It initially involves:

- Ben and Jack being checked weekly for bruising
- a social worker visiting Elsie weekly for a six-week period to complete a 'core assessment' and work with her on parenting issues
- Elsie being required to attend a family centre with Ben and Jack for a programme on parenting skills.

The social worker assigned to Elsie is Judy, aged 24, single and with no children.

Elsie knows several people who have had dealings with the CPT. A friend of Elsie's recently had a child taken into care.

What do you think the effect of this intervention will be on Elsie, and what consequences do you think it will have for Ben and Jack?

Comments on Exercise 10.3

This was a violent assault on a small child and there are some suggestions (though no hard evidence) that it was not an isolated incident. The professional agencies have legitimate concerns and have put in place a plan which will at least ensure that, if this sort of thing is a regular event, it should be picked up fairly quickly. What is more, the professional agencies might argue, this plan not only provides the safety net of monitoring but, in addition, it offers some help to Elsie to help her to cope in a different way in the future.

But if we put ourselves in Elsie's shoes – and it is important to do this, provided that we hold in mind the fact that the point of doing so is to help protect Ben and Jack – it may look rather less helpful.

What has happened is deeply humiliating for Elsie. She has never had a job. She has no qualifications. The most important work she does in life is to parent her children and her ability to do this work is now being called into question by powerful agencies who she knows sometimes take people's children away from them.

Elsie has found out for the first time that her health visitor and GP talked about her 'behind her back' to the CPT. (If I was Elsie this would make me feel angry and betrayed, and also make me feel that I was up against a powerful network of professional agencies, who valued each other's opinion more than they valued mine.)

She is being offered a 'core assessment'. This term would probably not mean anything to Elsie. Even if it is explained to her, it seems to me that the idea of an assessment carries an implication that the professionals are better able to understand Elsie's family than she is herself.

Elsie is also being offered 'work' with a social worker 'on parenting issues'. A phrase like 'work on parenting issues', though, is a very social work expression. What would Elsie make of it? And what does it actually mean? In my experience child protection workers often fail to explain these terms, and we are perhaps not always clear about what we mean ourselves. If what is being suggested is some sort of counselling or quasi-therapeutic work, then a clearer understanding with Elsie would be needed, and also her genuine consent. If something much more general and open-ended is being proposed then why not say so? (Perhaps: 'I'd like to visit you for a few weeks just to get to know you a bit better and see if there is any way we can help you to avoid hurting your children when you lose your temper'.)

I mean no disrespect to young or childless social workers, but in my experience, the fact that Judy is not much older than Elsie, and has no experience of parenting, is likely to be a significant issue for Elsie and an additional source of humiliation and resentment if it is not addressed in some way.

Parenting skills training at a family centre is a common response in such situations, but again is humiliating – it is like being sent back to school – and perhaps it is beside the point. Is it actually skills that Elsie is lacking? (If I drive badly when I am tired or stressed, it doesn't necessarily mean I am lacking in driving skills.)

In particular, the plan lacks any component aimed at reducing the stress on Elsie. For example, a simple, practical arrangement might be to provide some sponsored daycare to allow Elsie to do shopping without the children once a week. Although it is right and proper that a child protection plan should insist on Elsie taking responsibility for her violent behaviour, this should surely be balanced by some acknowledgement of the difficult task she faces? Otherwise the net effect of the whole approach is to locate the problem entirely inside Elsie, and thereby to amplify any feelings of self-doubt and low self-esteem which she already has.

Incidentally, plans like this often seem to ignore the fact that the children must have a father or fathers. It is rather hard that women in Elsie's position may have to undergo a humiliating scrutiny of their capacities and deficiencies as parents, while absent fathers, who may have abdicated any sort of parental responsibility, do not find themselves at the receiving end of any such scrutiny.

As to the effect on the little boys of this plan. In the short run it does provide a safety net, in that further assaults on Ben or Jack are likely to be quickly picked up. But in the long run a plan like this provides no practical help to Elsie, may well knock her confidence in her parenting, and is likely to embarrass and humiliate her. It is quite possible to imagine that such an intervention could, in the long run, leave Elsie somewhat less well-equipped to manage everyday stresses than she was before. Most parents at times feel trapped by their children, and resentful of the demands made on them. It is possible that the net effect of interventions of this kind might be to increase those feelings of resentment towards the children, so that they would experience a deterioration rather than an improvement in the standard of parenting they received.

How can social workers protect the children of poor people without contributing to the oppression that may be one of the major causes of child maltreatment in the first place? There are unfortunately no simple ways out of this dilemma, which sits at the core of social work practice. But the following are a few suggestions that are to do with being sensitive to power differences and avoiding the abuse of power. Most of these are relevant to work with people from any background, in fact, but are particularly important to note in relation to people who are poor or socially excluded, because of the greater power differences that exist.

- It is important, particularly for social workers who (like myself) come from comfortable, relatively affluent backgrounds, to be aware of the fact that parents in poor neighbourhoods are raising their children in vastly different circumstances, and raising them to cope with vastly different realities. To give an instance of this: middle-class parents in Britain, finding themselves in the 'catchment area' of state schools which have the reputation of being 'rough', typically take evasive action, either by sending their children to private schools, or by lobbying to get their children into other, less 'rough' state schools further away, or even by moving house so as to get into the catchment area of those less 'rough' schools. For poor parents, there may no alternative to letting their children attend the local 'rough' school, and therefore one of the tasks of the parents may be to equip them to cope in that environment. The author of an Israeli study comparing the attitudes of low- and middle-income parents, makes the point that some child-rearing practices, which might seem questionable from a middle-class perspective, 'could be adaptive mechanisms within the social context of a low income deprived neighbourhood' (Shor, 2000: 175).

- It is a good practice to check whether your own conduct, and the conduct of your agency, would be acceptable to you should you find yourself on the receiving end. For example, would you expect your children's school to inform you if they had concerns about your children, prior to contacting other agencies? What would your attitude be if a professional who had never met your children before, told you that she wished to interview them without you being present? As a general rule, poor people are used to a relatively powerless position and are often resigned to official scrutiny and compliant with official requests. When poor people do raise objections or do refuse to fall in with the wishes of child protection agencies, they can easily be labelled as 'uncooperative', 'difficult' and 'anti-authority'. We should be very careful about this. It's also important to be aware that people who feel in a powerless position may resort to aggressive behaviour more easily than those who are confident that they will be listened to.

- All parents and (depending on their level of understanding) all children need to be informed about what is going on, how things have been left, what is being recorded, who is being consulted, and what the possible outcomes are. People who are in a relatively powerless position may not ask questions (or alternatively, may do so in an aggressive rather than an assertive manner), but child protection agencies should treat them the same as they would treat more powerful and assertive people. Social work and child protection jargon ('assessment', 'core group', 'key worker', 'child protection register') should be carefully explained.

- It is important to avoid making people 'jump through hoops' just for the sake of doing something. An example that I have already mentioned is the practice of requiring parents to attend 'parenting skills' sessions. Any intervention with parents is only justified if it will enable them to parent their children better. For an agency to require parents (or children) to do something simply so as to make the agency feel *it* has done something is an abuse of power. Anything which makes parents feel humiliated and infantilized is unlikely to help them feel confident about being parents, and is therefore unlikely to help their children.

- Clearly there are some practices by parents and carers which are not acceptable, and it is entirely legitimate for a child protection agency, when such lines have been crossed, to insist on parents stopping these practices, and to take other action if parents do not comply. However, child protection workers should be very careful not to engage in 'nagging'. There are many parenting practices which childcare professionals may dislike – 'smacking' for instance – but which are not illegal and which would not constitute grounds for removing a child. There is no purpose to be served by 'insisting' that parents stop such practices, if in fact, there is nothing that the agency can do if they carry on. Being subjected to constant criticism is not a good way of getting better at anything, particularly if your self-esteem is already low, and you are already being subjected to stresses from other sources.

- In particular, child protection agencies should not make threats – such as the threat to take a child into care – if they are not in fact going to carry that threat out. It is the awareness that child protection social workers can and do on occasions take children away from their parents that makes them feared in poor communities. Of course, it is sometimes necessary to remove children from their parents to protect them against serious harm, and it is impossible to take away completely the fear that this causes. But the fear should not be exploited.

- In Exercise 10.3, I suggested that practical help would often be more effective than interventions that simply label a parent as failing and require her to prove her ability to change. I believe this to be the case. But it is worth bearing in mind that targeted help of the kind mentioned is still stigmatizing, because a parent must in effect prove that she is failing before she can gain access to it. ('Are you telling me I have to batter my kids before I can get any help?', as more than one parent has observed when trying unsuccessfully to get help from a social work agency.) For resource reasons, social work agencies often have no choice but to ration services in this way, although it would be much better if services such as daycare were provided on demand, or perhaps on financial criteria alone, so as to avoid parents having to experience failure before getting help.

Social workers are trained to work in an 'anti-oppressive' way. Of course this does not mean that social work on its own can counteract oppression. Poverty, unemployment and homelessness are the result of economic and political forces far, far beyond the reach of individual casework, though ironically they are partly the results of policies made by the very same governments that employ social workers. In their practice, social workers can only try (a) to mitigate to a small extent the effects on a few individuals of structural oppression, and (b) to avoid being oppressive themselves.

However, while social workers at work cannot expect to be able to change society, they and other child protection professionals are very well-placed to witness to the reality and extent of poverty and social exclusion, something which is largely invisible to the majority of citizens of the affluent 'West'. While they may not be able to change things at work, therefore, they do perhaps have a useful contribution to make *outside* the workplace to the wider political debate.

In this chapter I have discussed poverty, along with the closely related, overlapping issues of social exclusion, unemployment and homelessness, and explored its relationship to child maltreatment. I have considered:

- evidence that links poverty statistically with child maltreatment, making poverty a 'predictor' or 'risk factor' in child maltreatment, and discussed the nature of this connection
- the nature of poverty, including the concepts of relative and absolute poverty and of environmental poverty, the meaning of 'social exclusion', and the links with unemployment and homelessness
- the psychological consequences of poverty and social exclusion
- the idea of poverty as a stressor – a source of stress which can push some parents who might otherwise cope into abuse or neglect
- intervention by social workers and the child protection system and the danger that intervention intended to protect child may become, in effect, another kind of oppression of the poor. I made some suggestions about ways of avoiding this.

In the next chapter I will look further at the ways in which child protection interventions can actually be harmful, and will consider how the child protection system, intended to protect children from abuse, may actually perpetrate abuse in its own right.

Abusive Systems 11

. . . the practice of child protection can be as abusive as the behaviour of the parents which has brought the situation into the child protection arena in the first place. (Velleman, 2001: 42)

In the previous chapter, I suggested that the actions of child protection agencies can be a source of additional stress to poor families, which means that they may actually at times increase rather than reduce the risk of child maltreatment. In this chapter I will look at more direct ways in which the child protection system, and the system of public care for children (called the 'looked-after' system in England and Wales), can themselves be harmful to children, to the point where they could accurately be described as abusive.

Most of the abuse that is perpetrated by the child protection and looked-after systems is not deliberate and much of it is not easily avoidable. Although there are dangerous and abusive individuals in social work and in the looked-after system, as there are in every part of society, they are the exception. But systems can be abusive in effect, even when the individuals who operate them are acting with the best of intentions. Professional child protection and childcare systems have their own particular complex dynamic created by (a) the particular psychological motivation that leads people to become social workers and helping professionals; (b) the expectations – some of them unrealistic – that are placed upon the child protection system by the public at large, and by the powerful; (c) limited resources, which often bear no relationship to the scale of those expectations; and (d) the very human need of professionals and their managers to protect *themselves*. In the child protection system, as in any other type of human system, these competing pressures can result in consequences that are not intended by any individual.

Many child protection social workers are motivated by a strong desire to rescue children from situations in which they are suffering and being harmed. On one level this is a very appropriate motive for doing the work. But the danger of being a 'rescuer' is that you can become so taken up with the harm that a child needs protecting from that you can forget to consider the harm that you yourself might do. It is important for child protection social workers to recognize that there is no such thing as absolute safety, and that the likely or possible benefits of any intervention – whether or not this involves removing children from their parents' care – must be weighed against the likely or possible harm that it might do. Decisions about intervention should be based on what actually one can *realistically* hope to achieve, not on what one would ideally like to achieve.

I would suggest too that this need to be realistic about what can be achieved is important not only at the level of individual practice, but also at the policy level. Those who create policy, draft laws and write books (like this one) need to be guided by what is possible, rather than what would be ideal. Simply writing an objective down on paper does not make it happen, and attempting to meet laudable but unattainable goals can result in all sorts of unforeseen and undesirable consequences.

Abuse in public care

All the kinds of abuse and neglect that happen to children in their own homes, can happen too to children who are in public care, including, tragically, to children who have been removed from their own families precisely for the purpose of protecting them against abuse. Indeed, children who have been abused in their own homes may be particularly vulnerable to abuse elsewhere. They may accept abuse as the norm; they may have been taught that it is dangerous to complain about abuse; they may even have learnt to invite abuse as a way of getting attention. Some sexually abused children, for instance, may behave in a very sexually provocative way. Some children who have been physically abused may have learnt to think of violence and its aftermath as a way of getting intimacy, and may behave in ways that seem to invite violence.

On the other hand, children who have experienced emotional rejection may behave in ways which seem calculated to alienate themselves from their carers. (I quoted an example of this on p. 113.) This may be because it can feel safer to such children to reject others before they have a chance to reject them. Or perhaps it is because when we fear something in the future we sometimes find it easier to 'get it over with', rather than live in anticipation.

The behaviour of looked-after children is, therefore, one stressor which may contribute to the risk of abuse in the care system. Another is the difficulty on both sides of forming an attachment to someone who has their own separate history. Placing a child in an adoptive family or a foster-home is a little like the horticultural practice of grafting a branch from one tree onto another. When this is done skilfully, it can 'take' very successfully, but there is always a risk that the two different stocks will not bond together. This may help to explain why being an adoptive, foster- or step-child is one of the eight 'characteristics of the child' identified by Cyril Greenland (1987) as risk factors in fatal child abuse, and may be connected too with the finding of Anderson et al. (1993) that step-parents were roughly 10 times more likely to sexually abuse than parents.

The latter, however, may also be connected with the fact that paedophiles can be highly predatory and will actively seek opportunities to have contact with children, and this includes establishing relationships with single mothers in order to gain access to their children, like the narrator of the novel *Lolita*. Getting a job involving children is, of course, another obvious tactic, and it is not surprising that predatory paedophiles have been found operating in schools, churches, choirs, cub packs – and also in residential homes, foster-homes and adoptive families. Whatever checks and safeguards are put in place, it is difficult to see how they can ever be 100 per cent safe. Checking police records, for instance, will not be effective against paedophiles who have so far managed to keep their activities secret.

One of the facts of life that child protection workers have to live with, therefore, is that the system intended to provide a haven for children who would be unsafe in their own homes, does in itself contain a small minority of highly dangerous, abusive individuals. In the course of a career, a child protection social worker may be involved in investigations of alleged abuse that have occurred within the care system run by her own agency. (She would not normally *carry out* such an investigation however, as it is accepted practice that an independent agency should do this.) She may even have to deal with the aftermath of abuse that has occurred in a placement that she has herself arranged.

Exercise 11.1

Two sisters are placed with approved adopters Mr and Mrs Brown, after a period in foster-care. It has been decided that they cannot return to their own family. The older sister, Lynne, is 13; the younger, Kate, is 8. Lynne has experienced sexual abuse in her own family. She is restless and anxious, has difficulty concentrating on school work, and has difficulty getting on with her peers. She can be devious and manipulative at times. These problems continue in the placement, but it is hoped that the security of an adoptive home and the regular input of a therapist, who she has started seeing weekly, will help in time. Kate does not have a known history of abuse. She is a much more confident child, and much easier to like.

One month before the adoption is due to go through, Lynne tells her therapist that Mr Brown has been feeling under her clothes and getting her to masturbate him. This happens, she says, on a Saturday morning, when Mrs Brown takes Kate to a ballet class.

The therapist contacts the social services department, as a result of which both children are questioned by a social worker and the police. Lynne repeats her allegation in detail. Kate says nothing has happened to her and that she is very happy with Mr and Mrs Brown. Both girls are moved to a foster-home while investigations continue, though Kate very much resents this.

Mr Brown indignantly denies the allegation, saying that he and his wife have always known that Lynne is a 'lying, spiteful, vicious girl', but that they will fight 'tooth and nail' to get back Kate. Mrs Brown supports him.

You are the social worker responsible for Lynne and Kate, and you placed them with Mr and Mrs Brown. Imagine your reaction if you were to return from your summer holiday to find that all this had unfolded in your absence.

Comments on Exercise 11.1

As the social worker who made this placement you will have got to know both the girls and the Browns and will have a working relationship with all of them. You will probably have found things to like about all of them, and will certainly have decided that both Mr and Mrs Brown have something to offer these girls as parents.

What has happened would therefore be a severe blow to you, including your confidence to make judgements about other people. If the allegations are true, as seems probable, then you (and the social worker who assessed the Browns as adopters) have clearly seriously misread Mr Brown. Even if the allegations were not true, the reaction of Mr Brown perhaps reveals a side of him that you have not seen before.

A range of difficult decisions lie ahead, but it is clear that your own involvement up to now will make this especially difficult for you (as a social worker in this position you may be able to glimpse how it might feel to be the non-abusing parent in a family where the other parent is accused by a child of abuse). Although you may have a very important role to play in this case, I would suggest that this sort of situation does clearly indicate the need for support from another worker who is not encumbered with guilt and baggage from the past. Your own decision making is likely to be affected by this history.

Abusive foster-parents and adoptive parents

In July 1998, Sion Jenkins, the deputy headmaster of a school in Hastings, Kent, was found guilty of murdering his 13-year-old foster-daughter Billie-Jo with a tent spike. This happened outside his home where Billie-Jo had been living for five years (BBC News Online, 2 July 1998). In March of the same year, in North Wales, Roger Saint, the former manager of a children's home, and a foster-parent for many years, pleaded guilty to charges of indecent assault against five boys placed with him and his wife by the London Borough of Tower Hamlets. These boys, aged between 9 and 14 at time of placement, had all been subsequently adopted by the Saints. All of them complained, after leaving the Saints, of having been sexually abused by Roger Saint (Waterhouse, 2000). Saint also pleaded guilty to sexual assaults on a step-son, a foster-son and two pupils at an establishment where he once worked.

Although these cases are exceptional, they serve to make the point that foster- and adoptive homes are not necessarily havens from abuse. They also, of course, raise questions about the way that foster- and adoptive parents are assessed and placements are monitored. Saint, for instance, had a 25-year-old previous conviction for indecent assault on a 12-year-old boy, which, for whatever reason, had not prevented employers from offering him jobs in children's homes, or fostering and adoption agencies from placing children with him: the case has led to a tightening of the law. But although in individual cases, we may, in hindsight, see mistakes that were made or procedures that can be tightened up, the fact remains that there will always be an element of risk involved in child placement away from home. (And even the tightening up of procedures in the aftermath of tragedies may carry its own risks and have negative consequences for children in the long-run, as well as positive ones.)

A US study (Benedict et al., 1994) looked at reports of child abuse and neglect made about 285 foster-carers in the city of Baltimore, comparing them with allegations made against birth families in the same period. They found that, although there were proportionately fewer allegations of neglect against foster-parents than against birth-parents, in the case of physical abuse, the rate of allegations was *seven times higher* than that against birth-parents over the same period, while in the case of sexual abuse the rate was four times higher. When they looked at the rate of allegations that were actually felt to have been confirmed by subsequent investigation, the picture changes – with confirmed physical abuse dropping to a lower proportion in the case of foster-parents than in the case of natural parents. But, even though 60 per cent of allegations of sexual abuse were felt not to have been substantiated, this still left 40 per cent that were, and this remained a higher proportion of confirmed allegations of sexual abuse against foster-parents than against birth-parents.

Caution is advised before jumping to conclusions about figures like this because they reflect the likelihood of allegations being made as well as the likelihood of actual child maltreatment – and foster-parents may be more vulnerable to unfounded allegations than are birth-parents. Bray and Hinty (2001: 56), in a much smaller British study, found that only 2 out of a sample of 22 allegations against foster-parents to have been confirmed, and they point out that 'it is not unlikely that some birth parents, from motives of either guilt, resentment or parental concern, are very ready to seize upon any sign of failure in the care provided by foster-parents'. They also point out that some forms of parental behaviour, such as smacking, might not be treated as abusive if done by natural parents, but would be regarded as unacceptable when done by foster-parents.

However, it is also important to note that, even if we accept that most of the allegations made against foster-parents are not substantiated, a significant proportion *are* (nearly ten per cent in the case of the Bray and Hinty study). This indicates a need for vigilance on the part of professionals working with children in substitute families, something which can be difficult when foster-parents may, with justice, also see themselves as childcare professionals, and expect to be worked with by social workers and others as colleagues and parts of a professional team.

The risk of abuse within the system, I would suggest, is also an element of the calculation that must be made when considering the removal of children from their birth families. Social workers are sometimes placed under pressure to remove children from situations where there is some risk and place them 'in care'. It is important to be aware that care too carries risks, and that the risk of further abuse is part of this, though a greater risk is probably the likelihood of placement breakdown and the experience of rejection by carers who are unable to cope, something which I will return to below.

In the UK context, one form of fostering that is currently causing particular concern following the murder of Victoria Climbié, is so-called private fostering. Victoria Climbié died in the care of her great-aunt, Marie Thérese Kouao, who was fostering her as a private arrangement with Victoria's parents. There have been many reports (see Philpot, 2001) of children, often of West African origin, being abused or exploited in such private arrangements, which are frequently undeclared. It is interesting that there are some parallels between what is called private fostering and the eighteenth- and nineteenth-century practice of 'baby farming', which, as I discussed in Chapter 1, led to the very first pieces of child protection legislation in English law.

Abuse by residential staff

No one who reads the newspapers in the UK can fail to be aware of the long catalogue of cases where residential care workers have been accused of abusing children in residential establishments. Corby et al. (2001: 77–8) list no fewer than 18 public inquiries held in the UK over the period 1967–2000 into such cases. Among the better-known cases are

- the Kincora working boys hostel where, in the 1980s, there were allegations not only of sexual abuse of boys by a staff member, but of access being obtained to boys by members of a paedophile ring (Department of Health and Social Security, Northern Ireland, 1985)
- the Pindown inquiry in Staffordshire held in 1991, where there were concerns about cruel and degrading methods of punishment (Staffordshire County Council, 1991)
- the case of Frank Beck, accused of both sexual and physical abuse of children in his care while head of a children's home in Leicestershire (Leicestershire County Council, 1993)

- a series of allegations about physical and sexual abuse in a number of residential establishments (and foster-homes) in North Wales, resulting in the Waterhouse inquiry (Waterhouse, 2000).

Such cases are not confined to the UK. Similar concerns have arisen in the USA, Canada, the Irish Republic and elsewhere about abuse of children in public care and also in establishments operated by various religious organizations, such as the Christian Brothers in Ireland, whose residential establishments are now the subject of a large number of abuse allegations. In Canada the Episcopal (Anglican) Church has actually been brought to the point of bankruptcy by law suits brought by former pupils of residential schools for Native Canadians (*Episcopal News*, 25 May 2000).

As with allegations of abuse by foster-carers (and indeed any other allegation) we should of course be aware that not all allegations are necessarily true. In the case of residential social workers, the methods involved in obtaining evidence for convictions in the UK have, at times, been seriously questionable. They have typically included inviting adult former care residents, many years after the event, to make allegations, and there are instances of demonstrably false allegations being made as well as of allegations that seem pretty clearly to have been motivated by the possibility of substantial financial compensation (see Webster, 1998, for a detailed analysis of the process). I believe that it is likely that a significant number of imprisoned former residential workers may have been wrongfully convicted (Beckett, 2002b).

All the same, there really can be no doubt that abuse by staff has gone on and no doubt continues to go on in residential establishments, as it does in other contexts where adults work with children. In fact, it would be incredible if paedophiles were not found in residential establishments, given what we know about the driven single-minded pursuit of gratification that characterizes paedophilia, in common with other addictive behavioural patterns, and given that paedophiles may be impossible to detect in advance if they do not already have convictions.

Of course not only paedophiles but other kinds of abusive personalities, such as those who like to dominate and control others (in short, bullies) are inevitably to be found among those who work with vulnerable young people. There are also dynamics in residential environments, as in fostering, which may result in some individuals who might not otherwise be abusive, behaving in an abusive way. Children and adolescents in residential care may come from homes where they may have experienced violence, rejection, high levels of family conflict, abuse, neglect, a breakdown of parental authority. They may have had experiences at school and elsewhere that alienated them from authority in general, and which have encouraged them to adopt highly confrontational styles. They may have learnt to get what they want by threats or manipulation. Working in such a context is a difficult, emotionally demanding task and it would not be surprising if some individuals end up behaving in inappropriate ways, as do some parents who are under stress.

Once again, then, it is important that child protection workers are vigilant and that they do not imagine that residential care necessarily represents a safe haven from abuse.

Abuse by fellow-residents or other foster-children

Abuse by other children or adolescents occurs within and outside of families, but it is a particularly significant risk within residential and foster-care. By their nature residential care and foster-care will tend to bring together children and adolescents who have suffered maltreatment of one kind or another, and a significant minority of these children will have developed abusive behaviour patterns of their own. Indeed a proportion of children and adolescents are brought into public care *because* of their abusive behaviour.

Children coming into public care are therefore being brought into an environment where the risk of being exposed to other children who are abusers can often be quite high.

System abuse

I have been discussing abuse that is carried out by abusive individuals in responsible positions. More insidious and difficult to grasp, though, is the idea that child protection and childcare systems may be abusive in effect, *even when the individuals involved may not be abusive and may be acting with the best of intentions.*

In fact, having discussed sexual abuse, physical abuse, emotional abuse and neglect in earlier chapters, I want now to introduce a new category of abuse. System abuse, according to the National Commission of Inquiry into the Prevention of Child Abuse, occurs whenever the operation of legislation, officially sanctioned procedures or operational practices within systems or institutions is avoidably damaging to children and their families. (Williams et al., 1996: 5)

The relationship between system abuse and the other forms of abuse is analogous to the relationship between the behaviour of racist individuals and what is called *institutional racism*. When an organization is described as institutionally racist this does not mean that everyone employed by that organization is a racist, but that the structure of the organization and the way it operates has the effect of discriminating against people of certain ethnic backgrounds, whether or not that is the wish or intention of those who work for it.

Another analogy that might be drawn is with the notion of *iatrogenic illness*, which is illness that is actually caused by medical intervention.

There are a variety of interacting factors which exist in child protection and childcare work that may lead to the system itself being harmful to children. I will briefly list some of them before looking at some of the ways in which harm can be done.

- Professionals and agencies are interested in their own survival and their own reputation, as well as the well-being of children. Decisions are often to some extent motivated by self-protection. Procedures are to some extent designed to allow agencies to 'cover their backs'.
- Staff shortages and high staff turnover may result in some cases going for long periods without receiving any attention, or in cases being passed on again and again from one temporary member of staff to another. The latter can result in children and parents having to get to know – and explain themselves to – a succession of strangers, each of whom will have her own different ideas. Since any new caseworker has to 'get up to speed' on a complex case, rapid turnover of staff can lead to effective paralysis of decision making.
- Stress and overload experienced by professionals may result in poor decision making and, particularly, in short-term, reactive thinking. The cases of children perceived as not being at immediate risk, for instance, may be ignored, even if there are important decisions to be made about their long-term future. Cases where there is an immediate risk, on the other hand, may be dealt with in a 'firefighting' style, which rushes from one crisis to the next without addressing underlying problems or forming long-term plans.
- Professionals may be reluctant to make painful decisions, such as the decision to remove a child from a parent (or the opposite: a decision to allow a child to remain in a situation where there are some risks),

and may be prone to finding reasons to keep putting off such decisions, even though this has the result of children and parents being left 'in limbo'.

- The resources available in a given area may simply be inadequate for the task. This can be true in relation to material resources (having identified a serious problem and intervened in a family, the child protection system may then be unable to offer more than a metaphorical Band-Aid), but it can also be true in relation to human resources. For example a child could be removed from her family and placed with a new family intended to be her permanent home. But the new family might find her behaviour impossible to cope with, with the result that she may be subjected to placement breakdown.

- Interventions by professional agencies may be unrealistic and not sufficiently informed by evidence as to what actually works.

- Resource-rationing systems operated by public agencies may mean that it is necessary to have a crisis in order to obtain a service. In order to gain help, a family may have to prove decisively that it is failing. On the other hand, improvement in function can lead to withdrawal of support. To some extent such systems may actually promote 'dysfunctional' family behaviour (because, in terms of obtaining help, such behaviour is actually *functional*).

- It is difficult in some circumstances for child protection agencies to do nothing. This can mean making families 'jump through hoops' for the sake of doing something as much as for the benefit of the children in the family.

- Professional rivalries and boundary disputes between agencies can lead to children and families being passed to and fro or to protracted delays while disagreements are thrashed out.

System abuse by the child protection system

Exercise 11.2

Micky, a boy of six, is reported by his school to the child protection agencies because of a series of suspicious bruises, culminating in a group of clear grip-mark bruises on both his arms. His mother insists that she has done nothing wrong and that he has always bruised easily.

A social worker arranges to take mother and son to a doctor to look at the bruises. The doctor finds that the bruises seem to indicate very excessive force being used not just once but on a number of occasions, but says that it is just possible that the boy might bruise easily as a result of a 'bleeding disorder', and arranges for him to be seen in hospital by a specialist. Social worker, mother and child then find themselves waiting for an hour and a half in a hospital corridor to see the specialist doctor.

The doctor is exhausted after a long shift, and is not good with children in any case. He makes no eye contact with Micky, offers no reassurance, but pushes a large hypodermic needle into the back of his hand to take a blood sample. It is now eight o'clock in the evening.

How might all this be experienced by Micky?

Comments on Exercise 11.2

Waits in hospital corridors are tedious at any age but to a child of six they can feel like an eternity. This eternity of waiting takes place in a very frightening context where his mother is almost certainly agitated and distressed, and where she seems to be powerless against the demands of other more powerful strangers. And hospitals in themselves are frightening places.

Exhaustion and awkwardness are not necessarily interpreted as such by a small child. The specialist doctor, a complete stranger in a frightening environment, may well seem hostile and malign to Micky. Most children are frightened of needles in any case. The syringe used for a blood sample is larger, more alarming and more frightening than those used for injections, and in this context the whole experience probably feels like a violent assault. I would suggest that this sort of event can become the stuff of a child's nightmares.

It is also a good example of system abuse, because none of the participants set out to maltreat Micky. The GP and the social worker doubtless felt that the second medical opinion was in Micky's interests (to help establish whether he was safe at home). The specialist doctor was tired and lacking in social skills, rather than deliberately unkind.

The experience of being on the receiving end of a child protection investigation must often be a very frightening experience for a child. As in the example above, children are placed in unfamiliar environments and face unfamiliar demands from people who may be complete strangers. They may be subjected to intrusive physical examination.

They may be asked to 'tell tales' about their own parents (and may fear the possibility that what they say could result in parents going to prison or themselves going into care). They are placed in the position of witnessing their parents' authority being overruled by strangers.

Of course there are plenty of children who nevertheless welcome child protection investigations, because they are being abused and very much want the abuse to stop. But many children who are subject to investigations are not being abused, or at any rate are not being abused to the extent that they welcome this kind of intervention. In fact, even children who are being seriously abused may be so frightened by what they have set in motion that they decide to withdraw the allegation that set the whole thing off, a sequence of events that was described by Roland Summit in the 'Child Sexual Abuse Accommodation Syndrome' (Summit, 1983). A case of this kind was described in Exercise 6.3 (p. 123). In such a scenario not only is the intervention disturbing, but it fails to prevent parental abuse from continuing.

Not only the initial investigation but the protective steps subsequently taken can, in some instances, actually have a harmful impact on a child. In cases of serious concern about a child's physical safety, removal of a child from a parent's care may be indicated. But this may come at a price. One of the reasons why professional agencies may have become concerned in the first place is that there did not seem to be a secure attachment forming between parent and child, and separation of mother and child is not usually helpful with this, even if regular – even daily – contact is arranged. In fact, if the effect of the removal of a baby is to disrupt the formation of a mutual attachment between child and parent, it is possible that in the long run this may actually have the effect of *causing* harm, even if the intention was to *prevent* it (and even if, in the short run, prevention of harm was actually achieved).

Any decision to separate a child and parents needs therefore to be carefully weighed in the balance to ensure that the net benefits exceed the possible risks. Indeed any plan of action (including decisions to *return* children to parents) should be subjected to a cost-benefit analysis of this kind. And any intervention in family life should be proportionate to the benefits to be gained. (Was it necessary for Micky in Exercise 11.2, for instance, to have a blood test on the same day as the initial investigations, or was the benefit of doing this off-set by the distress that it caused?)

These points may perhaps seem obvious, and yet it is very easy for experienced child protection workers, involved in this kind of work on a daily basis, to become inured to the impact that their interventions can have.

Exercise 11.3

Melanie was aware that she might have difficulty in bonding with a baby who was the unplanned child of an abusive, one-off encounter, but had made the decision to have the baby. In particular she was very keen to use breast-feeding as a natural way of establishing a bond.

After the birth of baby Jade, a suspicious injury, seen in the context of her mother's known ambivalence, led the professional agencies to decide to remove her from Melanie and place her with foster-parents pending further investigations. Later a reasonable non-abusive explanation for the injury was found and Jade was returned, but Melanie had had to abandon breast-feeding and did not feel able to re-establish it.

What do you think the net effect of the professional intervention might be?

Comments on Exercise 11.3

Of course in such situations it is never possible to know what would have happened if different decisions had been made. Small babies often cope quite well with changes of carers – and bottle-fed babies can be content as well as breast-fed ones – so it may be that the disruption had little direct impact on Jade. But it seems to me that, by disrupting Melanie's own strategy for establishing a bond with her baby, this intervention could well have weakened her own confidence in her ability to do so, and resurrected fears of alienation from her own child. The effect of such things is incalculable, yet they may be the final straw that prevent the growth of a mutually satisfactory attachment. If so they could have lifelong effects on a child's development.

Clearly when a small baby is injured in suspicious circumstances, child protection agencies must be extremely concerned, because small babies are extremely vulnerable and are more likely than older children to suffer permanent damage or death as a result of physical abuse. If it had emerged that Jade's injury had been deliberately caused by her mother, then the decision to remove her might well have been vindicated. As so often in child protection work, hindsight is needed to know for certain whether or not the decision made was the best one.

But, as the outcome of enquiries could not be known at the start, it would have been better in this case if a way could have been found to monitor Melanie's care of Jade without separating the two of them.

Multiple placements

Children in public care can suffer abuse at the hands of their carers, as I've already discussed. But even when a child is looked after by carers who do not abuse them, public care can have an effect that amounts to a form of emotional abuse. The *Working Together* guidelines include the following in the definition of emotional abuse:

> It may involve conveying to children that they are worthless or unloved, inadequate, or valued only insofar as they meet the needs of another person. It may feature age or developmentally inappropriate expectations being imposed on children. It may involve causing children frequently to feel frightened or in danger. (Department of Health, 1999: 6)

One of the experiences that is commonly faced by children in public care is that of repeated placement moves. An American study, for instance, found that children waiting for decisions from the Boston Juvenile Court went through more than two foster-placements on average just during the 18-month average period that their cases were before the court (Bishop et al., 1992). A British government report (Department of Health, 1998b) found that in some local authority areas, as many as a third of all children in public care were going through three or more placements per year.

Placement moves can occur for a variety of reasons. Carers may have other commitments which prevent them from carrying on, or they may find it difficult to cope with the behaviour of particular children. Some moves are planned from the outset, with foster-parents or residential establishments taking on children for an agreed timescale in order to carry out a specific task. I suggest, however, that the niceties may often be lost on children and that the cumulative message that children receive from multiple placement moves is that they are not wanted or cared about very much.

This will be the case particularly if the moves are the result of a child's own behaviour. There are children who have experienced a long series of rejections within the care system, and have had to face, again and again, alienation from their carers, placement breakdown and then perhaps a move to one or two short-term placements before another long-term placement is found, only for the cycle of alienation and breakdown to begin again. I would suggest that such children do pick up very powerful messages about being 'worthless or unloved, inadequate, or valued only insofar as they meet the needs of another person', they may well experience themselves as being expected to meet 'developmentally inappropriate expectations', and they almost certainly will feel frightened and in danger, although they are likely to do their best to repress such feelings.

I would suggest that even children who are moved for reasons unconnected with their own behaviour are likely to pick up a lot of these messages. And when, as often occurs now in the UK, changes of placement are paralleled by equally rapid changes of social workers, then the experience of being 'in care' may actually be one of being alone in the world – a profoundly disturbing and harmful experience for a child.

This is another very good example of system abuse, in that it can occur without any of the participants having anything other than good intentions, and yet may do real long-term harm.

It is important that care agencies do everything possible to reduce this form of abuse and the UK government has recognized the importance of this by choosing as the very first of the sub-objectives of its *Quality Protects* programme: 'To reduce the number of changes of main carer for children looked after' (Department of Health, 1998b: 12). But I would suggest that it is important that we do also recognize that it is in the nature of public care that such things happen, and that social workers should therefore be wary of assuming that the removal of children into public care is necessarily a solution to the problems of neglect and abuse, or that it will necessarily provide children with security and stability.

Exercise 11.4

Kelly was taken into care on an emergency protection order at the age of seven, after she was found to have been left on her own in her mother's flat for the better part of a day. This was the fourth reported incident of her being left on her own. Her mother is a heroin user, who insists she is very committed to Kelly, but finds it difficult in practice to prioritize Kelly's needs over her own need to finance and feed her habit.

Kelly was initially placed with Mr and Mrs Brown, the only foster-parents with space available, but the Browns were about to go on holiday so, within a week, she was moved to Mr and Mrs Thompson. The plan at this stage is to return her quickly to her mother, but a decision is then reached that she should remain in foster-care for four months, to allow her mother to go through a programme of rehabilitation and put her life in order prior to Kelly's return. Mr and Mrs Thompson are unable to commit themselves for four months, so Kelly is moved to another set of foster-parents, the Rogers. There are a number of meetings with the Rogers who are very keen to work with Kelly during this difficult period and to provide her with a home until she can return to her mother.

Kelly stays with the Rogers for seven weeks, but during this time there are increasing tensions surrounding Kelly's behaviour with the Rogers' daughter, Emma, aged four, whom the Rogers feel Kelly picks on. This is brought to a head by a particular incident in which Kelly breaks a favourite toy of Emma's. The Rogers demand her immediate removal. She is placed back with Mr and Mrs Brown while another family is found. She is then informed that she will be moving to a new family, the Youngs. Kelly's social worker tells her that the Youngs are very keen to have her and to help her during the remaining period while her mother gets her life in order (a period which now looks like being longer than originally anticipated).

How would Kelly react to this news?

Comments on Exercise 11.4

Kelly is a child who has been let down more than once before entering public care. I would suggest that to Kelly the assurance that the Youngs really are going to provide her with stability will ring very hollow indeed. Indeed, she would be right to be sceptical on the evidence of her care history already. The Rogers, too, were supposed to be providing her with a stable base.

One cannot blame the Rogers for choosing to put the needs of their own daughter first. Quite possibly Kelly's treatment of Emma was a deliberate attempt to test the Rogers out, aimed at their area of greatest vulnerability. But such testing-out behaviour is commonplace, normal even, among children in Kelly's position. If the care system is unable to stand up to it, then it is pretty inevitable that children such as Kelly will regularly experience placement moves.

Other moves in this scenario were unconnected with Kelly's behaviour, and were to do with the logistics of the system, but this is not a distinction that will make much sense to a seven-year-old. Indeed even an adult would pick up the message from such treatment that her own needs and her own convenience was relatively unimportant compared with the needs of others.

Prevarication as neglect

Related to the problem of multiple placements is the form of system abuse – or perhaps 'system neglect' – that is sometimes known as 'drift'. In *Children who Wait*, Rowe and Lambert (1973) exposed the plight of large numbers of children in the public care system who spent long periods of time in supposedly temporary placements, or placements whose duration had not been defined, without any clear plan for their long-term future being made.

This is harmful to children because it deprives them of the security of carers with whom they can safely form a firm attachment. The child must hold something back. The carers, as human beings, probably hold something back too. And the child may experience a lack of something which is terribly important for children: someone with whom she can really feel she belongs. The fact that no one seems able to offer this must also for many children be a profound blow to their sense of self-worth – a message yet again that they are 'worthless or unloved, inadequate, or valued only insofar as they meet the needs of another person'. These feelings, and the psychological defences that a child inevitably constructs in order to ward off such feelings, may do harm to a child's capacity to form relationships. 'The longer a child spends in temporary care before being placed with permanent carers,' as a Department of Health circular puts it, 'the more difficult it is likely to be for that child to make the necessary social and emotional adjustments within the new family' (Department of Health, 1998a).

Although it is thirty years since Rowe and Lambert's book came out, the problem of children spending long periods in supposedly temporary care arrangements (or worse, as I've just discussed, long periods in a *series* of temporary care arrangements) still persists. A British government White Paper on adoption observed, in 2000, that 'decisions about how to provide a secure, stable and permanent placement . . . are not addressed early enough, focussed clearly enough, or taken swiftly enough' (Department of Health, 2000b: 15), and found that 80 per cent of adopted children have spent a year or more in the looked-after system before being adopted.

I would suggest, though, that the idea of drift is not just relevant to children in the care system. There are situations in which families are under intense professional scrutiny and where the possibility of children no longer being able to live in their family is continuously present. And I would suggest that if such situations are allowed to persist for long periods of time they too must be harmful.

One area in which drift has grown steadily worse over the last 10 years is in the courts. The 1989 Children Act was the first piece of legislation in England and Wales to require parties to court proceedings about children to avoid delay. But, ironically, the average length of care proceedings has grown longer, year on year, ever since the Act came into effect (Beckett, 2000). At the time of writing, children in England and Wales who are made subject to care proceedings must wait in temporary care arrangements for an average of nearly a year, and in one local authority sample I looked at, about 10 per cent were waiting for two years or more (Beckett, 2001b). This is an extremely long time for a child to be deprived of a secure home.

Once again this is a classic instance of system abuse in that it occurs without any deliberate intention to do harm. One of the factors that causes delay may even be an anxiety about making the wrong decision and a determination to be absolutely sure that the final decision, when it is made, is the right one. And yet, waiting for so long must be extremely difficult for children, and must have the potential to do long-term harm (two years, after all, is more than a tenth of an entire legal childhood). As I have pointed out elsewhere (Beckett, 2001a), in some respects waiting for a court is harder than other kinds of 'drift':

- When a case is still before the courts, the long-term future is inevitably uncertain. This is in contrast to delays caused, for example, by waiting for suitable carers to be found, where there is a definite future to be worked towards. The combination of high anxiety situations with the absence of stable attachment figures is uniquely difficult for children because it is *precisely* in those situations that a child needs – and instinctively seeks – the security that comes from the support of an attachment figure.
- In a situation where a court has yet to decide between several different long-term plans proposed by different parties, it is necessary to keep all options open. This can mean maintaining highly complex contact arrangements with a number of interested parties, or children and their families being subjected to series of intrusive assessments.
- While care proceedings are going on, the child in question is typically in the interim care of a local authority, which is in direct conflict with her own parent or parents. There may, additionally, be conflict between family members who are parties to the proceedings. The court process tends to promote adversarial stances and the child has to move between adults for whom she is an object of contention.

- Placement planning is difficult where the timescale of the placement is not known, or has become much longer than was originally envisaged. Court delays can result in children being moved from one temporary placement to another, or in sibling groups having to be split up.

It is important to remember – and this applies to *all* decision-making processes about children, and not just those that occur in court – that children need decisions to be made in a *reasonable timescale*. Of course it is important, too, to try to get decisions right and to collect as much relevant information and advice as possible to that end. But there can never be absolute certainty in this area of work, and after a certain point the pursuit of certainty becomes simply an excuse for avoiding taking the risk that is inevitably entailed in making a decision. The inevitability of risk taking in child protection work is something that I will return to in the next chapter, but I will conclude this one with some comments from a book that, like *Children who Wait*, first came out in 1973:

> Procedural and substantive decisions should never exceed the time that the child-to-be-placed can endure loss and uncertainty.
> The courts, social agencies, and all the adults concerned with child placement must greatly reduce the time they take for decision. . . . Whatever the cause of the time-taking, the costs as well as the benefits of the delay to the child must be weighed. Our guideline would allow for no more delay than that required for reasoned judgement. By reasoned judgement we do not mean certainty of judgement. We mean no more than the most reasonable judgement that can be made within the time available – measured to accord with the child's sense of time. Therefore, to avoid irreparable psychological injury, placement, whenever in dispute, must be treated as the emergency it is for the child. (Goldstein, et al., 1980: 42–3)

In this chapter I have looked at the ways that child protection systems, and childcare systems, can in themselves cause harm to children. I have considered:

- abuse perpetrated by abusive individuals in the public care system: foster-parents, adoptive parents, residential workers and other children in care
- the idea of *system abuse*, and the ways in which the practices and processes of organizational systems can be abusive in effect, even if the individuals within them are not abusive

- ways in which the child protection system itself can be harmful to children
- the problem of multiple placements for children in public care as an instance of system abuse
- the idea of prevarication and 'drift' being a form of system abuse, or neglect, when it delays decisions being made for children.

System abuse occurs because organizational systems are driven and shaped not simply by the needs of children but by a complex set of pressures and constraints. Among the pressures on child protection workers are public expectations, and perhaps their own expectations of themselves. In the next and final chapter I will ask what can reasonably be expected of a child protection system.

The Limits of Possibility 12

Reaching for the stars •
Prediction and hindsight •
Resources, resources •
Concluding comments •

In the previous chapter I considered the ways in which systems intended to protect children could themselves end up doing harm. This can happen for a variety of reasons. Sometimes there are abusive individuals within the system, sometimes the wrong decision is made, through incompetence or simply bad luck. But, as I said in the previous chapter, complex dynamics are at work within the child protection and childcare systems, which mean that many factors other than a purely rational consideration of a child's best interests will play a part in the making of decisions and the formation of policies and procedures. I mentioned the psychological needs of professional workers, the expectations that are placed upon the child protection system by society at large, and the inevitably limited resources that are made available by society at large for the work – resources which are not necessarily well-matched to expectations. ('Paradoxically, while the public continued to demand greater efforts to be made to curb child abuse, it was increasingly unwilling to fund those efforts,' writes Duncan Lindsey, 1994: 97, of the American scene.)

In this final chapter, I want to draw on my own experience in family social work to consider the real pressures and constraints that child protection social work operates under, and to consider what realistically can be expected of child protection social work and of the child protection system.

This chapter is written as the Victoria Climbié inquiry completes its work in London, and there is a widespread expectation of major changes afoot for the child protection system and family social work. I will not, however, attempt to predict what those changes may be. Instead I will offer some thoughts about what is, and what is not, possible and the dangers of asking for more from a child protection system than it can realistically achieve.

Reaching for the stars

It is commonly supposed that it is a good thing in life to 'think positive', to 'set your sights high', to 'reach for the stars'. And so it is, in many respects. But to set objectives, or to raise expectations, which cannot possibly be achieved can be very destructive indeed. This is true in respect of parenting. Good parents encourage and challenge their children, but it is a recognized form of emotional abuse to impose 'developmentally inappropriate expectations' on children (Department of Health, 1999: 5, 6). It is true too of work *with* parents. I have discussed before in this book the dangers in child protection work of demanding unrealistically high standards from parents.

It is also true, I suggest, that if child protection workers are expected to deliver more than they are realistically capable of, then the result will not be an improvement in practice but the reverse, a practice based on defensiveness and fear. This danger is succinctly summarized by a British government minister as follows:

> We must not pretend that actions taken by child protection agencies can ever guarantee that parents will not harm their children. The danger of trying to give such guarantees and of pillorying those agencies when harm does occur is that inappropriate interventions may be made out of fear. (John Bowis, OBE, MP, *Foreword* to Department of Health, 1995)

Mr Bowis might have added that a culture of fear also contributes to staff sickness, poor staff retention and difficulties in staff recruitment, and that striving after unrealistic goals can distort practice in other ways, for example by deflecting resources from areas where they might be more useful. Unrealistically high expectations can result in things getting worse.

It is reasonable to expect that a child protection system will reduce the incidence of child maltreatment, and help the victims of maltreatment, just as it is reasonable to expect the police to reduce the incidence of crime and arrest criminals, or doctors to save lives and reduce disease. But we do not expect the police to eliminate crime, and we do not expect doctors to abolish death, and we should not expect child protection systems to eradicate child abuse or neglect.

There are a number of reasons why this would be an unrealistic expectation. For one thing there are limits to the level of surveillance and state intervention that is desirable or practicable in a democratic society. We could probably detect more child abuse, for instance, if closed circuit television was installed in every home, but most people would feel that these benefits would be outweighed by many drawbacks to such an arrangement. In fact, beyond a certain level it must be the case that state intervention would actually be counterproductive, since the level of abuse and maltreatment within the state system would eventually be as great as the level outside it, in all the ways discussed in the previous chapter.

Another reason why it would be unrealistic to expect the child protection system to be able be eradicate child maltreatment is that so many of the underlying factors in child maltreatment lie outside the control of social work and other child protection agencies. Poverty, unemployment, drug abuse and mental illness are a few obvious examples.

In addition:

- It is in principle impossible to predict human behaviour with any degree of certainty. This makes it impossible to predict abuse in every case, and impossible too to predict with certainty the outcome of any intervention.
- The ability of child protection professionals are also limited – and always will be limited – by the resources that they are given to do the job.

The rest of this chapter will develop these last two points.

Prediction and hindsight

In the natural sciences it is accepted that complex natural phenomena, involving a very large number of variables, cannot be predicted except in a probabilistic sense. The following discussion, for instance, describes the difficulties involved in accurately predicting the weather:

... suppose the earth could be covered with sensors spaced one foot apart, rising at one foot intervals all the way to the top of the atmosphere. Suppose every sensor gives perfectly accurate readings of temperature, pressure, humidity, and any other quantity a meteorologist could want. Precisely at noon an infinitely powerful computer takes all the data and calculates what will happen at each point at 12.01, then 12.02, then 12.03.

The computer will still be unable to predict whether Princeton, New Jersey, will have sun or rain on a day one month away. At noon the spaces between the sensors will hide fluctuations that the computer will not know about. . . . By 12.01, those fluctuations will already have created small errors one foot away. Soon the errors will have multiplied to the ten-foot scale and so on up to the size of the globe. (Gleick, 1988: 21)

In practice, of course, meteorologists attempt to predict the weather with *far* less detailed data than this (using sensors separated by tens of miles), and we all know that the predictions they make, even a single day in advance, are often wrong. This does not reflect incompetence on the part of the meteorologists, or even lack of knowledge about the workings of the weather, but simply the impossibility of ever knowing what is going on in every single bit of the atmosphere.

This might seem a far cry from child protection, but in fact child protection professionals are in the business of making predictions too. From the many referrals that they receive, social work agencies have to decide which cases to allocate, which to prioritize, which to deal with as 'in need' and which to deal with as 'in need of protection'. The child protection system as a whole has to decide which cases to place on the register and what would be an appropriate protection plan. Social work agencies, in conjunction with others, have to decide which children should be removed from their families and which can stay in their families. All of these decisions involve trying to interpret limited information about what is going on at present behind the closed doors of families, and to predict what the future might hold. In other words: all of these decisions involve a risk assessment.

In practice, as in meteorology, the predictions have to be based on limited information. But even supposing that vast quantities of information were available about a given family – and even supposing that child protection agencies possessed a very precise and reliable tool for processing all that information and arriving at an objective measure of risk – it would not be possible to know for certain which situations were going to end up with a child being harmed and which would not.

I have illustrated this point elsewhere (Beckett, 2001c) by suggesting, for the sake of argument, that we possessed a formula into which we could insert information to come up with a positive score for parents who would kill their children, and a negative score for those who would not. Let us suppose that this formula had been tested and shown to work with 100 per cent of families who would otherwise go on to kill a baby, correctly giving them a positive score, and with 99 per cent of those who wouldn't, correctly giving them a negative one. This would leave a mere 1 per cent 'false positive' group, identified as dangerous by the formula, though not dangerous in fact, and no 'false negatives' at all. This would be an extraordinarily reliable tool, *far* more precise than any that actually exist. Out of every million babies born, it would accurately identify every single one of the five or so who would die without protective intervention.

Yet even such an exceptionally reliable formula would still be of very limited practical use. The problem would be that the five correctly identified true positives would be hidden among *ten thousand* others who would wrongly be identified as at risk of their lives. This is because, with something as rare as child murder, the apparently tiny 1 per cent false positive rate would still be big enough to swamp the accurate predictions.

In fact, of course, child protection work is not just about predicting child deaths but about predicting a whole range of different kinds of behaviour and different kinds of harm. But the principle remains the same. We do not possess formulas for predicting human behaviour which are as accurate as the imaginary one in my illustration, any more than weathermen possess sensors at one-foot intervals. (And of course, human behaviour is *far* more complex than the weather.) But, even if we did, pinpoint precision is not possible in risk assessment. *Risk assessment itself involves taking a risk of being wrong.*

I suggest that this is not always well understood by those who make child protection policy. There remains a tendency to believe that when something goes wrong a mistake must have been made, and with the benefit of hindsight it is always possible to identify decisions that seem to have been mistaken. The truth is, however, that:

> If a decision involves risk, then even when one can demonstrate that one has chosen the unarguably optimal course of action, some proportion of the time the outcome will be suboptimal. It follows that a bad outcome in and of itself does not constitute evidence that the decision was mistaken. The hindsight fallacy is to assume that it does. (Macdonald and Macdonald, 1999: 22)

The trouble with the hindsight fallacy is that it can lead to an anxious and fruitless endeavour to ensure that 'mistakes' are never made. This does not prevent tragedies from occurring, but it does mean that the system is actually less useful than it might be. It may result, for instance, in:

- A culture of fear, as described in the quote from John Bowis MP above, in which there is an unnecessarily high level of state intervention in family life and an unnecessarily high level of removal of children from their own families. This may help to explain the rapidly increasing number of children being taken into public care annually in England and Wales (Beckett, 2001a).
- A disproportionate investment of limited time and resources into information gathering, at the expense of actual services for children and families. Describing this problem as it exists in the USA, Neil Guterman speaks of 'an increasingly narrowed focus on screening, decision making and monitoring activities, driving out any remaining capacity to provide direct services to families' (Guterman, 2001: 44). I will return to this later.
- A paralysis of decision making resulting from a quest for a level of certainty which can never actually be achieved. This can and does result in all kinds of 'drift' and prevarication such as I discussed in the last chapter, including the increasing levels of prevarication that occur in court proceedings about children.

We cannot have a system that will always be able to anticipate abusive behaviour. In fact we probably cannot have a system that will reliably anticipate any comparatively rare and extreme form of human behaviour. A number of researchers into suicide, for instance, have concluded that 'prediction of suicide at an individual level is impossible' (Langan, 1999: 156).

Exercise 12.1

Look at the cases below referring to an imaginary social work team somewhere in London. For the sake of this exercise please imagine that, due to staff shortages in the team, it is only possible to follow up on one of these referrals immediately. The others will only be able to be followed up when more staff time becomes available.

Decide which of these referrals should be the one that is followed up immediately and the order in which you would follow up the others. Assume that the information below is all that is available to make this decision. After all, getting more information itself requires staff time.

Case (a)
Children: David aged 6, Wayne aged 4, Michael aged 2
Mother: Susan Smith – aged 22

Susan came into the social work office herself seeking financial help and help with accommodation. The children were observed to be unwashed and exceptionally wild. Susan paid them almost no attention at all (no eye contact, no reassurance, no explanation as to what was happening) other than continuously giving them sweets from a bag.

The story Susan told was that she had newly arrived in the area fleeing a violent partner in Leeds. Subsequent enquiries have shown that she and the children had a room at the local Women's Aid Refuge, but she was evicted from there when she let two men into the hostel and into her room.

Information obtained from Leeds is that she arrived *there* saying that she was fleeing a violent partner in *Sheffield*. Before Sheffield, it seems, she was in York. She was evicted from the refuge in Leeds also, again for letting men into the house, and she then lived briefly in bed-and-breakfast accommodation with the children. Other residents there were concerned that the children were being left on their own in the room. There were also several unsubstantiated allegations (in Leeds and York) of Susan being involved in prostitution and using the room shared with the children for this purpose. A child protection conference on grounds of neglect had been under consideration when she suddenly left Leeds.

Susan is asking for financial help and assistance with accommodation. She says that if this is not forthcoming she will go to Wales with the children.

Susan seems agitated, restless and evasive.

Case (b)
Children: James (5) and Matthew (4)
Mother: Mandy Baker (25)

Neighbours have been very worried about the environment in which the boys are living. Mandy keeps open house to local teenagers who come and go at all hours. There are loud noises – shouting, music and quite often fights – until the early hours.

The house is described as dirty and bare. The garden fence has been broken up for firewood. The front door was kicked in during a fight and never properly mended. Several windows have likewise also been broken. On one occasion, neighbours report, a young man who visited the house brought a horse right into the living room, which was the subject of a lot of excitement in the house.

The boys' school are also worried about them. They are absent about one day in five and late on most days. When in they always seem very tired (quiet, withdrawn, with rings under their eyes) and sometimes hungry. Their clothes are often not changed for a week.

Mandy often seems to teachers to be under the influence of drugs or alcohol and frequently does not come to collect them from school, several different friends of hers (some very young) coming in her place. Mandy has recently been asked to collect them herself or to let the school know who will be collecting them – and she agreed to do so.

But today a young friend of Mandy's, a girl of about 16, arrived to collect the boys from school, saying that Mandy was unwell. Teachers have seen her before with Mandy but the boys did not seem to know her very well. Teachers wonder if they made the right decision in letting them go with her and want the social work team to check the boys are alright.

Mandy is known to have suffered abuse as a child and to have grown up in care. The boys' father has never had contact with them.

Case (c)
Child: Hazel Maddox (13)
Mother: Tammy Maddox (34)
Father: Bill Maddox (32) (parents separated)

Hazel was admitted to hospital as a result of a paracetamol overdose. This is thought to have been a para-suicide rather than a real attempt on her own life. Hazel had been living with her mother but her mother now refuses to have her home, saying that she is fed up with her daughter's aggressive and difficult behaviour.

Hazel has a history of unexplained absences from school. Her health record includes enuresis to age 10, a hearing impairment for which no organic cause has ever been found and numerous urinary tract infections. When at school she is said to be rather isolated, and to find it difficult to make friends.

She is now medically ready for discharge.

Her father, Bill, who lives on his own, is willing to have her to stay with him, but Hazel is adamant that she does not want to go to him. The only reason she is able to give for this, however, is that he nags her a lot. Her contact with him has been somewhat erratic. She had little contact as a small child, but quite a lot in recent years until about six months ago, and since then has consistently refused to go.

Case (d)

Child: Annette Foster (4)

Mother: Judy Young (26)

Step-father: Mike Young (28) (father has no contact)

A referral has come from a Debbie Johnson, who is Judy's sister (Annette's aunt). Annette has a learning disability and attends a special school where she has a male one-to-one helper who is also her regular babysitter. Debbie is concerned that Annette has (according to Judy) recently been displaying a lot of behaviour that is overtly sexual and seems inappropriate for her age. For example getting dolls to enact sex, masturbating with objects.

Debbie says that Mike was very angry with Judy when he heard that Judy had talked about this with her, and has since tried to prevent the two sisters from having contact.

Debbie and her husband have themselves noticed some of this sexual behaviour for themselves. When Debbie visited with her husband, Annette climbed onto her husband's lap and rubbed up against his groin.

Mike and Judy married six months ago after quite a brief previous relationship.

Case (e)

Child: Daisy Wilcox (4 days)

Mother: Yasmine Wilcox (21)

Father: Tommy Green (19) (has on-going relationship with mother but does not live with her)

At 2 days old Daisy, while still on the maternity unit, showed some symptoms associated with opiate withdrawal. A blood test showed the presence of traces of opiates.

Yasmine denies any current usage of opiates, though she admits having used heroin in the past and to having served a short prison sentence for a drug-related offence. Yasmine insists that a strong non-prescription headache medication must be the source of the drug traces. She insists that she and the baby are fine and that she intends to take the baby home tomorrow.

Little is known about Yasmine's background, but the doctors insist that her explanation for the drug traces in Daisy's blood is implausible, and suggest that Yasmine should be prevented from taking her home until more enquiries can be made and until Daisy's symptoms have been monitored for a longer period.

Comments on Exercise 12.1

I don't believe there is a 'right' answer to this. There are long-term risks to children and immediate dangers in all of the cases, but the dangers are different in each one and difficult to weigh up against one another. In case (a), for instance, there are clearly reasons to be concerned about the neglect of these children. The immediate danger is that Susan will once again move on, so that the child protection agencies are once again unable to move forward. In case (b) there are again reasons to believe that the boys are being neglected, but no definite immediate danger, although James' and Matthew's teachers are understandably worried that they are being picked up from school by someone they seem to hardly know. In case (c) I would bear in mind the possibility of sexual abuse, though there is no firm evidence of this. The immediate issue is that Hazel has one parent who refuses to have her home and another parent who she refuses to go to. The immediate danger is that a clearly very unhappy 13-year-old, who has already taken one overdose, running the risk of permanent liver damage if not death, may do so again.

In case (d) there is clearly a possibility of sexual abuse, with some suspicion being attached to the step-father, though the male helper is also in a position to abuse Annette. There is no new danger today, but if Annette is being abused, then she will probably have to endure more abuse the longer the case is left. In case (e) a young mother, about whom there is little information, is proposing to discharge from hospital a 4-day-old baby who seems to be suffering Neonatal Abstinence Syndrome (see page 154) which can cause abnormal heartrate, prolonged screaming fits, feeding difficulties and even convulsions.

There are also features of these cases which might, with the benefit of hindsight, become significant, but which, in advance, it is impossible to accurately weigh. For example, you probably did not choose case (b) as your highest priority. However, suppose you were to discover, after the event, that Mandy had not collected the boys because she was too drunk to stand, that there were a group of about a dozen teenagers at home with her, also drunk, and that later the same evening the two little boys were made to simulate sexual acts with each other and with some of these teenagers for the amusement of the whole gathering. You might then look back again at the information you had received and notice, for instance, how it suggested a complete absence of boundaries in this household: the horse, the burnt fence, the noise, the constant coming and going. . . . But there is no formula which could tell you in advance that sexual abuse was going to take place.

On the other hand it is clear that there are a number of risk factors in case (b), as there are in cases (a), (c), (d) and (e). What is not always appreciated by those not actually involved in doing the job, is that child protection agencies are not so much in the business of picking out risky cases from cases where there are no risks, but of trying to make choices *between* risky cases.

Resources, resources

The task in the above exercise is, in essence, a task that I myself used to carry out on a regular basis as the manager of a children and families team. Duty social workers would take new referrals and collect together information about cases, and I would then decide which of these cases could be allocated to social workers within the team, which could be dealt with by 'no further action' and so on. Although in real life the constraints are seldom quite so cut and dried as in the exercise, essentially the same difficulties arose.

I could not realistically allocate all new referrals – not even all new referrals where there were significant risks – because the team's social workers were already busy and the more cases they took on, the less they would be able to do on each case. The arithmetic is simple. If a social worker has twenty cases, she has less than two hours per week per case to spend on all the visits, telephone calls, recording, travelling, completing forms, going to court and attending meetings that the case requires. If just one of her twenty cases is currently before the courts, or is in crisis, it may well take up half of her working week, leaving less than one hour per week for all her other cases. Bringing about change in a family is a complex task, and one that it is simply not worth taking on unless you are able to commit some time to it.

Another option open to me was to hold less urgent cases for allocation later. This was useful at times when members of the team were busy or absent for temporary reasons, but in the long run it is not sensible to place cases on the 'awaiting allocation' list at a faster rate than they are coming off it, because otherwise the list gets longer and longer, and children and families end up waiting longer and longer for a service. (I heard recently of a child psychiatry clinic where the normal waiting time for families seeking help with children with behaviour problems was 44 weeks, an absurd position to get into, since behaviour problems will tend to become more entrenched and probably more severe the longer the pattern is allowed to continue.)

One more option open to me was to defer a decision by asking a social worker to obtain more information. This was tempting but, of course, it carries its own costs, since information gathering (that is: assessment) itself takes time, and therefore takes away from other tasks, just as does actual allocation of cases for the purpose of providing a service. Recall the comment from Neil Guterman, quoted earlier, that a narrow preoccupation with 'screening, decision making and monitoring activities' can drive out 'any remaining capacity to provide direct services' (Guterman, 2001: 44).

For the sake of simplicity I will leave aside other manoeuvres that were sometimes open to me, such as referral on to another agency, or to another part of my own agency. The point I want to make, drawing on my own experience in this way, is that with limited resources it is simply impossible to 'cover all the bases'.

I appreciate that the system within which I operated was a relatively unsophisticated one, and that nowadays the various operations that I have just described are commonly undertaken by different teams or units, rather than within the confines of a single team, but essentially the same constraints still apply. For example, if a social work agency has separate 'assessment teams' undertaking assessments under the Lilac Book framework (Department of Health, 2000a), and 'continuing care' teams working with families identified as needing a service, the managers of that agency still have to determine how to divide their resources between assessment and service provision. It is just that this decision will be made not on a case-by-case basis, as I described it, but as a policy decision about the respective sizes of the two teams, and about the point at which cases are passed from one to the other.

Whatever the organizational structure, it remains the case that resource constraints, taken together with the fact that many events are, in principle, impossible to accurately predict, mean that it is not only likely but actually inevitable that child protection agencies will often fail to protect children – even children who are drawn to their attention as at risk – from subsequent abuse.

Viewing such events as being necessarily failures on the part of the system, and attempting to prevent them by imposing organizational changes, or additional procedures, may in fact have the effect of *increasing* the risk of more children 'slipping through the net', if they deflect resources and staff attention away from their primary task.

Concluding comments

It may seem rather negative to have ended this book with a chapter in which I insist that there are severe limits to the ability of child protection agencies to prevent child maltreatment, and in which I question the assumptions on which reform of the system is commonly based. In fact I believe that every day social workers, and other professionals, help many children to escape from intolerable abuse and neglect, and many families to steer themselves onto happier, less self-destructive paths. I believe that this is important work, essential in any civilized society, and I hope that this book will have offered a few useful insights to those who are embarking on it, or are already engaged in it.

The purpose of this chapter, therefore, has not been to cast doubt on the value of child protection work, but to suggest that child protection work would be able to help more children and more families if we were more honest about its limitations. We do not question the value of doctors because they cannot abolish death or anticipate every disease. Mistreatment of children is not something that can be abolished or always anticipated either. There are limits to what can be predicted, and there will always be limits to the resources that society is prepared to put into the task. And also, like much disease and many deaths, a good deal of child maltreatment is the product of wider social and environmental factors that fall well outside the power of individual professionals to address.

However, I suggest that child protection work would be more effective if it were able to be more imaginative and positive in its approach, and would not have to be constantly, anxiously contemplating failure.

In this chapter I considered the practical and theoretical constraints under which the child protection system operates. In it I have:

- warned about the negative consequences of imposing unrealistic expectations on the child protection system
- discussed the inherent uncertainties that exist in any attempt to predict human behaviour, and the limitations that this places on our ability to anticipate abuse
- considered the difficult, and inevitably risky, choices that are imposed on child protection agencies by resource constraints.

In conclusion I argued that child protection work, in spite of these constraints, has been helpful to many children and families, and suggested that its helpfulness would increase if it could be less preoccupied by the fear of failure.

References

Abel, G., Mittleman, M. and Becker, J. (1985) 'Sexual offenders: results of assessment and recommendations for treatment', in H. Ben-Aron, S. Hucker and C. Webster (eds) *Clinical Criminology*. Toronto: MMGraphics.

Alison, L. (2000) 'What are the risks to children of parental substance misuse?' in F. Harbin and M. Murphy (eds) *Substance Misuse and Child Care*. Lyme Regis: Russell House Publishing. pp. 9–20.

Alison, L. and Wyatt, S. (1999) 'Outcomes for infants of drugs addicts', *Abstracts from Proceedings of Royal College of Paediatrics and Child Health Annual Meeting*, York.

Allen, N. (1998) *Making Sense of the Children Act: A Guide for the Social and Welfare Services*, 3rd edn. London: John Wiley and Sons.

Anderson, J.C., Martin, J.L., Mullen, P.E., Romans, S.E. and Herbison, P. (1993) 'The prevalence of childhood sexual abuse experiences in a community sample of women', *Journal of the American Academy of Child and Adolescent Psychiatry*, 32: 911–19.

Ashworth, K. and Braithwaite, I. (1997) *Small Fortunes: Spending on Children, Childhood Poverty and Parental Sacrifice*. London: Joseph Rowntree Foundation.

Bagley, C. and Thurston, W. (1995) *Understanding and Preventing Child Sexual Abuse – Critical Summaries of 500 Key Studies*, Vol 2. Aldershot: Arena.

Batchelor, J. (1999) *Failure to Thrive in Young Children: Research and Practice Revisited*. London: The Children's Society.

Beckett, C. (2000) 'Waiting for court decisions: a kind of limbo', *Adoption and Fostering*, 24 (2): 55–62.

Beckett, C. (2001a) 'The great care proceedings explosion', *British Journal of Social Work*, 31 (3): 493–501.

Beckett, C. (2001b) 'The wait gets longer: an analysis of recent information on court delays', *Adoption and Fostering*, 25 (4): 60–7.

Beckett, C. (2001c) 'Social workers knew . . .' *Professional Social Work*, December: 3.

Beckett, C. (2002a) *Human Growth and Development*. London: Sage.

Beckett, C. (2002b) 'The witch-hunt metaphor: and residential workers accused of abuse', *British Journal of Social Work*, 32 (5): 621–8.

Beitchman, J.H., Zucker, K.J., Hood, J.E., da Costa, G.A., Akman, D. and

Cassavia, E. (1992) 'A review of the long-term effects of child sexual abuse', *Child Abuse and Neglect*, 16: 101–18.

Benedict, M.I., Zuravin, S., Brandt, D. and Abbey, H. (1994) 'Types and frequency of child maltreatment by family foster care providers in an urban population', *Child Abuse and Neglect*, 18 (7): 577–85.

Bennett, T. and Sibbitt, R. (2000) *Drug Use Among Arrestees (Home Office Research, Development and Statistics Directorate)*. Research Findings 119. London: Home Office.

Beresford, P., Green, D., Lister, R. and Woodard, K. (1999) *Poverty First Hand: Poor People Speak for Themselves*. London: CPAG.

Bishop, S., Murphy, M., Jellinek, M., Quinn, Sister D. and Poitrast, Judge F. (1992) 'Protecting seriously mistreated children: time delays in a court sample', *Journal of Child Abuse and Neglect*, 16: 465–74.

Blackburn, C. (1991) *Poverty and Health: Working with Families*. Buckingham: Open University Press.

Booth, T. and Booth, W. (1993a) 'Parental adequacy, parenting failure and parents with learning difficulties', *Health and Social Care*, 2: 161–72.

Booth, T. and Booth, W. (1993b) 'Parenting with learning difficulties: lessons for practitioners', *British Journal of Social Work*, 23: 459–80.

Booth, T. and Booth, W. (1994) *Parenting under Pressure: Mothers and Fathers with Learning Difficulties*. Buckingham: Open University Press.

Booth, T. and Booth, W. (1996) 'Parental competence and parents with learning difficulties', *Child and Family Social Work*, 1: 81–6.

Booth, T. and Booth, W. (1998) *Growing up with Parents who have Learning Difficulties*. London: Routledge.

Bowker, L.H., Arbitel, M. and McFerron, J.R. (1988) 'On the relationship between wife beating and child abuse', in K. Yllo and M. Bograd (eds) *Feminist Perspectives on Wife Abuse*. Newbury Park, CA: Sage.

Bowlby, J. (1980) *Attachment* (Vol. 1 of *Attachment and Loss*). London: Pimlico.

Bray, S. and Hinty, B. (2001) 'Allegations against foster carers and the implications for local authority training and support', *Adoption and Fostering*, 25 (1): 55–66.

Bureau of Labor Statistics (2002) www.stats.bls.gov

Burke, P. and Cigno, K. (2000) *Learning Disabilities in Children*. Oxford: Blackwell Science.

Burton, S. (1997) *Where there's a Will there's a Way. Refocussing Childcare Practice: A Guide for Team Managers*. London: National Children's Bureau.

Butler-Sloss, Lord Justice E. (1987) *Report of the Inquiry into Child Abuse in Cleveland*. London: HMSO.

Calder, M., with Hanks, H., Epps, K., Print, B., Morrison, T. and Henniker, J. (1997) *Juveniles and Children who Sexually Abuse: Frameworks for Assessment*. Lyme Regis: Russell House Publishing.

Carter, B. and McGoldrick, M. (eds) (1989) *The Changing Family Life Cycle*. Boston: Allyn and Bacon.

Chaffin, M., Kelleher, K. and Hollenberg, J. (1996) 'Onset of physical abuse and neglect: psychiatric, substance abuse, and social risk factors from prospective community data', *Child Abuse and Neglect*, 20 (3): 191–203.

Christofferson, M.N. (2000) 'Growing up with unemployment: a study of parental unemployment and children's risk of abuse and neglect based on national longitudinal 1973 birth cohorts in Denmark', *Childhood*, 7 (4): 421–38.

Clarke, A. and Clarke, A. (2000) *Early Experience and the Life Path*. London: Jessica Kingsley Ltd.

Cleaver, H., Unell, I. and Aldgate, J. (1999) *Childrens Needs – Parenting Capacity: The Impact of Parental Mental Illness, Problem Alcohol and Drug Use, and Domestic Violence on Children's Development*. London: HMSO.

Cohen, F. and Densen-Gerber, J. (1982) 'A study of the relationship between child abuse and drug addiction in 178 parents: preliminary results', *Child Abuse and Neglect*, 6: 383–7.

Community Care (2002) 'Crucial moments in a tragic case', 21–27 February, pp 18–21 (reporters L. Revans, S. Gillen and R. Downey).

Cooper, A., Hetherington, R., Baistow, K., Pitts, J. and Spriggs, A. (1995) *Positive Child Protection: A View from Abroad*. Lyme Regis: Russell House Publishing.

Corby, B., Doig, A. and Roberts, V. (2001) *Public Inquiries into Abuse of Children in Residential Care*. London: Jessica Kingsley Ltd.

Corner, R. (1997) *Pre-Birth Risk Assessment in Child Protection*. Norwich: Social Work Monographs.

Cox, B.D., Huppert, F. and Whichelow, M. (1987) *The Health and Lifestyles Survey*. London: Health Promotion Research Trust.

Cross, S.B., Kaye, E. and Ratnofsky, A.C. (1993) *A Report on the Maltreatment of Children with Disabilities*. Washington DC: National Center for Child Abuse and Neglect.

Delaney, R. (1991) *Fostering Changes: Treating Attachment-Disordered Children*. Fort Collins: William J. Corbett Publishing.

Department of Health (1995) *Child Protection: Messages from Research*. London: HMSO.

Department of Health (1997) *National Treatment Research Outcome Study*. London: Department of Health.

Department of Health (1998a) *Adoption – Achieving the Right Balance*. Local Authority Circular (98) 20. London: Department of Health.

Department of Health (1998b) *The Quality Protects Programme: Transforming Children's Services*. Local Authority Circular (98) 28. London: Department of Health.

Department of Health (1999) *Working Together: A Guide to Interagency Working to Safeguard and Promote the Welfare of Children*. London: HMSO.

Department of Health (2000a) *Framework for the Assessment of Children in Need and their Families* (the Lilac Book). London: HMSO.

Department of Health (2000b) *Adoption, a New Approach*. London: HMSO.

Department of Health and Social Security, Northern Ireland (1985) *Report of the Committee of Inquiry into Children's Homes and Hostels*. Belfast: HMSO.

Dowdney, I. and Skuse, D. (1993) 'Parenting provided by adults with mental retardation', *Journal of Child Psychology and Psychiatry*, 34 (1): 25–37.

Eckenrode, J., Laird, M. and Doris, J. (1993) 'School performance and disciplinary problems among abused and neglected children', *Developmental Psychology*, 29: 53–64.

Episcopal News Service, 25 May 2000, http://www.episcopalchurch.org/ens/2000-087.html

Erickson, M.F., Egeland, B. and Pianta, R. (1989) 'The effects of maltreatment on the development of young children', in D. Cicchetti and V. Carlson (eds) *Child Maltreatment*. Cambridge: Cambridge University Press. pp. 647–84.

Erooga, M. and Masson, H. (eds) (1999) *Children and Young People who Sexually Abuse Others*. London: Routledge.

Family Policy Studies Centre (2000) *Family Poverty and Social Exclusion (Family Briefing Paper 15)*. London: Family Policy Studies Centre.

Farmer, E. and Owen, M. (1995) *Child Protection Practice: Private Risks and Public Remedies*. London: HMSO.

Fergusson, D.M. and Mullen, P.E. (1999) *Childhood Sexual Abuse: an Evidence Based Perspective*. London: Sage.

Finkelhor, D. (1998) 'The trauma of child sexual abuse: two models', in G. Wyatt and G. Powell (eds) *Lasting Effects of Child Sexual Abuse*. Newbury Park, CA: Sage. pp. 61–82.

Finkelhor, D. and Browne, A. (1986) 'The traumatic impact of child sexual abuse: an update', *American Journal of Orthopsychiatry*, 55: 530–41.

Fisher, D. (1994) 'Adult sex offenders: who are they? Why and how do they do it?' in T. Morrison, M. Erooga and R.C. Beckett (eds) *Sexual Offending Against Children: Assessment and Treatment of Male Abusers*. London: Routledge. pp. 1–24.

Forrester, D. (2000) 'Parental substance abuse and Child Protection in a British sample', *Child Abuse Review*, 9: 235–46.

Franklin, C. and Jordan, C. (1999) *Family Practice: Brief Systems Methods for Social Work*. Pacific Grove, CA: Brooks/Cole.

Fryer, D. (1992) 'Psychological or material deprivation: why does unemployment have mental health consequences?' in E. McLaughlin (ed.) *Understanding Unemployment: New Perspectives on Active Labour Market Policies*. London: Routledge. pp. 103–25.

Furniss, T. (1991) *The Multi-Professional Handbook of Sexual Abuse*. London: Routledge.

Gath, A. (1977) 'The impact of an abnormal child upon the parents', *British Journal of Psychiatry*, 130: 405–10.

Gaudin, J.M. (1999) 'Child neglect: short-term and long-term outcomes', in H. Dubowitz (ed.) *Neglected Children: Research, Practice and Policy*. Thousand Oaks, CA: Sage. pp. 89–108.

Gibbons, J., Gallagher, B., Bell, C. and Gordon, D. (1995) *Development after Physical Abuse in Early Childhood*. London: HMSO.

Gilman, M. (2000) 'Social exclusion and drug using parents', in F. Harbin and M. Murphy (eds) *Substance Misuse and Child Care*. Lyme Regis: Russell House Publishing. pp. 21–6.

Glaun, D. and Brown, P. (1999) 'Motherhood, intellectual disability and child protection: characteristics of a court sample', *Journal of Intellectual and Developmental Disability*, 24 (1): 95–105.

Gleick, J. (1988) *Chaos: Making a New Science*. New York: Viking Penguin.

Goldstein, A. (2001) *Addiction: From Biology to Drug Policy*. Buckingham: Open University Press.

Goldstein, J., Freud, A. and Solnit, A.J. (1980) *Beyond the Best Interests of the Child, New Edition with Epilogue*. London: Burnett Books.

Green, J. (1995) 'Children and accidents', in B. Davey (ed.) *(1995) Birth to Old Age: Health in Transition*. Buckingham: Open University Press, pp. 77–91.

Greenland, C. (1987) *Preventing CAN Deaths: An International Study of Deaths due to Child Abuse and Neglect*. London: Tavistock.

Guardian Society, 1 October 2001 '"Ineffective" authorities failed to protect Lauren'. http://society.guardian.co.uk

Guterman, N. (2001) *Stopping Child Maltreatment before it Starts: Emerging Horizons in Home Visitation Services*. Thousand Oaks, CA: Sage.

Hansard, House of Commons, 29 June 1987, Col. 257.

Harbin, F. and Murphy, M. (2000) *Substance Misuse and Child Care*. Lyme Regis: Russell House Publishing.

Harlow, H. (1963) 'The maternal affectional system', in B.M. Foss (ed.) *Determinants of Human Behaviour*. London: Methuen. pp. 3–33.

Henning, K., Leitenberg, H., Coffey, P., Turner, T. and Bennett, R.T. (1996) 'Long term psychological and social impact of witnessing physical conflict between adults', *Journal of Interpersonal Violence*, 11: 35–51.

Herrenkohl, R.C., Herrenkohl, E.C., Egolf, B.P. and Wu, P. (1991) 'The developmental consequences of child abuse: the Lehigh longitudinal study', in R.H. Starr and D.A. Wolfe (eds) *The Effects of Child Abuse and Neglect*. New York: Guilford. pp. 57–81.

Hester, M., Pearson, C. and Harwin, N. (2000) *Making an Impact: Children and Domestic Violence, A Reader*. London: Jessica Kingsley Ltd.

Hodapp, R.M. (1996) 'Down syndrome: developmental, psychiatric and management issues', *Child and Adolescent Psychiatric Clinics of North America*, 5: 881–94.

Hodapp, R.M. and Krasner, D.V. (1995) 'Families of children with disabilities: findings for a national sample of eighth-grade students', *Exceptionality*, 5: 71–81.

Holden, G.W. (1998) 'Introduction: the development of research into another consequence of family violence', in G.W. Holden, R. Geffner and E.N. Jouriles (eds) *Children Exposed to Marital Violence*. Washington DC: American Psychological Association. pp. 1–18.

Howard, M., Garnham, A., Fimister, G. and Veit-Wilson, J. (2001) *Poverty: The Facts*, 4th edn. London: CPAG.

Howe, D. (1993) *On Being a Client: Understanding the Process of Counselling and Psychotherapy*. London: Sage.

Howells, G. (1997) 'A general practice perspective', in J. O'Hara and A. Sperlinger (eds) *Adults with Learning Disabilities*. Chichester: John Wiley and Sons. pp. 61–80.

Hughes, H. (1992) 'Impact of spouse abuse on children of battered women', *Violence Update*, 1 August: 525–31.

Hutson, S. and Jenkins, R. (1989) *Taking the Strain: Families, Unemployment and the Transition to Adulthood*. Buckingham: Open University Press.

Kelly, L. (1994) 'The interconnectedness of domestic violence and child abuse: challenges for research, policy and practice', in A. Mullender and R. Morley (eds) *Children Living with Domestic Violence, Putting Men's Abuse of Women on the Child Care Agenda*. London: Whiting and Birch. pp. 43–56.

Kempe, C.H., Silverman, F.N., Steele, B.F., Droegmueller, W. and Silver, H.K. (1962) 'The battered child syndrome', *Journal of the American Medical Association*, 181: 17–24.

Kennedy, M. (2002) 'Disability and child abuse', in K. Wilson and A. James (eds) *The Child Protection Handbook*, 2nd edn. London: Bailliere Tindall, pp. 147–71.

Langan, J. (1999) 'Assessing risk in mental health', in P. Parsloe (ed.) *Risk Assessment in Social Work and Social Care*. London: Jessica Kingsley Ltd. pp. 153–78.

Leicestershire County Council (1993) *The Leicestershire Inquiry 1992: Report of an Inquiry into Aspects of the Management of Children's Homes in Leicestershire between 1973 and 1986*. Leicester: Leicestershire County Council.

Leopold, B. and Steffan, E. (1997) *Special Needs of Children of Drug Misusers: Final Report, 1997*. Brussels: Commission of the European Union.

Lindsey, D. (1994) *The Welfare of Children*. New York: Oxford University Press.

London Borough of Brent (1985) *A Child in Trust: Report of the Panel of Inquiry Investigating the Circumstances Surrounding the Death of Jasmine Beckford*. London: London Borough of Brent.

Lynch, M. (1992) 'Child protection – have we lost our way?' *Adoption and Fostering*, 16 (4): 15–22.

Macdonald, K. and Macdonald, G. (1999) 'Perceptions of risk', in P. Parsloe (ed.) *Risk Assessment in Social Work and Social Care*. London: Jessica Kingsley Ltd. pp. 17–52.

Macrory, F. and Harbin, F. (2000) 'Substance misuse and pregnancy', in F. Harbin and M. Murphy (eds) *Substance Misuse and Child Care*. Lyme Regis: Russell House Publishing. pp. 67–78.

McGaw, S. (1996) 'Services for parents with learning disabilities', *Tizard Learning Disability Review*, 1 (1): 21–8.

McGaw, S. and Sturmey, P. (1993) 'Identifying the needs of parents with learning disabilities: a review', *Child Abuse Review*, 2: 101–17.

McGaw, S. and Sturmey, P. (1994) 'Assessing parents with learning disabilities: the Parental Skills Model', *Child Abuse Review*, 3: 36–51.

Middleton, L. (1992) *Children First: Working with Children and Disability*. Birmingham: Venture Press.

Middleton, L. (1999) *Disabled Children: Challenging Social Exclusion*. Oxford: Blackwell Science.

Miller-Perrin, C. and Perrin, R. (1999) *Child Maltreatment: An Introduction*. Thousand Oaks, CA: Sage.

Minnes, P. (1988) 'Family stress associated with a developmentally handicapped child', *International Review of Research on Mental Retardation*, 15: 195–226.

Morris, J (1999) 'Disabled children, child protection systems and the Children Act 1989', *Child Abuse Review*, 8: 91–108.

Morris, K., Marsh, P. and Wiffin, J. (1998) *Family Group Conferences – A Training Pack*. London: Family Rights Group.

Murphy, J.M., Jellinek, M., Quinn, D., Smith, G., Poitrast, F. and Goshko, M. (1991) 'Substance abuse and serious child mistreatment: prevalence, risk and outcome in a court sample', *Child Abuse and Neglect*, 15: 197–211.

Murphy, M. and Harbin, F. (2000) 'Background and current context of substance misuse and child care', in F. Harbin and M. Murphy (eds) *Substance Misuse and Child Care*. Lyme Regis: Russell Home Publishing. pp. 67–78.

Nabokov, V. (1992) *Lolita*. London: Everyman.

National Research Council (1993) *Understanding Child Abuse and Neglect*. Washington DC: National Academy Press.

NCCANI (National Clearinghouse on Child Abuse and Neglect Information) (2002) *Reporting Laws, Number 1, Definitions of Child Abuse and Neglect*. http://www.calib.com.nccanch

Oates, R., Forrest, D. and Peacock, A. (1985) 'Self-esteem of abused children', *Child Abuse and Neglect*, 9: 159–63.

Office of National Statistics (2002) www.statistics.gov.uk

Painz, F. (1993) *Parents with a Learning Disability*. Norwich: University of East Anglia, Social Work Monographs.

Pantazis, C. and Gordon, D. (1997) 'Poverty and crime', in D. Gordon and C. Pantazis (eds) *Breadline Britain in the 1990s*. Aldershot: Ashgate. pp. 115–33.

Parton, N. (1991) *Governing the Family: Child Care, Child Protection and the State*. Basingstoke: Macmillan.

Parton, N. (1994) 'Problematics of government, (post)modernity and social work', *British Journal of Social Work*, 24 (1): 9–32.

Parton, N. and O'Byrne, P. (2000) *Constructive Social Work: Towards a New Practice*. Basingstoke: Macmillan.

Payne, M. (1997) *Modern Social Work Theory*, 2nd edn. Basingstoke: Macmillan.

Philpot, T. (2001) *A Very Private Practice: A Report into Private Fostering*. London: BAAF.

Pithouse, A. (1998) *Social Work: The Social Organisation of an Invisible Trade*. Aldershot: Ashgate.

Rowe, J. and Lambert, L. (1973) *Children who Wait: A Study of Children Needing Substitute Families*. London: Association of British Adoption and Fostering Agencies.

Russell, D. (1986) *The Secret Trauma: Incest in the Lives of Women and Girls*. New York: Basic Books.

Rutter, M. (1974) *The Family in Society: Dimensions of Parenthood*. London: HMSO.

Rutter, M. and Rutter, M. (1993) *Developing Minds: Challenge and Continuity across the Lifespan*. London: Penguin.

Rutter, M. and the English and Romanian Adoptees Study Team (1998) 'Developmental catch-up, and deficit, following adoption after severe global early privation', *Journal of Child Psychology and Psychiatry*, 39 (4): 465–76.

Schofield, G. (1996) 'Parental competence and the welfare of the child: issues for those who work with parents with learning difficulties and their children. A response to Booth and Booth', *Child and Family Social Work*, 1: 87–92.

SCODA (Standing Conference on Drug Abuse) (1997) *Drug Using Parents:*

Policy Guidelines for Inter-agency Working. London: Local Government Association.

Shor, R. (2000) 'Child maltreatment: differences in perceptions between parents in low income and middle income neighbourhoods', *British Journal of Social Work*, 30: 165–78.

Silbert, M. and Pines, A. (1981) 'Sexual child abuse as an antecedent to prostitution', *Child Abuse and Neglect*, 5: 407–11.

Silvern, L., Karyl, J., Waelde, L, Hodges, W.F., Starek. J., Heidt, E. and Min, K. (1995) 'Retrospective reports of parental partner abuse: relationships to depression, trauma symptoms and self-esteem among college students', *Journal of Family Violence*, 10: 177–202.

Solnit, A. and Stark, M. (1961) 'Mourning and the birth of a defective child', *Psychoanalytic Study of the Child*, 16: 523–37.

Sperlinger, A. (1997) 'Introduction' in J. O'Hara and A. Sperlinger (eds) *Adults with Learning Disabilities: A Practical Approach for Health Professionals*. Chichester: John Wiley and Sons.

Staffordshire County Council (1991) *The Pindown Experience and the Protection of Children: The Report of the Staffordshire Child Care Inquiry 1990*. Stafford: Staffordshire County Council.

Stark, E. and Flitcraft, A. (1985) 'Woman-battering, child abuse and social heredity: what is the relationship?' in N. Johnson (ed.) *Marital Violence*. London: Routledge and Kegan Paul. pp. 147–71.

Straus, M.A. (1992) 'Children as witnesses to family violence: a risk factor for life-long problems among a nationally representative sample of American men and women', in *Children and Violence: A Report of the Twenty-third Ross Roundtable on Initial Approaches to Common Paediatric Problems*. Columbus, OH: Ross Laboratories.

Summit, R. (1983) 'The child sexual abuse accommodation syndrome', *Child Abuse and Neglect*, 7: 177–93.

Summit, R. (1988) 'Hidden pain: societal avoidance of child sexual abuse', in G. Wyatt and G. Powell (eds) *Lasting Effects of Child Sexual Abuse*. Newbury Park, CA: Sage. pp. 39–60.

Townsend, P. (1979) *Poverty in the United Kingdom*. London: Penguin.

Tucker, M. and Johnson, O. (1989) 'Competence promoting vs. competence inhibiting social support for mentally retarded mothers', *Human Organisation*, 48 (2): 95–107.

Tymchuk, A. (1992) 'Predicting adequacy of parenting by people with mental retardation', *Child Abuse and Nelgect*, 16: 154–78.

Tymchuk, A. and Andron, L. (1994) 'Rationale, approaches, results and resource implications of programmes to enhance parenting skills of people with learning disabilities', in A. Craft (ed.) *Practice Issues in Sexuality and Learning Disabilities*. London: Routledge. pp. 202–16.

Velleman, R. (2001) 'Working with substance misusing parents as part of court proceedings', *Representing Children*, 14 (1): 36–48.

Waldfogel, J. (1999) *The Future of Child Protection*. Cambridge MA: Harvard University Press.

Wang, C. and Daro, D. (1998) *Current Trends in Child Abuse Reporting and Fatalities: The Results of the 1997 Annual Fifty State Survey*. Chicago: National Committee to Prevent Child Abuse.

Wang, C. and Harding, K. (1999) *Current Trends in Child Abuse Reporting and Fatalities: The Results of the 1998 Annual Fifty State Survey.* Chicago: National Committee to Prevent Child Abuse.

Warr, P.B. and Jackson, P.R. (1983) 'Self-esteem and unemployment among young workers', *Le Travail Humain*, 46: 335–66.

Waterhouse, Sir Ronald and the Tribunal of Inquiry into the abuse of children in care in the former county council areas of Gwynnedd and Clwyd since 1974 (2000) *Lost in Care.* London: HMSO.

Watson, G. (1989) 'The abuse of disabled children and young people', in W.S. Rogers, D. Hevey and E. Ash (eds) *Child Abuse and Neglect.* Buckingham: Open University Press. pp. 113–18.

Watts, P. (2000) 'Solution focussed brief therapy used in a substance misuse setting', in F. Harbin and M. Murphy (eds) *Substance Misuse and Child Care.* Lyme Regis: Russell House Publishing. pp. 95–110.

Webster, R. (1998) *The Great Children's Home Panic.* Oxford: Orwell Books.

Weir, A. and Douglas, A. (eds) (1999) *Child Protection and Adult Mental Health.* Oxford: Butterworth Heinemann.

Westcott, H. and Cross, M. (1996) *Thus Far and No Further: Towards Ending the Abuse of Disabled Children.* Birmingham: Venture Press.

Williams (Lord Williams of Mostyn, Chair) (1996) *Report of the National Commission of Inquiry into the Prevention of Child Abuse.* Vol 1, Rhe Report. London: HMSO.

Wolf, S.C. (1984) 'A Multifactor Model of Deviant Sexuality'. Paper presented at the Third International Conference on Victimology, Lisbon.

Index